Organizations:
Cases, Issues, Concepts

Organizations:
Cases, Issues, Concepts

Edited by Rob Paton, with the assistance of
Suzanne Brown, Roger Spear, Jake Chapman, Mike Floyd and John Hamwee

Harper and Row Publishers
in association with
The Open University

Harper & Row, Publishers
London

Cambridge
Hagerstown
Philadelphia
New York

San Francisco
Mexico City
Sao Paulo
Sydney

This selection and editorial matter © 1984 The Open University

First published 1984
All rights reserved

Harper & Row Ltd
28 Tavistock St
London WC2E 7PN

British Library Cataloguing in Publication Data
   Organizations.
      1. Organization
      I. Paton, Rob
      II. Open Systems Group
      302.3'5   HM131

   ISBN 0-06-318264-5

Typeset by Gedset, Cheltenham.
Printed and bound by Butler & Tanner Ltd., Frome
and London

Preface & Acknowledgements

In preparing this Reader I was closely assisted throughout by colleagues in the Open University Systems Group. Since the term 'systems' has many connotations it may be worth saying that the Systems Group is not a collection of Operations Researchers, or computer analysts, or O & M practitioners, or general systems theorists; it is a multi-disciplinary group, located in the Faculty of Technology, whose members share a common interest in the development of appropriate methods for action and policy-oriented studies. Those of us who produced this Reader were working as a team to produce the course entitled 'Managing in Organizations'. It was a team in far more than the formal sense.

Suzanne Brown's enormous contribution deserves special mention: it ranged from suggesting and commenting on innumerable articles through to the really formidable task of preparing 'clean copies' for our publishers. Although not a member of the Course Team, John Hughes gave us considerable assistance. In the face of absurdly overdue manuscripts, June McGowan, Sue Snelling and other secretaries saved us from the wrath of the University's publishers.

Finally the publishers have also earned our appreciation. Even more important than Marianne Lagrange's charm and competence, they were prepared to back our belief that the sort of material we were gathering for our course would constitute a viable Reader making some useful material easily accessible to other teachers and students.

Rob Paton
Walton Hall, September 1983.

Contents

Introduction

This collection of readings was designed as a resource for courses on organizations. It will support courses in management education, broadly conceived — including not just administration but any practically-oriented concern for organizations and their problems — rather than social-scientific courses. It embodies the view that there is considerably more to managing in organizations than some popular notions of management suggest. The material is intended to promote an understanding of organizations and the things that go on in them, and explores issues that face managers, employees and specialist staff in the organization and conduct of their work.

The readings are intended for introductory or basic courses on organizations at degree level. So the material was selected to be appropriate for first or second year students (or equivalent on non-degree courses) in business studies and for those whose principal subject of study would lie elsewhere — in computing, engineering, accounting, operations research, or whatever.

Although this is certainly not the sort of Reader that aims at a comprehensive treatment of the subject, the readings were selected to provide a rudimentary coverage. So in Section I the Cases cover large and small, public and private, organizations; and in Section III the Concepts range from interpersonal to interorganizational levels of analysis. In Section II, by contrast, our aim was much more to present some topics that concern people in organizations in a stimulating form. Taken together, the need for basic coverage and the attempt to maintain a fairly consistent level of treatment, meant that on occasions we had to fall back on providing material ourselves, and on other occasions we had to edit articles heavily. The argument that it is good for students to learn to tackle 'real' academic writing in this field is only sound if they are going to need that ability; otherwise, it's much more important that they learn the content. On this basis, our choice of articles was often swayed by the prose style.

The central difficulty in teaching about organizations and their problems is to provide ideas that have the generality to be useful in a myriad of different circumstances and then to ensure that students can bridge the gap from what will often be somewhat unfamiliar and abstract terms, to their own particular experience. Unless the ideas are applied to realistic contexts and students gradually find they can make them work, the teaching remains, literally, an academic exercise. The catch is that, often, the more general and potentially valuable the ideas, the wider the gap becomes. The division of the Reader into three sections (Cases, Issues, Concepts — though the last distinction is less clear cut) reflects a strategy for addressing this basic teaching dilemma. The three sections represent progressively higher levels of abstraction and generalization and the essential point is to draw the connections *between* the material in the three sections — and from that material to the student's own experiences (in which respect most of our Open University students, combining work and study, are at an enormous advantage compared to full-time students).

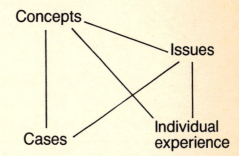

In brief, the Issues provide middle-level generalizations about particular problem areas; they can be fairly easily related to students' own experiences, and further discussed and analysed using the Concepts. The Cases can provide illustrations of particular issues, and also provide examples of, or practice at, the application of concepts. The Concepts represent more theoretical ideas selected for their contribution to a practical understanding of issues and particular cases (as opposed to their value in research). Teachers (and indeed students) should be able to see the scope for numerous connections between the sections of the Reader, and this was another consideration in selecting pieces.

I CASES

I Cases

Case studies are a step towards the real world, a substitute for it that can be readily shared, a way of learning from *other people's* experience. They demonstrate the richness of organizational life and the inadequacy of simple formulas. In many ways, stories of failure, of things going awfully wrong, make good material: disasters are not just interesting but demand explanations, in a way that success or normal competence do not. Two of the studies are of that sort but they should be read sympathetically: would you or I really have been able to foresee and avoid the problems? Organizations are easy to knock, particularly with hindsight, and difficult to change. But success, and (most common of all) outcomes which are neither one nor the other, can also be interesting and instructive, as the two other studies show. The cases were chosen because they 'ring true', they have the 'richness' of real events — in particular, they all display something of the variety of points of view that existed in the events recounted. And that variety of viewpoints is, ultimately, what makes organizational work difficult.

1 Changing Complex Information Systems: Medical Records at Anersley Hospital

J. Berridge

This name and the entire case study are fictional, while based upon real-life problems that may be met in health service administration. The case was written as a basis for study and discussion, rather than to illustrate effective or ineffective handling of an administrative situation.

The background

Anersley Hospital is a long-stay psychiatric and geriatric hospital of some 600 beds which sprawls across an extensive site in a suburb of a large town. Its many piecemeal additions over the past seventy years have no architectural distinction. Many of them are wooden and metal huts and buildings erected during the 1939-45 war. During the last three years, the hospital has become a centre for psychiatric treatment for the town and surrounding area, as small peripheral hospitals and wards are closed down in a rationalization drive. In numbers of beds, the hospital has declined as more patients are treated on an out-patient basis, and the concept of community care spreads. So out-patient clinics have conversely become a more major part of Anersley's activities, and new facilities have been built to cater for the greatly increased number of out-patients.

The changing role of medical records in the hospital

The rather unplanned and erratic nature of Anersley's expansion over a period of years was reflected in the haphazard siting of facilities and departments. Perhaps medical records illustrated this type of growth particularly clearly. The medical records filing section was at the end of a long corridor on the extremity of the hospital, and was accommodated in a wooden hut — one of a series of large huts leading off the corridor, and now mainly used as stores. The hut was dilapidated on the outside, but inside it had been made cheerful by colourful posters and cartoons that the staff had pinned on the walls, and other touches of homeliness and individuality. An example of this was the hand-painted sign on the door, above the official name plate of 'Medical Records Department'; it simply read 'The Shack'. The desks and equipment of the medical records filing section were worn and out of date, and the actual racks and shelves for the storage of patients' records were a selection of miscellaneous designs and various ages that had just accumulated over the years. The physical layout is shown in Figure 1.1.

The function of medical records has changed greatly in Anersley Hospital over the past years. For a long period it had been little more than a storage activity to aid the medical and nursing staff, who made manuscript notes on fairly straightforward forms. These were then filed in manilla folders and in box files on long shelves, subsequently to be located through a set of dog-eared index cards. While the record still remains traditionally the responsibility of the consultant, for any one patient it is now a much more complex set of documents, containing, in addition to clinical information, a variety of observations from other practitioners such as midwives, health visitors, social workers, physiotherapists, radiographers and laboratory staff. At the same time, the functions of medical records departments have become more complex. They include medical secretarial activities, as well as clerks and receptionists on wards and clinics. They receive a range of demands for information, not only from within the hospital, but also much more widely for uses as diverse as national statistics for central government, or for specialized research into clinical and social aspects of health care.

Working methods in the filing section at Anersley Hospital had evolved over time, and there were few rigid procedures or methods. Patients' records were collected and returned quite informally by a variety of staff — nurses, orderlies, clerks, porters. The only security seemed to be whether they were known to the staff of the medical records department. Sometimes clerks or porters who came regularly for records and knew the methods of filing would ask permission to look out records themselves, if the records clerks were particularly busy. Appointments clerks from out-patient clinics would often come down casually to the department two or three days before a

This case study was originally published in an abridged form in J. Child (1977) *Organisations — a guide to problems and practice*, Harper & Row. The author expresses his thanks for assistance with the case study to Peter Tebbit in respect of the original version, to John Child for suggesting improvements in drafting, and to Ted Starks for much advice on the technical aspects of medical records practice. All these persons acted in a personal capacity and not in an official role; responsibility for mistakes in the case study is that of the author.

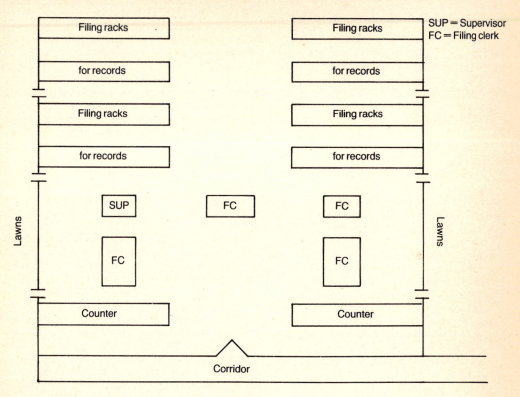

Figure 1.1   *Physical layout of original medical records filing section.*

clinic and, jointly with the records clerk, search out the records needed, having a pleasant talk at the same time. Reciprocally, it was not unknown for a records clerk to make a private arrangement with an appointments clerk to assist with the running of a clinic, if things were busy at that end of the hospital. The surprising thing to a stranger was that the records department worked markedly well. The success rate in finding records was very high — even those old, odd, elusive ones. The degree of cooperation with medical and nursing staff was also high. There was never any quibbling about demands for records at awkward times or at the last minute when extra patients attended a clinic. Undoubtedly the department worked on good memories and easy personal relationships, but it *did* work!

For the past ten years Mrs Price has been in charge of the filing section of the medical records department, as senior medical records clerk; in all she has spent nearly thirty years in this department of the hospital. Hence she has seen medical records expand from little more than a filing activity employing a small handful of people to the present complex function involving more than thirty staff, including medical secretaries, receptionists, appointment clerks, clerical and statistical staff. Partic-

ularly over the last ten years, these newer sections of the medical records department have grown much faster in numbers of personnel than the original filing section, which has almost remained static in staff numbers. The new sections, as they evolved, had supervisors appointed, and they reported directly to the Hospital Secretary, as did Mrs Price. With an administrative reorganization of the National Health Service, the Hospital Secretary was redesignated as Unit Administrator, but Mrs Price and the other section heads continued to report to him as before. Everybody in the hospital seems to know Mrs Price, and she is liked for her equable temperament and pleasant disposition. Four filing clerks report to her in turn, and they perform the filing activities.

Although Mrs Price was in charge of the section, in practice she and her four assistants all used to do the same work, allocating it among themselves approximately equally by mutual agreement. There never seemed to be any problem of keeping up with the constant stream of filing and requests, even as the volume of work built up as out-patient clinics became more numerous. In a busy period, people would work through tea breaks, and in slack spells they would liaise (that is, gossip) with their counterparts in other departments. At tea-time, mornings and afternoons, one of the clerks would slip down the road to the local bakery, and bring back cream doughnuts for all of the staff, plus any visitors who happened to be there. Not surprisingly, visitors were frequent! The doughnuts were financed through a peculiar custom. In the corner of the working space was a large waste-paper basket, into which the staff would throw from time to time crumpled balls of scrap paper from their desks; if they missed the waste-paper basket, they had to pay a fine of one halfpenny into the doughnut fund. Other clerical workers in the hospital regarded the medical records clerks with some envy as having a nice job.

The move

About a year ago, with the decision to centralize many of the psychiatric and geriatric out-patient clinics for the catchment area of Anersley Hospital, and with the drive to reduce the number of in-patient beds, a greatly increased load of out-patient clinic work resulted. To cope with these new demands, new clinic facilities were built or rebuilt, new equipment was purchased, and new staff appointed, often from large integrated hospitals of the District General Hospital type. Such staff seemed to the old staff to show a tendency to be less friendly, more impatient for results, and less inclined to build up easy working methods through the slow process of first creating bonds of friendship and trust. Medical records staff in 'The Shack' sensed some of this slight strain, isolated as they were on the edge of the hospital; but with increasing work loads, they cooperated and worked even more closely together, and counted themselves fortunate to be part of a small but good team, and to have still the goodwill of their old colleagues in wards, clinics and departments.

Medical records functions were also included in the reorganization. A study by the Regional Management Services Department's Organization and Methods (O & M) team had confirmed suspicions about the inefficiency of the old scattered medical records department. The filing section had been at one end of the hospital, while the out-patient clinics and the appointment clerks had been at the other end of the hospital, where they were much under the influence of nursing staff. The medical secretaries had been located in various offices around the hospital, for instance, in small rooms attached to wards where they could be at hand for medical staff. Often they were underoccupied, due to lack of work in their particular area. The O & M team's report had indicated the administrative advantages to be gained by the centralization of many of the medical records activities, on the lines of similar exercises carried out by the team in other hospitals of the region. A standard form for an integrated medical records department therefore already existed, and the team was able to suggest its adoption at Anersley, with certain minor modifications to meet local conditions.

Thus the three main functions of the medical records department (records filing, appointments and secretarial) were gathered together into an integrated department for reasons of economy and convenience in obtaining and processing records. A fourth section was created in the medical records department; this was the records administrative office, to handle the many requests for statistical data arising from patients' records. A spare pavilion was found (recently vacated by long-stay patients) and the two large wards were comprehensively converted, one into an extra out-patient facility and the other into the new integrated medical records department.

As is customary, the planning and design work was carried out at the Regional Health Authority headquarters, in liaison with administrative staff of the Health District in which Anersley Hospital was situated. The pavilion was completely rebuilt internally, tastefully decorated, carpeted, air-conditioned and equipped with modern furniture, office equipment, and records storage methods. The old storage racks from 'The Shack' were completely replaced with new equipment designed by a well-known firm specializing in records' storage. Patients' information would still be held in folders using the standard forms, but the old tiers of shelves were replaced by a modern space-saving system involving purpose-built metal staging exactly fitting the size of the folder and running on tracks so that one rack could easily be slid back by hand to reveal a second rack behind, holding less frequently requested files. The capital cost of the new equipment for the department was high, but the O & M team's main criterion for its adoption was whether it could cope with all demands for the foreseeable future.

Shortly before these alterations were completed, and with the increasing complexity of the medical records function, a new post of hospital Medical Records Officer (MRO) was created. The MRO was to be in charge of the new integrated department, with the various section heads reporting to him. A major responsibility for him was to supervise the change-over of records to the new building and to organize the start-up of the new procedures. The person appointed was Mr Fraser, who had held various posts in medical records in different parts of the country; he was in his early forties, and was well informed about the technicalities of medical records and keen to set up a new service to good standards. Before coming to Anersley Hospital, his job was as a Deputy MRO in a large hospital where he had gained a good reputation. Mr Fraser impressed the interviewing panel at his appointment as having drive, being keen to be in charge of his own medical records department, and wanting to show his capabilities, possibly as a basis for a future promotion to a coordinating post in medical records at District level. Mr Fraser reported to the Unit Administrator at Anersley Hospital, Mr Littlewood, who could be regarded as middle management.

Since Mr Fraser's arrival at Anersley was some two years after the planning period, the decisions had all been taken regarding the physical facilities and equipment for the new medical records department. Nevertheless, he reviewed the future needs for the reorganized hospital, using the O & M team's data bases and research studies in other hospitals which had undergone similar changes of function to that proposed for Anersley. When he studied the records filing section in 'The Shack', he found that (after making allowances for their outdated equipment and unrationalized working methods) the section was unlikely to be able to cope with the projected increasing volume of records since it was already working at some 110 per cent of normal expected output. Although Mr Fraser took care not to give the members of the section this information, it did enable him to assure them that the change to the new building would mean less hard work for them, as a result of the new lay-out and improved equipment. He was a little disappointed to find that this news did not produce any marked enthusiasm among the staff of the section.

In the early days after his arrival at Anersley, Mr Fraser spent a considerable amount of time with the O & M team and the Architect's Department at regional headquarters, so that he appreciated their proposals and recommendations and could use the equipment to the full. He was particularly impressed with the elegance and logic of the plans, which would improve access to records for key users, and provide a much faster processing of information on a reliable basis. Subsequently he worked out master plans for the transfer of equipment, records and personnel to the new office, and for the detailed operation of the new department and Records Library, as he renamed the filing section, in line with current practice. He then converted these plans into working instructions for each member of staff to follow after the transfer, and he issued these instructions some ten days in advance of the move via supervisors and section heads to each person. Like others in charge of groups of staff, Mrs Price received a substantial sheaf of instructions from Mr Fraser, and, after a short briefing, he entrusted her

with the task of instructing her staff. The group of five in 'The Shack' worked meticulously through the detail and did their best to understand the new procedures. A few days before the actual moving day Mr Fraser checked with the staff in order to ensure a smooth change-over; neither Mrs Price nor her staff had any questions in advance and they acknowledged that the instructions certainly were thorough. Mr Fraser was a little disappointed at this passive response to his new instructions; he had put a great deal of painstaking work into them, and had hoped that staff would react with more recognition. He put the lack of involvement down to Mrs Price's limitations as a supervisor in leading her staff, and to their lack of concern for and knowledge of proper standards of good practice in medical records.

The actual movement of the records to the new department was Mr Fraser's masterpiece of planning, to such an extent that the Unit Administrator congratulated Mr Fraser on the continuation of the records service, scarcely with any disruption. Friday clinics were cancelled that week, and the records staff cleared up all outstanding documents on Friday morning — and then were given the Friday afternoon off as a holiday. At 1 p.m. a veritable army of porters and helpers descended on 'The Shack' to perform the heavy task of moving every document right across the hospital to the new office. With Mr Fraser and another administrator in charge and following the master plan, everything was correctly filed by 4 p.m. on the Sunday after-

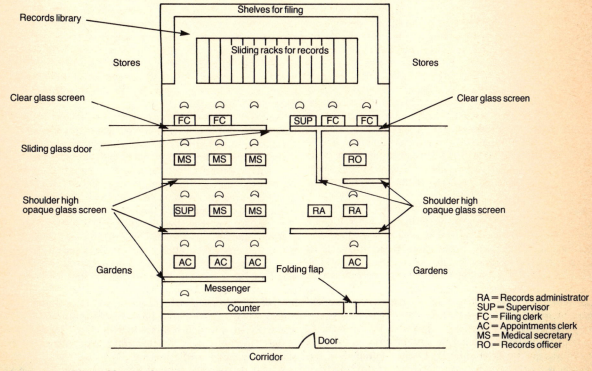

Figure 1.2   *Physical layout of new integrated medical records office.*

noon. At all times Mr Fraser was at hand to check the removal team's instructions and to give supplementary orders. On the Monday morning, the new medical records department started up, almost as if the change had never occurred, and disruption was minimized.

The new integrated department

Although filing procedures were not very different in the new department, the overall mode of operation of the department was considerably streamlined and more efficient in concept. Mr Fraser felt that his concern before the move in getting people trained in advance had helped them to get used quickly to the changed physical layout and conditions, and to the new standards which he hoped to inculcate. A diagram of the new department is shown in Figure 1.2

So that a real measure of security could be retained over records, a floor-to-ceiling glass screen had been erected at the end of the Records Library. All the staff in that section had desks behind the screen and behind them were the filing racks, shiny and new. The only entrance to the Records Library was through the one sliding door next to Mrs Price's desk, and she had instructions only to admit persons designated on a list which Mr Fraser had drawn up. The Records Library staff were expected in their turn to leave the office only at specified times, unless in special circumstances. A messenger was appointed for the department, and his duties included collecting and receiving clinic lists and requests for records, transmitting them to Mrs Price, subsequently collecting records from her and conveying them to wards and clinics. Anyone outside the department making a single request for records, would pass the details via the messenger or sometimes directly to Mrs Price, and she would either find the file herself or allocate the work to one of her staff. The Records Library staff queried the need for these procedures when Mr Fraser was explaining methods at a post-move training session. He explained its logic with two reasons: first, it would prevent excessive interruption of their work by a constant flow of requests; secondly, it helped introduce a suitably professional standard of security with records — and he cited the unfortunate case that had befallen him some years earlier when a drunken porter had recited some rather explicit case notes to an enthralled audience in the 'spit and sawdust' bar of a local pub!

In many ways, the new methods introduced by Mr Fraser began, as he put it, to 'get a grip' on the Records Library. Gone were the piles of unfiled records that sometimes used to lie on desks overnight at times of rush; all work had to be cleared before the night records clerk/telephonist came on duty. The use of tracer cards was made mandatory whenever records were removed, even for use within the medical records department. The master index was no longer treated in a 'cavalier fashion' that had prevailed before — Mr Fraser's expression for everyone working on it; it was made the responsibility of one member alone of the staff. An attempt to paste pictures on the glass screen was quickly checked by Mr Fraser on grounds of unsightliness. Tea break now consisted of a fixed period of fifteen minutes in the staff dining-room. At the same time, Mr Fraser

was able to keep a general supervisory eye on proceedings, and he felt it his duty to squash some rather irresponsible behaviour involving attempts to throw paper balls through the sliding glass door when it was open. He explained to Mr Littlewood that, in all, he was slowly instilling professional pride and standards into the staff of the Records Library. He also made a point of building up Mrs Price's supervisory position, and he gave her the opportunity to show such skills by making certain that changes and instructions always reached her as requests, for her to pass on as instructions to her staff.

Problems encountered

During the six months that followed the move the service provided by the Records Library deteriorated. Records were obtained far less reliably than previously; there were frequent delays and sudden requests at the last minute were often the subject of argument. Filing of records began to get behind, and so Mr Fraser instituted a rule that any records unfiled at the end of the day should be returned to Mrs Price for safe-keeping. The stock of such records grew alarmingly. Mrs Price attempted to file them the following day, in addition to her normal work, but never seemed to catch up. It became assumed that once records had been passed over to Mrs Price, they ceased to be the responsibility of the clerk to whom they had originally been assigned. The old habit of team effort in helping to find apparently missing records seemed to disappear, and problems were experienced with deficiencies in the master index.

Faced with such issues, Mrs Price requested Mr Fraser to let her staff work half an hour's overtime each evening for a week to clear the back-log. Mr Fraser refused, with the words 'If the staff spent less time chatting and got on with the job they're paid to do, there'd be no problem — the O & M team didn't recommend any overtime'. Although her staff several times again mentioned this solution to her, Mrs Price was never willing to raise the matter again.

Staff in clinics which were experiencing difficulties in getting patients' records in good time complained eventually through consultants to Mr Littlewood, the Unit Administrator. His wide range of responsibilities meant that he had little time to exercise day-to-day control over medical records — or any other section. He believed in delegation, and thus his contact with departments occurred mainly when problems or changes arose. As a result of the complaint, Mr Fraser made a ruling that records must be passed over to clinics even earlier, to allow for errors and omissions to be corrected. Even the easy relationship within the department between records clerks and medical secretaries began to suffer with the increasing workload and pressure for a faster turnround of work. All the staff felt real concern that their service was deteriorating, and tried hard to retrieve the position, even to the extent of working through tea-breaks. Mr Fraser perhaps did not see all the problems, as he was often out of the office at meetings, or in outlying hospitals in the District, preparing for their integration into a comprehensive scheme for medical records.

Within the Records Library work became slower due to missing or misplaced records, and the back-log became larger than ever. In an attempt to speed up the pace of work the clerks began to omit the tracer cards when records were removed — on the grounds that they had always managed well enough without them in 'The Shack'. When he discovered this habit, Mr Fraser used to carry out periodic checks; there were hard feelings on both sides when (inevitably) he discovered missing cards, and the staff used to refer to him as 'the bloodhound'.

Certain vague reports that all was not well in medical records reached Mr Littlewood again. Still believing that Mr Fraser should have a full chance to sort out teething troubles without interference from above, he did not intervene. Mr Fraser, in his view, was showing energy and determination, implementing a major change in the hospital's procedures, and, in any case, it might well not be prudent to involve the hard-pressed O & M team again in sorting out matters at Anersley, before every effort had been made within the hospital to resolve the problems.

The crisis

Matters came to a head one evening at about 11.30 p.m., when Mr Littlewood was called from bed to the telephone by an icily-polite consultant who wished to inform him that he had been waiting for exactly three hours for the records of a patient who had just been admitted under a section of the Mental Health Act 1959. It was known that the man had been both an in-patient and an out-patient of the hospital before, but three hours' search by the night records clerk/telephonist had failed to reveal any notes or reference at all. Mr Littlewood rang Mr Fraser and tersely asked him to come to the hospital at once to meet him.

It took Mr Fraser about twenty-five minutes to find the patient's records, which were wrongly filed, and, in addition, apparently incomplete to some extent. Mr Littlewood searched also, and was dismayed with what he found. There were piles of case notes stuffed in desks, bundles of reports from departments lying, weeks old, in the innermost racks, there were missing or incomplete tracer cards and the master index seemed very inefficient. Beside Mrs Price's desk was a new addition — a small wooden rack from 'The Shack', with three shelves marked 'Pending' (all full) and one for 'Unaccountable' (part-full). As Mr Littlewood searched, the consultant stood beside him and related a series of carefully documented and heartfelt incidents about the shortcomings and failures of the new medical records department.

The consultant departed to the ward, bearing the records. Mr Littlewood regarded Mr Fraser sourly. 'We will meet at nine o'clock today in my office to find out why this has occurred, and what we are going to do about it. Goodnight'.

The aftermath

The meeting in Mr Littlewood's office was quite brief and, for Mr Fraser, relatively undistressing — perhaps reflecting the health service's tradition of civilized administration. It was agreed between the two men that 'serious teething troubles' still existed, that Mr Fraser would spend much more time in the hospital medical records office sorting out problems, and that, finally, he would report back formally to Mr Littlewood in three months' time.

Once back in the department (which was 'buzzing' with speculation and comment over the news of the previous night's events), Mr Fraser sat down to make his plans to get the service running more smoothly. After a couple of days' reflection, he set about energetically putting them into practice.

First he concentrated on technical difficulties with the records storage equipment and in the identification and tracing of individual patients' records. Then he reviewed all routines adopted by clinics, wards and departments for requesting and returning records, reconsidering the deadlines, the internal movement of records between sections in the medical records department and instituting a procedure for emergencies. Thirdly, he endeavoured to involve Mrs Price more in the exercise of her supervisory role, through playing a greater part in the allocation and control of work, through insisting on strict observance of the deadlines for requests, and through trying to get her to take a more consistent approach to dividing the 'trouble-shooting' activity between herself and her staff. Finally, he tried to ensure that each of the medical records filing clerks knew the procedures and routines exactly and adhered to them, especially in respect of handling problems of missing, incomplete or unidentifiable records. As a result of all these activities, Mr Fraser felt that an additional full-time appointment was necessary to the Records Library on the grounds of the increasing volume of work; a school leaver with clerical training was duly recruited.

On balance, Mr Fraser felt that from these measures he could detect an improvement of service in many respects, especially in the response time for records, in the night service and in the level of complaints from users of records. The department seemed to be settling into a routine of operation and was developing smoother relationships with other departments — as he was able to report to Mr Littlewood. Yet Mr Fraser could detect other matters which concerned him a little. Staff turnover had risen from the previous extremely low level, and staff seemed to work without any conspicuous enthusiasm. Mrs Price continued in her post, but never made any original contribution to improving standards or solving problems. It was generally accepted among staff that she would seek retirement at the earliest permissible point, in a year's time, and that her replacement would be a much younger person, with professional training in medical records and a career orientation towards middle or senior management in the health services.

Mr Fraser reflected one day on the direction of the change, on the manner in which it had been conducted, on the present standard of service, and on the present capacity of his department to respond to future demands — and he wondered whether he was as confident still in his own knowledge and abilities as he had been on appointment! He began to think about taking advice . . .

2 Little Women
E. Tynan

This case describes an organization that is unusual: not only is it an out-and-out success story, but it is owned and controlled by its members. However, the fact that it did succeed shouldn't make one imagine it was bound to succeed. Self-help schemes of this general form are often contemplated and sometimes attempted — why did this one succeed where so many others fail?

History

The idea and the planning

At 24 Margaret Elliot found her role as a young mother keeping a modern house oppressive. She needed an outlet but was reluctant to return to the kind of work she had done before marriage. Margaret Elliot had no qualifications, she had left school at 14; 'it was one of those schools that you leave then. There was no further fifth or sixth form — you left at fourth form. No talk of going on to college'. She began work on her fifteenth birthday, as a clerk, and waited to get married, which she did four years later.

She had two children and a home, which her husband was buying on a mortgage, when he joined Sunderlandia, a common ownership building firm in the town. The common ownership structure — in which ownership and ultimate control lay with the working members — seemed to offer scope for Peter Elliot's energy and his ambition to change working relationships in the building industry. Margaret Elliot met Robert Oakeshott, one of the promoters of the building firm and he encouraged her to think of setting up a venture herself, with a group of friends.

She enlisted married friends and relatives in the same impasse for discussions. They needed to get out of the 'four walls' but without losing their children to baby minders whom they could not afford anyway. Their meetings in a local pub called the Dun Cow evolved the idea of a shop with a nursery above it. They wanted to work without the discomfort of supervision. The shop would have a relaxed atmosphere and provide a bench to rest on. The poor could buy small portions without embarrassment. The shop would stock dried goods in bulk as well as the normal range of groceries. A rota would be deliberately arranged to eliminate the possibility of cliques developing and malicious gossip poisoning the group morale.

As secretary of the group, Margaret Elliot had written to several organizations requesting finance but had met with no success. Traditional sources were not sympathetic to them.

Next, Margaret and another of Little Women travelled to London to attend the annual general meeting of the Industrial Common Ownership Movement. There they canvassed for funds.

The financial prediction described a capital investment of £4,000 and a weekly turnover of £500 based on the probable market of 100 families of four, rising to £1,000 after three months. Their wages would be £11 a week, representing 20 hours at 60p with £1 reinvested. Travelling expenses would be paid where necessary. On their return from London, Margaret Elliot and her friend were able to report to the next meeting that money would be available.

The meeting was a long awaited fillip to several downcast spirits. They had already been discussing the project for a year, and even at this stage they were finding strength in numbers. One despondent member could always be cheered by another whose mood was different. This was just as well. They were to wait another year.

They registered themselves under the Industrial and Provident Legislation calling themselves Little Women. The original intention had been to rent a shop but it proved difficult to find premises. At last, late the following year, an interesting property appeared for sale. It was purchased and a deadline set for opening on 2 December to capture the seasonal trade. This left less than five weeks for repairs, decorations, rewiring, installation of a fridge and cool cabinet, and purchase of stock.

The night before

Christian Elliot laughed and tossed empty boxes at his sister. They and the other children of Little Women played beyond the counter while their mothers and some friends unpacked the stock. The wealth of items was exhilarating and the variety bewildering. Cling peaches, gravy thickeners, detergents and baby goods, biscuits and mashed peas, Shredded Wheat and Smash . . .

'Christian, put that down!'

'It's not like me, I feel like committing suicide!'

Margaret Elliot had hardly slept last night. She'd signed the biggest cheque of her life that day, £930.32 to Joblings Cash and Carry. A promised £500 loan had not come in but at least the bank manager was sympathetic and agreed to increase the overdraft to £1,500. The sums made her dizzy.

They had done everything on the cheap. Friends and family had renovated the shop. They had bought everything second-hand and now the bacon-slicer would not work. The blade was rusty and would be condemned outright by any Health Inspector, said the sales rep who urged them to invest in a new machine. Their first roll of bacon lay pressed in muslin in the cold cabinet. The cabinet hummed and gave off a dangerous smell. Who could tell what might happen in the night? And the morning — would the breadman come in time? They had not been able to get any German butter. The freezer should be on for at least twelve hours before any frozen food went into it. The flex was broken and where was that bloody masking tape?

'Christian, put that down!'

After the filling of the shelves and the labelling of the prices, their shrewd shoppers' eyes cringed at the aggressive figures they had copied out in red magic markers. Would people come? Would they buy? Would the first customer want 'half a pound of bacon, sliced thin and not too fat, please. And I'll take half a pound of butter . . . oh, haven't you got the German?'

Jimmy Austin had not come to lay the last of the lino like he promised. Here was Peter straight from work and ready for his tea. 'And who's going to get the husbands' dinner?' he asked. Margaret had fed her family and sat down for the first time that day.

'Will we never give the shop up, never, mam?' asked Vicky Elliot.

'No, never, pet!'

They had worked very hard, and not only on the shop. During the weeks before the opening volunteers had decorated the upstairs so that when the public finally came into the shop the children were ready upstairs in clean, fresh rooms.

Learning to cope

Some instinct for survival had told them that the predicted turnover of £500 was too optimistic. They therefore decided to show their commitment to the enterprise by working for nothing for the first month and going on half wages after that. They would still aim for the original wage but the immediate concern was to allow trade to pick up gradually.

Their two years' meeting together had cemented their friendship, but it was to be tested severely in the first week of their existence. Of the seven women only five lasted the first week. Family and friends were now enlisted to serve in the shop. The weather was cold and trade was poor but none of them felt confident enough to manage alone behind the counters. For Mary Evans, who had not worked for ten years, the confrontation with the customers was particularly nerve-racking.

The problem of staffing was compounded by the misery of the children upstairs. The solid fuel boiler didn't work. Radiators were cold and there was no hot water in the shop. The Health Inspector warned them about the standards of hygiene. One of the first meetings which Margaret Elliot attended after the opening was to decide on the purchase of an expensive item; £140 was to be spent on a new boiler which one of the husbands would install. Things seemed a little brighter after that. There were a few more customers, the wages were ridiculous, but the children were able to sleep in the warm and there was hot, soapy water at night to clean the bacon slicer.

Staff recruitment was a pressing problem. Their original wage of 50p seemed small incentive, but on 25p they felt their chance of attracting people was slim. They were wrong; women existed who were glad to join. An informal ruling that each recruit be known to at least two of the group and should serve a month's probation resulted in the acceptance, by the end of February, of two new members.

Takings in the shop had been increasing gradually but the main problem was how to pass experience and 'feel' for the trade on to the new rota. Customer requests were recorded haphazardly on bits of paper. Making up the gaps on the shelves was relatively simple but the policy of 'special offers' which they were bombarded with by their suppliers was confusing. They were nervous of losing profit on the one hand, and losing customers on the other. The problem was brought up repeatedly at their meetings, where it was emphasized again and again that proper checks must be made by those on duty when the stock came in and was priced, and that a wall chart of dates must show the duration of the special offers and the stages in their climb back to the original price.

The establishment of a regular rota, now that they had the full complement of seven, made dealing with stock slightly easier. Each member was able, over a period of several weeks, to experience what each different day in the shop meant: ordering frozen foods, clearing the window displays, ordering dried goods, putting out the bins. The members began to take on areas of special responsibility. One drove a car and went regularly to collect from the Cash and Carry and was paid an allowance for petrol. Another would have a general interest in frozen food. Tasks such as washing the bacon slicer and cleaning the floor seemed to go easily to those inclined to the work. Where a job appeared the women did it spontaneously, much as they would at home.

As the weeks went by trade continued to improve. They hired a Saturday girl to give them free time at weekends. By mid-March the wages had been increased to 30p an hour and a stocktaking had revealed an overall gross margin of profit on turnover of approximately 28 per cent. The premises above the shop had been let to two students and should bring in £12 a week when a damp patch had been repaired. Until that time the tenants were on half rent.

At their meetings they often congratulated themselves on their survival. 'Can you imagine life without Little Women?' was a refrain. Behind it was the sneaking suspicion that they might have built a shop on sand. 'Are we in Queer Street?' An interest in the accounts was always shown by all members and while Margaret Elliot as secretary kept the accounts for the first month and went regularly to consult with Robert Oakeshott about them, she intended to hand over to successors.

Thereafter, each Little Woman should deal with the moneys for three months at a time. Each and every one would understand the process in which they worked. That no one should develop a skill at the expense of another's ignorance was a tenet of the group. By July takings reached almost £700 a week but the overdraft became too large. The shop then 'starved' for a week, no fresh stock was ordered. As each member bought at her own discretion this control appeared the simplest to devise and enforce.

The social fund to which they had contributed 30p each week for a celebratory outing was empty. They had hired a van and gone *en masse* to a dinner and disco in South Shields. They were surviving. Perhaps they were even succeeding; they were certainly full of confidence.

The shop was winning a share of the market. It was busy and complaints and requests for goods not in stock were rare. The original aim to keep dry goods was expanded imaginatively. A wide variety of dried fruits, lentils and cereals were on sale. So were spaghetti and spices, special flour and fresh yeast. Small portions were still offered. Garlic sausage graced the cool cabinet and pâté appeared on the counter. Ice creams, lemonade and 'ket' (cheap and cheerful children's sweets) vied for space with potatoes and rubber baseball boots from Hong Kong.

The sale of fresh sandwiches was introduced. Thirty flat cakes were made into fresh meat and salad sandwiches and sold every day. The demand was for more but the hands were not available. Expansion had brought with it increased responsibilities and problems of storage. Most of the Little Women were fatigued, but by the summer their sense of achievement was enormous. They were already able to deal with salesmen and representatives and they were now experienced in dealing with national press and television. Very early on it was decided that these agencies must pay. Little Women were approached by Guinness to figure in an advertising campaign. They conscientiously sampled the product and also looked forward to the additional refrigerator which they hoped the fee would buy. Funds from their broadcasting and journalistic fees had already purchased new heaters, a new blade for the bacon slicer and new bins for food storage.

While they were flattered and pleased by the publicity it was nevertheless an added strain and one which they coped with as a group. One Little Woman broke down and cried after a session of filming for television but the rest were there to comfort her.

New roles for women

Husbands

'Since time began, women have traditionally worked in the kitchens and reared children and more or less have been unpaid servants. Up here in the North East of England things are really, in most cases, still like that. Emancipation is taking its time arriving here.'

From the outset the planning meetings were held in spite of some husbands' suspicions. Allegations that meetings were not serious but merely a chance to break out were light-hearted but

also disturbing. It was a rare husband who would stay in with sick children to allow his wife to attend a meeting. The women relied on husbands' consent and support emotionally, and also in the hard matter of financial guarantee. Their husbands signed as guarantors for the bank loan at £450 each, a sufficient sign of real support, but sometimes forgotten in the wear and tear of new challenges.

They also relied on their husbands and fathers to renovate and repair the shop cheaply. While men that are joiners and bricklayers are usually ready at the end of the day to lay their tools down, they never stinted in the help needed at the outset.

The women had predicted that they would need slowly to adapt their husbands' expectations in the home. Long habits could only be altered slowly and the inevitable disruption of these habits led to friction. A proper wage for their wives' trouble might have justified the activity and certainly sweetened some of the initial wrangles at home.

However routine the new arrangements became, the pressure from husbands was nevertheless constant. The women's own definition of duty made them think first of their husbands and children. This is not a new constraint but it was highlighted during the period of adjustment and it brought issues to the surface, where they have been discussed in a way that would not be possible without the existence of the shop. The shop gave the women legitimacy; in the context of their outside responsibilities they could rearrange their older concerns.

The husband who most strenuously pressed his wife to leave the shop was also the one who, for the first time, washed the children's nappies before his wife got home from work. The husband that would not allow his wife to go on the celebratory dinner and dance outing became an item on the agenda and the target for a subtle process of reorientation.

Children

The children continued to make the same demands on their mothers. Sudden sickness cannot be predicted and in the initial weeks of trading the children's welfare was a major issue. Cold weather and the lack of proper heating meant that the children were unable to sleep. Furniture was inadequate and children took their meals perched on armchairs. Early meetings put the expenditure of £140 for a boiler as an essential item however unpalatable the cost. Chairs and tables were required. Posters put up on the walls and plasticine trodden into the carpet showed that the nursery had reached the required level of comfort; it now had to divert and control a set of children whose demands were more those of a small class in school than those of a family. The friction of children unused to one another's company was soon smoothed away, but more children can mean more trouble and there were days when the more disruptive of the children would create more havoc than would have been tolerated in some of their homes. Nevertheless, some mothers dealt well with the children and, depending on their energies, could serve the obligatory one hour in the nursery or longer. Those mothers who felt the need to escape childish chatter could do so down in the shop. This seems a natural process, simple and productive.

The autumn attendance at nursery school for the younger children taxed the ingenuity of the group. Many arrangements had to be made so that each mother could escort her children to the new surroundings and do so until they were confident enough to be taken there by anyone.

These responsibilities were not new for the women. What was new was their incorporation in a group activity. The proprietary nature of their involvement in the shop was now established and generated a strict sense of loyalty to one another. The Little Women were now experiencing the treadmill of duty, which in factory work they could avoid by taking a day off sick. In their present work their intimacy did not allow for deception of this kind.

Shopkeeping

An area of intense concern was that of stocking the shop and predicting customer demands. While their knowledge of shopping was a useful base it did not prepare them for the intricacies of pricing goods. Special offers were a particular problem. These items offered at a reduced rate for a limited period needed very careful monitoring, which the rota found difficult to effect. The timing of the arrival of 'special' stock and its gradual return to 'normal' prices was too complicated a procedure for a work pattern that was fragmented.

In the shop the special responsibility of collecting stock was taken by the member who had transport. She was paid for the trip she made each week to the Cash and Carry. As the bulk of goods increased another member was coopted to help her. The day before the collection the women on duty in the shop checked the shelves and prepared a list of items required. On the day of collection this was checked again and after discussion added to or altered. The goods were collected and checked and priced. As the member who performed this role was on a rota for two consecutive days she was able to control the pricing and unpacking.

The tasks of each day were now regularized so that each woman performed them once or twice during a three-week cycle. The responsibility to think of ways of developing the shop was likewise open to all. Personal preferences played a part in responsibilities. One was interested primarily in frozen goods, another in dried goods, another in cooked meats, and so on. In drudgery there was a good-natured ruling that Margaret Elliot would not wash the bacon slicer more than once a week. There were women, however, who preferred this task to others and so the jobs were usually done as the need arose.

The pattern of work was to open the shop and nursery simultaneously at 9.00 a.m. Fresh sandwiches were prepared for 10.00 a.m. The shop stayed open lunchtimes and on Wednesday, which was early closing in Sunderland. It opened all day on Saturday. The burden of this routine was alleviated by the hiring of a 'Saturday girl' who came all day during the winter but opted to do just the mornings in the summer.

The tasks for each day were written up on wall charts. The diary indicated the regular jobs: Monday — renew window display; Tuesday — rejects back to the wholesaler; Wednesday — prepare order for the market; Thursday — collection from the market; Friday — bin collection; every day — bread and pie man.

Wall charts showed the date on which special offers were bought, the duration of the time for reduced prices and intervals of price increases. A list of goods taken for consumption at lunch or tea time was kept and members reminded at meetings of the importance of paying for these as they were taken. There was a fear that profits could be nibbled away unnoticed.

Information was generally conveyed easily. Margaret and three other members lived round the corner and shopped as customers every day even if they were not on duty. The three members who lived further from the shop were on the phone and easily contacted if the need arose. The bookkeeping role was taken in turn, with each member doing the accounts for three months at a time. Margaret Elliot chose as her successor the person with the most clerical experience. As each member's turn approached she spent several evenings in the home of the girl dealing with accounts and watched as the entries were made. In one instance a member insisted that only by watching the process would she feel competent to take over.

While the customers certainly seemed partisan and enjoyed the support they gave, the publicity of the aims of the shop occasionally gave rise to: 'I thought this was supposed to be a cheap shop!' While they wished to trade fairly and generously, the women found the motive to maximize their profit was sometimes in conflict with this.

The provision of whole flours, yeast and a variety of dried goods attracted a clientele that travelled to buy them. Any slack time was spent weighing out and wrapping cheese and dried goods. This preparation meant that the service speeded up. As custom increased this efficiency was forced on the women.

The strength of the group

Margaret Elliot's leadership

Their confidence resided in the harmonious nature of the group. This developed from the leadership of Margaret Elliot and the closeness of her sister-in-law and her lifelong friend. These three constituted a nucleus and were in the project from its earliest beginning. They were indivisible and took on recruits whose work attributes could never shake their loyalty.

The nature of Margaret Elliot's leadership was pervasive. While she was self-effacing her concern was seen and felt to be total. As secretary she was the contact with the outside world. Not only the outside world of banking, cooperative organization and television and radio, but more immediately the friendship of Robert Oakeshott, promoter of Sunderlandia. His support was always in the background and for months of early trading Margaret discussed matters with him on a regular weekly basis. The financial calculations of a preliminary stock-taking done in March 1977 were done for Little Women by Robert Oakeshott.

When visitors came to the shop if Margaret was present, she dealt with them. She was interested to do this and the group probably deferred to her ability to deal with questions; she no longer felt threatened by such events, while most of the group were still apprehensive.

Agendas for the meetings which were held every fortnight were drawn up informally by Margaret and others presented items at the meeting itself. While every member contributed and felt able to suggest and disagree, Margaret's chairmanship of the meetings kept them to business matters until they were settled. The meetings were not merely concerned with business, however; each member took her own drink, cider or beer, and it was a social occasion which covered as much gossip, personal anecdotes, airing of worries and advice as could be crammed into three hours. One of the satisfactions claimed by the group was the high level of intimacy which they developed through these meetings; it was reassuring and comforting for them all. If Margaret Elliot influenced the group more than their equal status would suggest, she did so by listening and learning; she invited contributions and so strengthened morale.

Friction

Harmony resulted also from the way in which conflicts were dealt with. Friction arose from outside the group in the demands, prohibitions or complaints of husbands and the behaviour and health of the children. This usually resulted in crises of confidence in the women involved, who had to question their loyalty to the group and risk disturbing the delicate balance of energies there. The difficulty of dealing with the children was acknowledged by the ruling that each recruit to Little Women must bring her children with her. In this way a possible source of recrimination and comparison is guarded against.

The behaviour of certain children threatened the equality of the group and they tried to recruit women with, as it were, equal burdens. A woman with very underdisciplined children was not an equal proposition; she could make more demands on the group than those with tractable children, who would in turn be infected by the habits of the hooligans. This happened with the most recent recruit, but the problem was dealt with.

Internally the conflict showed itself in recruitment of staff. When there were only five in the group the discussions showed that jealousy and resentment existed if one relative or friend was preferred to another. The recruitment of the 'Saturday girl' was an instance. She was the girl who baby-sat regularly for one member of the group. She was watched carefully and prolonged conversations between her and her sponsor were noted and remarked on. Another member developed a style of conduct during the early months which even the customers noted. She was referred to as 'the manageress' and this led to a severe crisis in which the caucus of Margaret Elliot, May Evans and Sandra Robertson found that working with her was imposing an intolerable strain on them. All the women resented being told what to do by a colleague. They resented the assumption of superiority, which may just have been due to energy and enthusiasm on the part of the offender. The matter was never dealt with directly, but several personal remarks served the purpose. The girl changed her demeanour and also lessened her

commitment. She went on to serve only two days. Her previous history indicated that her energy and drive often resulted in her working too hard and not being able to adopt a steady pace. The response of the group to her conduct and her final capitulation could have been the solution that all were looking for. It certainly resulted in a much happier and more productive atmosphere in which 'the manageress' was regarded with more affection and esteem than ever, tempered with only a residue of suspicion.

Personal development

The personal development of each member varied. Margaret Elliot's achievement was the most outstanding. In her capacity as secretary she became used to dealing with outside agencies. She approached community action groups for help in supervising the nursery during the summer. She travelled to London to attend ICOM meetings regularly and the experience of independent initiative was novel and exciting. She took driving lessons so that there would be more than one member with transport at her disposal. The project, which she started, received national attention and interest and was widely acclaimed as a success. She was wary of such sweeping praise and guarded against future failure by insisting on the priority of the business and the details of running it, which she saw as crucial to its well-being.

Mary Evans faced the rigours of work after ten years at home looking after her children and to achieve that was her main intention. For the rest, the confidence that came from working with Little Women spilled over into a greater interest in themselves, their appearance and their general well-being.

The novelty of running their own shop may have worn off during the first six months and certainly there were signs of fatigue. Margaret Elliot was exhausted and her doctor prescribed a tranquillizer; she found its effects too soporific and gave it up. The fact that after eight months they had dealt with problems and developed an expertise and conduct together meant that they faced the future with some confidence. They had shown themselves to the public. They offered their analysis of what was needed and they seemed to have been correct in their assumptions. They were proved capable and clever in a public sphere, perhaps for the first time in their lives.

Postscript. Three years after it opened Little Women sold the shop as a going concern and paid off all their loans. Although takings in the shop had declined slightly so there was some financial pressure, this was not an important factor. Their children were now at school, and as Margaret Elliot said, 'We had put our lot into it and we were very tired.' It was time for something different. Margaret Elliot took a course in Community and Youth Work at Sunderland Polytechnic and played an active role in the Northern area of ICOM. During this time the Little Women group continued to meet and when last heard of they had all taken training programmes in preparation for the launch of a new cooperative venture under her leadership.

3 The Launch of the Centaur

A.N. *Other* with *R. Paton*

This case study has been reconstructed from some of the material contained in an internal company report. For obvious reasons the motor manufacturer and the individuals concerned have been disguised. Centaur is the name of the new model, and is also used to refer to the assembly facility which produces it. The Centaur is a replacement for the Paravel, and is being produced in a brand new section of the Workville Plant which also produces the Taurus and is one of a number of plants across the country. In dealing with problems, managers involved in producing Centaur have to liaise with specialist support services, either elsewhere on the large Workville site or based at the Company's administrative centre. The report was prepared by a member of one such specialist department.

Introduction

This report has been prepared in the hope that the problems described can be avoided or reduced when new models are launched in the future. As a measure of the seriousness of the problems, it can be reported that those involved estimated it was costing £14,000 to produce a car we were selling for £6,000. Of course everyone expects to lose money for the first three months while snags are ironed out, but it is nearly a year since the first line started and it may well take a further six months before we are making the car for a profit. Problems of this magnitude cannot be dealt with simply by changing the personnel concerned, as seems, at times, to have been the main response of the senior managers concerned. A simplified organization chart (Figure 3.1) indicates the departments and personnel involved.

Planning

Nobody had any recent experience of starting up a new facility and building a new car. Those people who remembered the Paravel remembered it as it affected their former, lower-level, job positions. Moreover, with measured day-work, stronger unions and a larger organization, the industrial relations scene had altered since the early 1960s.

In the early pre-operational days of Centaur, the plant director had to run the project along with his day-to-day responsibilities for Paravel and Taurus production. Since emphasis is always placed on output, the 'tomorrow's problems' of Centaur were regarded as of less consequence and could, or would have to, await resolution in the future. Since each departmental head was responsible for identifying and resolving his department's problems, nobody looked at the kind of problems that would be likely to develop at functional interfaces. Furthermore, since managers had little experience of solving the kind of problems that

a new project creates, as distinct from the kind of problems that occur in the day-to-day running of an established plant, it was unlikely that they would uncover many of the problems that arose when the plant started up.

Plans were made without reference to the finance needed to carry them out; hence some parts of the project have not been implemented. For example, racks necessary for the efficient subassembly of steering columns have still not been introduced. Maintenance problems provide a further example; when planning it was decided to provide maintenance outposts of fitters and mechanics so that response to equipment failures would be faster than if it was necessary to rely on the major workshop. These fitters/mechanics would have their own sets of tools and would work in relative independence from the main shop. This plan remains to be implemented, not because of industrial relations problems but because the finance is not available.

Insufficient regard was paid to final finish and rectification areas. Parking presented one problem: where to put unfinished cars that people needed to work on. Charlie Simmons (assembly line superintendent) feels in the light of experience that the objective of building quality into the car on the line was too ambitious. He feels that the planners decided on the level of quality without knowing how it could be achieved.

Another idea was to have a special area for the subassembly of facias but this was dropped. Facias are now assembled on a 'hotch-potch' basis and consideration is to be given once more to the idea of a special assembly area. Industrial engineers say it takes forty-five minutes to assemble a facia, the operators take about ninety minutes, while the former plant director says it can be done in twelve (that's the time he says it took him when he put one together for his own knowledge).

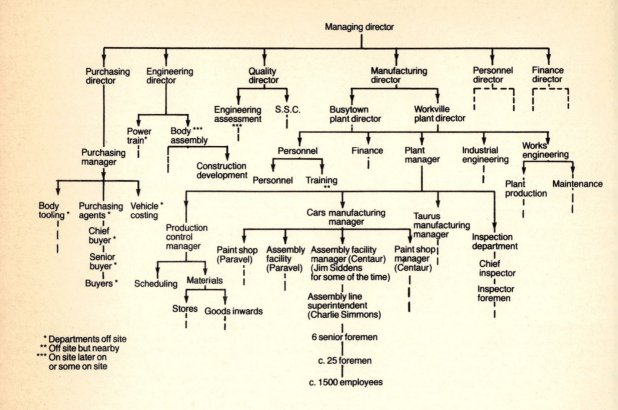

Figure 3.1 *Organization chart for Centaur.*

After they had been told of the plans for the factory — rest-area lockers, seat lockers by the track, tables and so on — operators and supervisors were disappointed to find that money for these had run out. Furniture was 'borrowed' from other parts of the plant.

My predecessor, it is alleged, promised the foremen offices. When the plant first started they complained about not having offices and threatened to go on strike. A review by works engineers took place and they suggested building offices in various parts of the factory. Finance said it was too expensive and couldn't be done. Personnel looked into the matter and were advised by me not to support the foremen's application on the grounds that the foremen should be 'on line', where they have desks and cupboards anyway, supporting their men. Six months later, Jim Siddens (then assembly facility manager) and the plant director agreed to build offices for foremen, but of course we don't know what was forgone by building the offices, since there was no attempt at opportunity costing. Now that foremen have been given offices they want furniture for them, but there is no money available so more 'borrowing' is taking place.

When foremen first entered the facility they had no telephones. This meant that before they could seek assistance in response to their problems, they had to find a telephone or walk to where assistance was available, perhaps a quarter of a mile away or more.

Management style

Neither the car manufacturing manager nor the assembly facility manager were trained in starting up a project. The plant was initially run along lines suggested by their experience in Paravel.

After the plant had been running in low volume (one track) for two months the assembly facility manager was replaced by Jim Siddens. Jim was an ex-HQ man, more extroverted than his predecessor, and he had had some success in overcoming launch problems in his area in the preceding months. Jim Siddens wanted to avoid 'people problems' so he discussed the problems occurring in Centaur with senior shop stewards. This was, so legend has it, done over drinks in the bar. His style of management however irritated those above him and those below. Foremen and superintendents would sometimes hear about management decisions from shop stewards. And supervisors felt that their decisions were likely to be overruled by more senior management (Jim) and so did not push discipline and control hard enough. In part this was due to their lack of experience. Foremen would suspend people or take them off the clock for breaking one rule or another, but then find themselves overruled because they were procedurally out of order. They didn't know the disciplinary procedure because it hadn't been taught to them.

Jim's style of management was participative, in that he regularly discussed current and future events with shop stewards, but it wasn't sufficiently participative in that foremen were (or thought they were) left out. After the publication of the management communications brochures, foremen were brought into discussions with their senior foremen, who have a face-to-face opportunity to discuss the operations of the plant with Jim. Increasingly Jim began to run the plant without the car's manufacturing manager, who was left to tidy up and run Paravel. At the time the plant manager was replaced, Jim was still seen as the key man. More recently Jim Siddens has also been replaced and this has meant a further change in management style — though his successor has at least succeeded in getting control over support services.

The changes in management and styles of management have led to cynicism and confusion, according to Charlie Simmons, the assembly line superintendent. At first emphasis was placed on getting out large volumes of cars; then it changed, after complaints about quality (Centaur has the lowest quality rating of any of our cars), to improving standards. Now the emphasis is once more on volume. Disciplinary standards have also wavered between attempting to be strict, to more easy-going exhortation.

Personnel and industrial relations

The position of clock stations hasn't helped discipline. These are positioned on the external walls, some distance from foremen. Because of the large numbers of people that foremen have had to supervise, they find it difficult to remember all of the people working in their section. Continuing transfers of labour throughout the plant, to cope with increasing volumes and the rectification work which was above expected levels, has not helped this problem of familiarity. As a result people have been leaving early in large numbers or have been clocked in by their work mates, but have not attended work. Because the lines are heavily overmanned, their absences have tended not to disrupt production. Security officers decided it wasn't part of their job to check people to see if they were leaving early.

The pressures for increased production exerted on local management by HQ improved the bargaining position of the shop stewards. Because management hadn't the time (or perhaps the skills) to develop certain features of running the plant, shop stewards stepped into the breach and then tried to maintain their new-found position. For example, job selection for each employee was carried out by the shop steward on the basis of seniority. In general they were quite sensible about this (according to all the superintendents I spoke to) although there were some isolated cases of difficulty. However, as the plant grew in operational size greater opportunities arose for less experienced people to take on more highly-skilled tasks. Also, many people having learnt to do one task would be 'shifted' to another task so that the learning curve was continually extended.

Personnel recruited, from outside, quite a number of people who were unsuitable for track work, and who then had to be found alternative work by superintendents. It was not that the skill level was too low but that the physical suitability of certain people was in question. Some people had heart conditions which although not immediately serious meant that they could be given certificates of excuse for certain types of work by their doctors. Others were deaf, too old or too fat. All of this contributed to the movement of labour.

Shop stewards arranged for transfer of labour from Paravel to Centaur because management hadn't actually got any plans on how to do this. This also contributed to overmanning. Personnel were recruiting when superintendents didn't know what to do with the labour that they had got. People would be released from working in Paravel without reference to the numbers coming through the gates. The supervisor with whom I shared an office once complained that he had two hundred men arriving and nothing for them to do.

When the Centaur plant first opened up, food supply was inadequate. Ten-minute breaks became twenty minutes as people queued up at the buffet and automat and the boiler. Delays were made worse by amenities — including toilets — being sited some distance from the working area, so encouraging people to add walking time into their breaks. Industrial relations were not improved by allowing operators to queue for ten or fifteen minutes for food when they then found that the buffet had run out.

Charlie Simmons says that it was normal to spend time discussing the shortage of bacon sandwiches with shop stewards. Since, at this time, he was the only member of management in the new works, his time was particularly valuable. Some people went to the older, more familiar, parts of the plant to get food. In the initial stages of launch people in the engine dress section at the furthest end of the factory had no seats, the buffet was hundreds of yards away and so was the boiler. They brought their own food to work and did the best they could. Had it not been that they were almost all new and didn't know what they should expect, industrial relations problems would probably have arisen. Industrial relations problems (such as storekeepers who say that they should have safety clothing) have contributed to the inadequate performance of the stores — but manufacturing also think that the stores are undermanned.

Training

There were inadequacies in the amount, type and timing of training offered to people who were to work on and organize the operation of the Centaur project. Many people at middle management level (superintendents) and at lower levels (foremen and senior foremen) received training in how to operate specific aspects of the plant some time before they actually needed to use it. By the time that the plant became operational, perhaps more than twelve months after training, some of the skills and knowledge imparted was no longer available. It had either been forgotten or the people had changed their jobs.

Senior foremen, foremen and superintendents alleged that they received no training on how to start up and run a new assembly area (the paint shop superintendent acknowledges that he did, but he isn't paint shop superintendent any more). The training school says that training was given before Centaur opened but if people changed their jobs or the project fell behind schedule it isn't their fault if the skills and knowledge aren't available. To my knowledge, new foremen and new senior foremen were selected and employed without being trained at all; any training was given months later. A senior foreman transferred from Paravel had to start the second line with 50 per cent fresh labour, two experienced foremen, and not one person (including himself) who knew how to put the car together, only bits of it. He learnt by going to construction development and building one himself. Training have a record of him attending their courses. My conjecture is that they tried to teach people how to run a factory, not how to start one up.

Foremen are responsible for training at Workville. In the early days foremen might be responsible for supervising sixty to seventy people (it is presently about forty). Since the new foremen had had no training, and the older ones had had no training in starting up or running this particular facility, their ability to train others was somewhat limited. Hence the training school recruited three operators to train people in carrying out skilled operations. A leading spokesman for foremen also applied for one of these positions but didn't get it. When one training school recruit boasted that he didn't have to clock in whilst foremen did, the foremen went on strike. The trainers were removed from Centaur; thereafter whatever training was given was once again provided by operators or foremen.

Insufficient numbers of people were trained to maintain the plant and equipment. Those who were trained were not always available to repair breakdowns and although maintenance workers in general are quite highly skilled, their unfamiliarity with the equipment led to delays in repairing breakdowns; electricians in particular took longer to repair damage than they probably would have if they had been more familiar with the equipment. Little preventative maintenance has been undertaken, except on transfer machines. Of course, new tools should not break down; but if untrained and inexperienced labour is used, what else can be expected?

Liaison with service departments

Service personnel outside Centaur (and some inside the facility) were uncertain who did what because appointments were not announced. Some people didn't know where to go anyway. No-one told them about the maps on the facility walls — let alone where they were located. Hence people did not know where or whom they were visiting. Charlie Simmons, as the first superintendent in the plant, wasn't able to acquire support services at all easily.

Nor was Charlie, as a young, relatively new (previously he was a graduate trainee) and unannounced member of management, able to use the informal network of aid and support that grows up in every plant to supplement or supplant the formal system. But the original assembly facility manager, a well-known, long-service employee, had similar difficulties, so this could be because people in other departments were used to doing the familiar and Centaur was still of lower importance, in terms of production, than Paravel or Taurus. Also, transport from other parts of the plant to Centaur is generally regarded as necessary, whilst people would often walk to older parts of the plant. Thus it was easier for them to solve nearby and familiar problems for people they knew, rather than try to solve more

distant, Centaur difficulties. Jim Siddens and the new plant manager complained to me about support problems and asked if there was some way of integrating them into manufacturing responsibilities. I told them how to do it (by setting up regular lateral face-to-face communication) but probably because of political reasons, what efforts they made weren't that successful.

Suppliers' quality was poor and some supplies inadequate; liaison between purchasing and goods inwards, who check deliveries for quality problems, is poor. Liaison between goods inwards and manufacturing is good, except that goods inwards aren't always in a position to give the kind of assistance manufacturing needs. Liaison between manufacturing and purchasing is to all intents non-existent.

Communication between engineering and purchasing is not always very good. Modifications take some time to be implemented by suppliers. Vehicle costing re-assess the cost of each modified component over thirty-five pence and purchasing must ensure that the new cost and tooling charges are within estimates before allowing the supplier to make a modification to his tooling. Financial approval is also required. If purchasing had some way of knowing which modifications were urgent from a manufacturing point of view this system could be circumvented in most cases.

Instead of telling the supplier by telling purchasing informally, Charlie Simmons uses the formal system (so do the other superintendents). When I have spoken to purchasing about some of manufacturing's problems they told me that it takes about six weeks to get information from Workville on their desks. If a foreman or an inspector at Busytown has a problem, for example, he goes and talks to the buyer. But at Workville the superintendents don't know any buyers. Since buyers get quality complaints from SSC (suppliers standards control) or engineering assessment or goods inwards in paper form there is not the pressure placed on them to resolve suppliers' quality problems that face-to-face meetings with superintendents or inspectors can provide. Anyway, purchasing don't always hear about quality problems — unless every delivery is faulty or the track stops or looks as though it's going to.

Engineering were asked to provide model variants before they had got the basic vehicle right; thus they were overworked. Their modifications system was not properly coordinated between manufacturing, quality, purchasing and the supplier. When manufacturing needed to change a design they used the formal system, raising a modification request note. These went into a system overloaded with design engineering sponsored 'mod notes' and no-one seemed to be able easily to trace any particular note. Manufacturing didn't always know who to approach to get around the system for urgent jobs. For instance, it is standard practice in many plants to get verbal approval for urgent design changes and let the paperwork follow in due course. This was not always done in the case of Centaur. Manufacturing didn't always know which delivery of components contained modified parts nor did they always know when to expect them.

Design engineering, during the initial launch period, were being reorganized and everyone was still trying to find their feet in the new organization. This only added to Centaur problems. Also the engineers placed a ban on working in Centaur in the period during which the car was launched and production expanded. After six months some engineers started working in Centaur, almost full time, and this has been of enormous advantage in resolving design/manufacturing problems.

At the time that Centaur was just beginning to get off the ground, Workville purchasing was relocated as part of the company reorganization. This had serious consequences. Firstly, though some staff did move to Busytown, all but two left or retired fairly quickly. The new people concerned didn't know Workville or its method of supply, inspection or design modification.

Secondly, and much more seriously, the run down of assembly tooling (part of the purchasing department) preparatory to its transfer to Busytown meant that the availability of checking jigs was poor and delays in modifications to these jigs also occurred. Buyers had no experience in procuring checking jigs, so the task fell onto the few remaining tooling engineers. The lack of availability of checking jigs affected supplies. Some suppliers had difficulty in accurately determining necessary standards and inspectors found it difficult to inspect incoming components. Some jigs are not only essential for gauging accuracy but are an essential part of the production process; hence quality suffered when jigs were not available. In the past Paravel were responsible for making their own jigs; resources for this, especially when building a completely new car with constant modifications, are now no longer adequate. Even when suppliers had produced a jig, the testing engineers didn't always know (in the beginning) where the completed jig should be sent (to engineering assessment, not inspection). As a result there were serious delays in getting approval for supplies. Buyers waited weeks to find out if a supplier's components were acceptable. In addition, the engineering assessment and laboratory area did not seem to have been expanded sufficiently to cater for the demands of approving thousands of components for a new car which was constantly being modified. Nor did they have sufficient clerical support.

4 Planning in Openshire

M. Floyd

The following material presents a fictionalized account of a planning controversy. Its purpose is not to explore the particular planning issues involved, but rather to use the controversy as a focus for considering the nature of strategic planning, the way in which an organization charged with planning goes about its work, and the sorts of difficulties it faces.

The following material is provided:

Item A Extract from the *Edgington Advertiser* of 10 February 1980

Item B Extract from the *Edgington Advertiser* of 2 March 1980

Item C The Structure Plan Policies for Edgington

Item D Extract from the *Edgington Advertiser* of 10 May 1980

Item E Memo from Mike Crail to Jean Grimsdyke of 20 May 1980

Item F (i) Memo from Jean Grimsdyke to Dick Roach of 22 May 1980
        (ii) Telephone message to Dick Roach

        (iii) Memo from Dick Roach to Jean Grimsdyke of 27 May 1980

Item G (i) Letter from Dick Roach to Ted Peel of 29 May 1980
        (ii) Letter from Ted Peel to Dick Roach 7 June 1980
        (iii) Letter from Dick Roach to Nigel Glemp of 8 June 1980
        (iv) Letter from Nigel Glemp to Dick Roach of 18 June 1980

Item H Extract from Transcript of the Public Inquiry into the Edgington Bypass (22 June 1980)

Item A Extract from the *Edgington Advertiser* of 10 February 1980

Bypass Needed to Keep Jobs

The Bypass is essential if Edgington's shopping and commercial areas are to avoid being choked to death. The only other alternative, according to Jean Grimsdyke, the County Planning Officer, is for large factories, shops and offices to close up and move out of town. So after 50 years of debate and procrastination something new has to be done to keep Edgington alive.

The first sign of something getting done has been the hive of activity at the old Town Hall over the last few days. No! It's not because the Council can't afford its new glass palace in Market Street. The Public Inquiry into the Bypass opens there today with a blaze of publicity. TV crews were in the High Street by nine o'clock. They left after filming the arrival of the Inspector and some of the objectors.

Some of the officials looked worried at the number of objectors filing their opposition to the scheme. Some recent inquiries have witnessed stormy scenes of protest over the criteria used to decide whether to build new roads. Since the oil crisis, the objectors say, there hasn't been the same growth in motor traffic, so the new roads are unnecessary and an infringement of local amenity. They have a good case here in Edgington. The bypass was first mooted almost fifty years ago. Twenty years later the Edgington Borough Development Plan contained a proposal for a bypass. Then in 1968 with traffic congestion becoming even more of a serious problem, especially in the city centre, a Transportation Study was initiated jointly by the County Council and the Edgington Borough Council. This study concluded that even with improved public transport and car parking constraint in the city centre, there would still be an urgent need for a bypass. Some of the objectors are certain to say that since 1973 and the oil-price rises, this study is largely out of date and irrelevant.

However the Council has gone ahead on the basis of this conclusion and in 1978 appointed consultants to examine the feasibility of alternative routes for the bypass. This resulted in the public exhibition of the two favoured routes three years ago. Ironically it was one of the last major issues the Council dealt with just before it moved out of the old Town Hall; now they have to go back to settle the matter once and for all.

It seems certain the Council will not waver in its support of the bypass, especially since the Tories regained control last year. The bypass was incorporated into the structure plan submitted to the Minister of the Environment. Support was affirmed in later 'Annual Position Statements' which made use of data emerging from the continuing Transportation Study. No one seems more committed to the bypass than Jean Grimsdyke. 'Take it away', she says, 'and major changes in the structure plan would be needed'.

Bypass needed to prevent economic decline

In particular she points out that the bypass had a 'vital role' to play in maintaining both the viability of the local Edgington economy and of its urban environment. Without the bypass congestion in the city centre would become even worse and this would eventually — if it had not already done so — lead to the commercial decline of the area.

I asked her about the traffic restraint and management measures the traffic engineers had recently brought in. Were they not working then? She insisted that they were, in fact, proving extremely effective, but on their own they are not enough, she says. Without the bypass the only way of reducing traffic to acceptable levels, and preventing Edgington's shopping and commercial areas from being 'choked to death' is for many factories, offices and large shops to close down or move out of town. Jean Grimsdyke conceded that a massive investment in public transport might 'do the trick' but that the level of investment needed was much greater than that required by the bypass and certainly beyond the limited resources of the county council. At the very least, she argued, it would be necessary to restrain still further the growth of jobs in Edgington and to allow more residential development, so as to reduce the need for workers to commute into the city from outside. Neither of these alternatives is regarded as acceptable by the council.

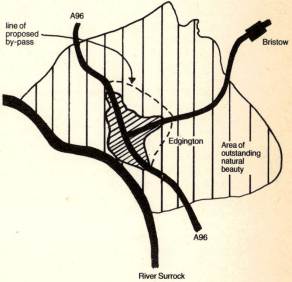

Item B   Extract from the *Edgington*
Advertiser **of 2 March 1980**

NOW IT'S TOO MANY JOBS!
Jobs Versus the Environment

The biggest problem facing Edgington over the next 10 years is having too many new jobs! This emerged at the Planning Inquiry yesterday as the Council set out its reasoning behind the proposed bypass. Apparently there will be an extra 8,700 jobs in Edgington over the next 10 years — good news for those on the dole queue. But bad news for the traffic planners. The problem, according to the Council, is that the people taking up these jobs will mostly live in the outlying towns and villages. The extra congestion caused by them travelling in to work each day could be the last straw for Edgington's traffic congestion.

The Chamber of Commerce greeted the prospect of more jobs with obvious pleasure. However they were obviously not so pleased by the disclosure that the planners aim to partly solve their problems by diverting new jobs from Edgington to the new town of Bristow. Bristow was developed to try to help disperse the population from the industrial conurbation further north. However the concern over inner city decay has led to a reversal of this policy by the Government who are now aiming to redevelop the inner city environment and keep the population there. The change means that there is a real danger that the infrastructure in Bristow New Town, the roads, and other general facilities, will not be fully used. So, argue the planners, let's kill two birds with one stone and shift some jobs from Edgington to Bristow.

But this isn't the only problem the planners face. Although we may often take it for granted, Openshire is a very beautiful county — especially when compared to those areas, no more than fifty miles to the north, whose scenery is devastated by the industrial developments of the nineteenth century and whose social landscapes are now blotted by levels of unemployment that make our own figure of just 8 per cent look insignificant. How our neighbours envy our picturesque hills and river valleys, Edgington's glorious cathedral and, perhaps even more, its thriving commercial sector and the carpet industry that makes us a major economic centre.

Unfortunately — at least for us — our neighbours do not just look enviously across our borders. Increasingly they are packing up their belongings and moving south, putting pressure on our housing, increasing our unemployment and, thanks to the many elderly people who come here to retire, Openshire is fast becoming burdened with a disproportionate number of old people. Thus in 1971 over a quarter of the population were over 65 — and in some areas they constituted nearly a third, or double the average proportion for the country as a whole. An unbalanced population is also an unstable one, so that, left to itself, the population of Openshire will decline and this could have an adverse effect on the supply of labour for commerce and industry.

This is where the jobs forecast comes in. Planning applications for office and industrial development show a likely increase of 8,700 jobs by 1991. This is a bit higher than another estimate, based on analysing trends in particular sectors, which comes out at 8,000 jobs. A reduction in unemployment in Edgington — currently only 7,000 — might go some way towards meeting this demand, but it is thought that a substantial increase in the total population, or in the amount of commuting into Edgington from outlying towns and villages, is inevitable. Furthermore a continuing fall in activity rates (the proportion of the population who are available for work) is likely to exacerbate the problem. A closely related problem is that of the level of wages in the country. In spite of the outward appearance of affluence and the low levels of unemployment, average wages are below the figure for the country as a whole, due to the low wages received by workers in Edgington's tourist industry.

Outside of the Edgington area the problems are seen to be the reverse, with employment failing to grow as rapidly as the workforce. At the same time there is considerable potential for additional housing development, which would lead to further increases in the population. This is why the planners in Openshire are seeking to divert some of the new industrial and commercial development from Edgington to Bristow.

The Structure Plan to the Rescue

Under the 1968 Town and Country Planning Act the planners in Openshire are required to submit to central government their proposals for dealing with problems such as these and, in particular, their policies regarding the future use of land, in the form of a structure plan for the county. In approaching this task the planners were faced with a number of difficulties. Foremost amongst these was the simple fact that there already existed a whole range of policies — not all of them publicised or even explicit — which bore upon the issues outlined earlier. There is always a temptation — and professional planners are perhaps more susceptible to it than most — to offer the kind of helpful suggestion made by the Irishman who, asked the way to Dublin, told the weary traveller that I would never have started from here! Our planners managed however to resist such a temptation and were especially mindful of the existing policy framework and the way it had evolved over the years.

They were very conscious too of the many constraints that limited considerably the options open to them. Perhaps the most significant of these was the designation of much of the area surrounding Edgington as an Area of Outstanding Natural Beauty. This would make it extremely difficult to permit any further expansion of the city.

They were aware too that apart from Bristow New Town the scope for diverting large-scale growth to other areas in the county was going to be limited to an increasing extent by the problems of financing the additional infrastructure of new roads, water supply, sewerage, schools and so on.

One possible source of additional labour for Edgington could be the towns outside Openshire in neighbouring Downshire. The Downshire plan is however less advanced than that of Openshire, and whether or not these towns will have a surplus of labour is not at all clear. Such a solution would in any case run up against the problems of coping with a large increase in commuting and traffic. It was generally felt that traffic congestion in Edgington was already unacceptable and that any major new road-building within the city area would encounter a great deal of opposition, on account of the large number of historic sites and buildings in Edgington.

The plan therefore came down in favour of restricting severely any further growth of housing and jobs in Edgington. The plan recognized though that outstanding permissions for industrial and commercial development would inevitably mean a growth of jobs in the short term and that additional housing would be needed in any case.

Thus while restricting the growth of jobs and population as much as possible, the planners were forced to accept that some growth would take place and that this will inevitably mean an increase in traffic in Edgington. According to Jean Grimsdyke traffic in the town is already at a level such that the economy of the town is threatened. If further increase is not accommodated or diverted, the consequences will, she says, be catastrophic.

A large number of amenity groups do not agree. They accept much of the reasoning behind the structure plan but question the claim that the bypass can solve the problem outlined above. Much hinges on quite technical arguments, including the interpretation of computer calculations. Hopefully though the enquiry will bring these out and make them comprehensible.

Item C   The Structure Plan Policies for Edgington

EMPLOYMENT POLICY

The policy is as follows:

It is intended to restrain employment increase in Edgington by means of the following policies, which will be relaxed if and when there is no longer any likelihood of a substantial rise in the total number of jobs in the area.

(a) *Offices and research establishments, and premises for Local Government, Health Authority, statutory undertakings, Government Departments, other public bodies, local business and professional services.* These types of development will normally only be acceptable where the predominant activity of the firm, business or organization is to serve all or part of the area. Moreover, any permission given will be restricted to a total increase in floor area not exceeding 50 per cent over that occupied by the firm, business or organization within the area on 1st January 1978. Additional provision will not be permitted where the cumulative total would exceed this 50 per cent increase within ten years of the date of the first permission.

(b) *Manufacturing industry and warehousing.* This type of development will be acceptable only when it is required by industrialists already located within Edgington whose proposals will not result in more than 100 new jobs or 2,000 square metres, whichever is the greater, or where the firm is not located within the area and the proposals will not result in more than 50 new jobs, or 1,000 square metres, whichever is the greater. In every case, the site or buildings must be allocated or suitable for industry and a further expansion within ten years will not be permitted.

(c) *Tourism.* Proposals which individually or collectively lead to an increase of more than 175 new jobs will be specially considered by the County Council in the light of the current employment and housing situation.

Wherever a proposal is acceptable the applicant or the owner will be expected to enter into an agreement not to sell or lease any premises to be vacated for a purpose which would lead to employment growth of a type prohibited by this policy.

HOUSING POLICIES

In 1969 the preservation policies of the former local planning authorities were strengthened by the designation of the Area of Outstanding Natural Beauty by the Countryside Commission. It is, therefore, intended that the following shall be readopted.

The general policy approach, common to all towns in the area, is that further encroachment of development on the Area of Outstanding Natural Beauty should be prohibited except in the areas mentioned below.

Whilst the number of jobs is increasing, the housing problem will be aggravated unless more land is released for development. Certain land is already committed for housing.

It is intended to release for development, land at Bradbury. The boundaries of this land and density of building will be settled during the preparation of local plans.

On the other hand, some land which was previously allocated for residential development on approved Town Maps, is no longer considered suitable and is therefore being deleted, because of the landscape importance and cost of servicing these areas.

The underdeveloped land allocated on existing Town Maps or which already has an effective planning permission will continue to be available for development with the exception of some of the land at Willow Valley. The revised boundaries of these development areas will be determined during the preparation of local plans for each. There will also be some infilling and redevelopment sites available.

It is anticipated that after allowing for a probable reduction in the average occupancy of existing dwellings, total allocation could result in a population increase of about 21,000. Hence the capacity population of the area is 114,000 or more, if occupancy rates cease to decline.

At present University students are competing in the housing market.

It is intended that any further growth of student numbers at the University should be housed in purpose-built student accommodation.

Despite these policies, and the likely availability of a limited amount of building land further afield, it is probable that the demand for housing will force up prices to the detriment of those on low incomes. This is a special local situation which could be aggravated by the growth of tourism and shopping which generally rely upon relatively low-paid employees. National measures to overcome the housing problem are likely to be insufficient. It is therefore intended:

To use the majority of undeveloped land for the erection of low-price housing for sale, or for rent from Housing Associations or Local Authorities.

To encourage the building of unsubsidized property for single people, whether working or retired, so that existing under-occupied properties can be made available for family use.

At the upper end of the housing market there are signs that the erection of substantial numbers of new flats is having the effect of making uneconomic the preservation in use of the fine terraces, squares and crescents which give these places much of their distinctive character. There is little possibility of these properties being properly maintained if they are vacated by easonably well-to-do occupants and further study is needed to determine the economics of their retention.

TRANSPORT POLICIES

t has already been indicated that the social and resource costs nd the dislocation to property caused by major road works, ufficient to remove all the present traffic problems, cannot be ccepted. At the other extreme, it may not be possible for a tour-st centre and major shopping service centre to thrive if there is total reliance on public transport. There may be a long-term ossibility of removing some traffic-generating activities to ites outside the towns, in order to relieve the problem, but gain the financial costs would be high, and the need to retain nspoilt Areas of Outstanding Natural Beauty means that the lternative sites available are very few. This possibility will be urther examined, but for the time being it will not be pursued, lthough restrictions on the establishment of new major traffic-enerating activities are desirable.

Within the area generally, it is intended to use traffic management and parking control measures so as to encourage the use of public transport and reduce congestion or environmental conflict. New facilities such as 'park and ride' will be provided, if found to be appropriate after further study.

The completion of a bypass to the east of the built-up area is an essential part of this policy, and other measures may be brought forward following the transportation studies now in hand. The establishment of new activities which would be major traffic generators or attractors, will not be accepted where these would substantially add to the traffic problems of the area.

LOCAL PLANS

Within the perimeter of each urban area new development is expected to accord with the character and predominant use of the area in which it will stand. Any change from this character and predominant use should take place only in accordance with an adopted local plan for the area concerned. The following considerations are basic to the preparation of such local plans:

(i)   The traffic generation effects of the proposed land uses.
(ii)   The effects upon schools, services and utilities of the proposed land users.
(iii)   The character of the area.
(iv)   The need to optimize use of land.
(v)   The access to job, school and social facilities.
(vi)   Other environmental factors such as the proximity of main roads.
(vii)   Any effects upon the employment pattern of the town as a whole.

It is intended that no development shall take place beyond the boundaries of areas allocated for development on the existing Town Maps except in accordance with an adopted local plan for the area concerned. If it is essential to consider individual proposals before this stage is reached, they will be examined by the County Council as departures from the Structure Plan. These local plans will take into account the general policies of the Structure Plan as well as those specifically referred to in the preceding paragraph.

Item D   Extract from the *Edgington Advertiser* **of 10 May 1980**

The Planners and the Bypass

With the Public Inquiry into the Edgington Bypass now in its thirteenth week, the Openshire planners are beginning to get used to the bright lights and publicity surrounding what has come to be called the 'Battle of the Bypass'. Some of them even seem to be liking it!

For their County Planning Officer, Jean Grimsdyke, the glare of publicity is, of course, not a new experience. A prominent figure in professional planning circles, she has acquired a reputation not only for holding strong views on the nature and the role of local authority planning, but also for her ability to convince elected members of the rightness of her approach and to carry it through in practice.

She believes that, if strategic planning is to be effective, it has to be locked in closely with the work of the other departments in the county council, especially those with more direct responsibilities for providing services, such as the Highways Department. Drawing on the experience of her deputy, Reg Watkins, she has ensured that the planning department is closely involved in the work on the authority's capital programme and provides information and research support to other departments, notably Transportation. A member of the planning department is in fact one of the team that prepared the Transportation Plan and Programme (TPP). The influence of the planning department on the authority is strengthened further by Jean Grimsdyke's membership of a powerful Chief Officers' group.

She also lays great stress on the importance of monitoring the plan and the importance attached to monitoring is reflected in the size of the Monitoring Unit, which is the largest of the four units in the department. Headed by Dick Roach it is responsible for most of the routine data collection and analysis, and for the work of the Annual Position Statement. Dick Roach also does most of the drafting of the statement, although Jean Grimsdyke and Reg Watkins are closely involved in the final stages of its preparation. The relationship between all three appears to be a good one, with a certain complementarity in styles and skills manifesting itself. If Jean Grimsdyke can be said to provide the drive and style of Openshire's planning, Dick Roach might be said to provide the diligence and calm managerial abilities that make it work. Dick, who is handling much of the detailed technical work at the Inquiry, is incidentally not a car-owner.

Another key figure is Jim Welch, head of the Economic Unit, with whom Jean Grimsdyke works very closely. His unit exists primarily to encourage industry into the county. One of the ways it does this is by collecting data on land which is available and suitable for industrial develop-ment and the unit publishes a quarterly bulletin on this. Much of Jim Welch's time however is spent in meetings with employers in the area and he stresses the importance of the 'soft' information he gleans from such meetings.

Finally, Mike Crail is the head of the policy unit, but is less involved in the mainstream of planning activity in the department. His unit is supposed to be responsible for the more in-depth and long-term investigation of issues, and the formulation of policy in new areas.

Modern Management Practices

The organization of the department is interesting too. Following a reorganization much of the work in the department is now done by project teams. Team leaders can be appointed from the members of any of the units and the team themselves often consist of members from all three units. The team leaders report to Reg Watkins for work on the projects. Consequently ultimate responsibility for the work being done by a single officer may rest in the hands of two or three people. According to Jean Grimsdyke these arrangements give staff more responsibility and most officers are enthusiastic about this way of working, saying that it makes for much better communication and a more interesting job.

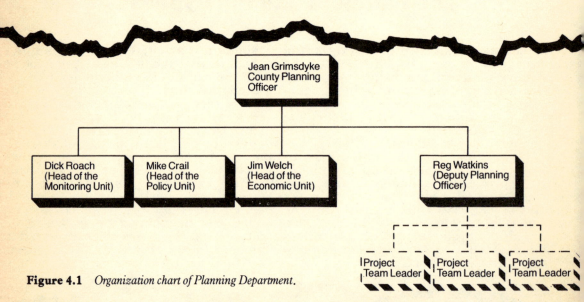

Figure 4.1 *Organization chart of Planning Department.*

Item E

From: Mike Crail, Head of Policy Unit   20 May 1980
To: Jean Grimsdyke
Re: The Reorganization of the Dept.

I want to set out, for the record, my views on the departmental reorganization now that it has been in force for a year. Although I have tried to make the so-called 'project management' work I feel that my original misgivings have been more than confirmed. Specifically, I am no longer in effective control of my staff and I believe important aspects of long-term policy are being neglected. I can cite several recent instances where individuals have devoted a quite disproportionate amount of time to tasks that they happened to have a personal interest in, to the detriment of far more substantive matters. No wonder the new arrangements are so popular! I appreciate that on this as on other issues I am the odd man out, and that your mind is made up; but I think you should know my views, even if you are no longer intending formally to review the arrangements, as I thought had been agreed a year ago.

Item F(i)

From: Jean Grimsdyke
To: Dick Roach

                                                 22 May 1980
I am very concerned that, when David Arkwright cross-examines me next month, he is going to ask some awkward questions regarding the relationship of the bypass to our structure plan policies, and especially those concerned with the Edgington economy. Could you please convene a meeting of unit heads so we can thrash out exactly where we stand on these issues? You had better also ask Reg along.

Item F(ii)

Phone Message

Time: 9.30

Date: 24th May

Dick - Big Jean called — Says sorry, but cannot attend the meeting on the bypass and the structure plan. She wants you to let her have a full account of what is discussed, as soon as you can.

Sandra.

Item F(iii)

From: Dick Roach
To: Jean Grimsdyke

27 May 1980

I was very sorry that you were unable to make the meeting on Wednesday. I did however take detailed notes as you requested and the following is a résumé of what was said.

Reg set the ball rolling in his usual abrasive fashion by telling me I had invited the wrong people along. We were all too interested in planning theory he said. The Inspector would be looking for something much more concrete and specific than anything we were likely to come up with. Why wasn't there someone from the districts, he asked. I pointed out that the districts were not exactly 'wild about our approach to planning', although they were beginning to understand it better. Mike then suggested that we move on but Reg angrily interrupted him to argue that it was crucial we maintain a line that Edgington Council supports 100%. (What are your feelings on this?)

Reg went on to suggest that we might find ourselves in 'deep water' if we present the bypass as an attempt to intervene in the local economy. 'There is a considerable body of opinion', he said, 'that believes government is incapable of doing anything ... it is a deep philosophical question'. At the same time, he admitted, there are many who criticize planners for not taking sufficient account of the effect of their policies on the local economy. The real problem though, he thinks, is that we are not really at all clear as to what we are trying to do. In theory of course we should merely be reflecting the wishes of the politicians in this respect. But, according to Reg, they would tell us we should be giving priority to helping small business. Technically speaking, of course, this may not be an issue.

At this point in the discussion, which seemed to be getting more and more philosophical (thanks to Reg as much as anyone!) Jim made one of his rare contributions. He proposed that we should argue that the plan is really designed to 'raise incomes in the county'. Reg observed that such an aim would be very acceptable to councillors. Mike asked whether people — and the Inspector in particular! — might not comment that the area already appeared to be very affluent. An increase in affluence would also result in more cars, as well as greater demand for land, said Mike. At which point he was well and truly sat on by Reg, who stated that he was 'not having that'. Mike added meekly that 'we must not lose sight of the consequences of prosperity', but Reg simply noted that 'all the places I have ever liked have been prosperous areas'. And that was that. The aim of raising incomes in the county was adopted as the primary rationale for the plan. (I must confess that on reflection I am not 100% happy with this. What do you think?)

Reg acknowledged though that such an aim did raise other issues. Was it, he asked, the social or the cash wage we should be maximizing. To illustrate the point he suggested that in the case of mining a large proportion of the wage was 'danger money'. Thus to bring mining into the area might increase the cash wage but not the social wage. The same might be said of car production, so that Openshire would not welcome either. According to Jim the kind of industries that would increase the social wage, and hence were desirable, were pharmaceutical and electronic industries — and especially those associated with the 'chip'. A further complication was then introduced by Reg who, arguing that the cost of housing in Openshire was high because the social wage was high, suggested that the real need was to identify the opportunities for 'wealth-increasing activities'. Simply reflecting existing needs 'gets us nowhere except a lot of work'.

At this point I thought it was time to remind everyone that we were there primarily to prepare for next week's Inquiry and that, important though aims were, there were a lot of other questions that we might be asked. The bypass might well contribute to these aims, but what about the distribution of benefits? There might be an overall increase in social wage, cash wage or whatever but the effect might be to benefit some but disadvantage others. In fact, I said, that is precisely one of the arguments that BEBAG have already referred to and we are likely to hear a lot more of it next week.

And, furthermore, haven't we been arguing that we want the bypass in order to solve the problem of present congestion, rather than to achieve some distant and possibly ephemeral aim? The others looked at me, a bit nonplussed, but Reg then looked at his watch and said he had another meeting to go to. Jim too said he ought to be preparing a paper for Friday's committee meeting so we adjourned. I have arranged another meeting for Thursday. (I really do think you had better attend.)

29 May 1980

Item G(i)

Mr Edward Peel,
District Engineer,
Surrock Area Water Authority,
High Street,
Bristow,
Openshire.

Dear Ted,

As you are no doubt aware the Public Inquiry into the Edgington Bypass is upon us and Jean Grimsdyke, our County Planning Officer, is becoming very concerned with regard to the 'state of play' on your plans to provide a water supply and sewerage for the Bradbury development.

You will recall that we assumed in the Structure Plan that development would probably go ahead in 1981. In our last Annual Position Statement we noted the cut-backs in your investment programme and proposed that the Bradbury land would not be released till 1985. If there are any further delays we can probably hold off the developer, though if they took an application to Appeal they might just win it in the current climate. But we're more worried just now with what we tell the Inspector at the Inquiry. If we tell him that the line of the bypass has to skirt the Bradbury land because there is going to be a big new housing estate there, we had better be pretty sure of it. If one of the objectors gets hold of the possibility that there might not be, our case is going to look a bit sick. You simply can't admit to being unsure of something like this, however sound the reasons for uncertainty.

So could you please let me have information on your new five-year capital programme or, better still, a letter from the Chief Engineer giving a firm undertaking that the work will be done within the next five years.

Sorry to put you to this trouble.

Best wishes.

Yours sincerely,

Dick Roach,
(Head of Monitoring Unit,
Openshire County Council)

Item G(ii)

Mr Dick Roach,
County Planning Department,
County Hall,
Edgington,
Openshire.

Dear Dick,   7 June 1980

Thank you for your letter of 29 May. I appreciate your anxiety over the water supply and sewerage for the Bradbury development. I'm afraid though you have rather put us on the spot. It's not only that we're unsure what resources are going to be available over the next five years, we're also still unclear regarding the growth in demand we can expect from increases in the present population and any further immigration as a result of developments already planned.

As you know we base our investment strategy mainly on population forecasts and although the Structure Plan does provide us with some of the information we need, we're still having difficulty because you have used a rather different approach to breaking down the population forecasts than we do.

If you could let us have a set of forecasts based on the districts and not on your 'policy areas', as you call them, I think I may be able to get the Chief to provide you with what you want, though I can't promise it of course.

Look forward to hearing from you.

Yours sincerely,

Ted Peel

Ted Peel
(District Engineer, Surrock Area Water Authority)

Mr Nigel Glemp,
Planning and Research Department,
Edgington Borough Council,
City Hall,   8 June 1980
Bristow Road,
Edgington.

Dear Nigel,

As you will recall from our telephone discussion a couple of weeks ago, we over here are very anxious that any uncertainty regarding the development of the land at Bradbury does not surface during the Bypass Inquiry. Ted Peel, at the water authority, has agreed to getting something in writing committing his authority to making the necessary investment in infrastructure, provided we provide him with forecasts of population growth in the districts.

Unfortunately our own population forecasts are based on our 'policy areas', and I was wondering if your work on the Edgington District Plan was far enough advanced for you to provide the figures Ted wants.

I'm afraid the timetable is pretty tight and I must get the forecasts to Ted by the 15th at the latest, to give him plenty of time to get back to us before Jean Grimsdyke's cross-examination by BEBAG on the 22nd.

Yours sincerely,

Dick Roach

Item G(iii)

Dick Roach
(Head of Monitoring Unit,
Openshire County Council)

Item G(iv)

Mr Dick Roach,
County Planning Department,
County Hall,
Edgington,
Openshire.

Dear Dick,

18 June 1980

Sorry to be so long getting back to you but the figures you need were not
immediately to hand. I was however able to arrange some runs of our small-areas
forecasting model and enclose the printouts. Hope they are what the See and Saw
are wanting.

I ought to mention, by the way, that in order to run the model we had to make one
or two rather dubious assumptions. To begin with we assumed the bypass would
be built! Also we had to make an estimate of how the activity rate is going to
change in the next twenty years. To be quite honest the figures we put in are not
much better than guesses. Still, you need not tell Ted Peel that!

Perhaps more to the point though our work on the Edgington Plan is beginning to
throw up some very real problems regarding the resources needed to implement
it. With things the way they are I am not at all sure that the plan is going to contain
any public sector housing on the Bradbury land. This could mean that the
proposed line of the bypass could go straight through the Bradbury land. But don't
worry, we'll sit on this for a while and I can't see the draft plan actually being
published till 1982.

Once again, sorry about the delay,

Your sincerely,

Nigel Glemp

Nigel Glemp
(Assistant Borough Planning Officer,
Edgington Borough Council)

Item H   Extract from Transcript of the Public Inquiry into the Edgington Bypass (22 June 1980)

CROSS-EXAMINATION of Jean Grimsdyke (Openshire County Planning Officer) by David Arkwright (representing the Bar the Edgington Bypass Amenity Group)

D.A.   Good afternoon, Miss Grimsdyke.

J.G.   Good afternoon.

D.A.   Now, could I ask you to turn to 1.20 on page 7 of your evidence. You say in your first sentence 'The underlying trend for many years has been for increasing amounts of traffic to use the principal roads in Edgington'. What in your view has led to that underlying trend?

J.G.   The increasing economic activity and prosperity of the county.

D.A.   'In consequence many roads have become overloaded', you go on to say. It may be possible in the future, may it not, for Edgington to have increasing prosperity without dependence on or having to suffer increasing amounts of traffic?

J.G.   Yes, I think that the fact that one thing caused another in one period of history does not mean to say that it would go on causing it in another period of history. Patently, before cars, increasing prosperity did not lead to more car traffic.

D.A.   The essence of planning is to affect trends, is it not? And, in a sense, to manipulate them in the interests of society and the nation. It is not just simply that the nation has grown richer and the people have wanted to drive their cars, is it? Has not society and has not the whole process of transportation planning gone to assist that trend that has led to increasing amounts of traffic? That is the point I am making.

J.G.   It would be open to society to forgo the benefits of personal travel and the traffic that goes with it if it wished to do this, and it would be wrong in these circumstances for those in authority to exert their forcefulness so to speak, I will not put it stronger than that, to prevent people owning and running their cars as a general principle, which does not mean to say that there are not cases where one might say, yes, we must prevent people owning and running cars. Indeed there are such cases. If such a policy were adopted we would not need a bypass. But it would also mean we would not have a tourist industry in Edgington.

D.A.   Is it not the case that planners, like so many people associated with making these kinds of decisions, tend to assume that everyone owns a car? The statistics in fact show that only half of the households in Edgington own a car.

J.G.   This statistic is one of the most misleading in current planning circulation. I do not know that exact figure off-hand but roughly one-third of the households in Edgington are single-person households so that of that half, the half of those which does not own cars, at least a half and maybe two-thirds are simply single persons living alone. Their need for a car is patently very different from the husband-wife-two-children type of household. I think therefore that it would be quite wrong to think that the lack of cars in half the households represents more than a very small proportion of people deprived of transport as a consequence of it. What is, of course, much more difficult to measure is the people in the households with cars who are deprived because the head of the household goes off with it each day or even for several days on end.

D.A.   I am grateful to you for mentioning such households Miss Grimsdyke. It is good of you to relieve me of mentioning the matter. I would like though to move on now and consider your view that the commercial decline of Edgington due to traffic congestion has already started and would have been more obvious were it not for the recession. But are you really sure that the commercial decline can only be arrested by the construction of the new bypass? Is that what you are saying?

J.G.   Yes.

D.A.   It is as stark as that?

J.G.   Yes.

D.A.   So we now look to the bypass construction date as beginning in 1985. We have two years of construction of it, with immense disruption of one kind and another and then we are told that we have fifteen years of gradual traffic growth and erosion of the advantages. Is that really how you see Edgington's future?

J.G.   I do not understand the second half, I do not understand that point at all. I am afraid I cannot see the erosion of anything. I do not understand what you are talking about.

D.A.   The erosion of traffic advantages in the centre of Edgington brought by the bypass.

J.G.   There will not be any erosion of traffic advantages.

D.A.   I see. It is no advantage to me to argue the point any further. Can I move on to section 4.20?

Inspector   I did not completely hear the last reply. I am not sure I got it down right. Could Miss Grimsdyke please repeat it?

J.G.   I think Mr Arkwright was suggesting that there would be an erosion of traffic advantages over the fifteen years after the bypass was completed.

D.A.   That is right.

J.G.   I am saying I don't think there will be any erosion of those traffic advantages during that time.

Inspector   I see. I may have misunderstood this and I should like to understand it. I thought we cleared up this morning that by 1999 we would have virtually the same traffic as at present.

J.G.   Only in the central area.

Inspector   Miss Grimsdyke is saying there might be gradual erosion in the central area?

J.G.   No.

Inspector   Not even there?

J.G.   No, I do not think the traffic advantages are reduced because you have a little more traffic on a road which had a little less traffic on it. As far as the main road is concerned there are substantial advantages for some short stretches. The traffic advantages come to the traffic that uses the bypass or uses the rat-runs.

Inspector   I see.

J.G.   Unless you consider the traffic advantage to be in a line of six cars instead of twelve cars at a traffic light. I do not see that as a significant advantage.

D.A.   Can we now move on Miss Grimsdyke, to 4.20, where you say that the more you tried to do this, that is the public transport dominated movement system, the higher the cost. You go on to say that vehicle users are not likely to be attracted to public transport even if it is free. Do you not think though that if Edgington established itself as a byword for splendid public transport, some of which is free, are you really suggesting that people would rush to go elsewhere? You are obviously; you say so. But are you really saying so on mature consideration?

J.G.   Yes. I am saying that I think the notion that there would be large numbers, a large increase in the numbers of people using public transport if it were free is misconceived. People use transport for convenience rather than marginal cost reasons.

D.A.   Would you then deny that Sheffield established itself as a major attraction for shoppers largely because of its low cost transport?

J.G.   I do not believe that was the reason.

D.A.   You do not think that it would very rapidly be known in the country that Edgington was a place where you could hop on buses almost anywhere at low cost, you do not think that would attract people in this country, in the present climate of opinion and the future we now seem to be facing?

J.G.   I think it would be very neglectful of my duty to advise any authority to run the risk of that speculative possibility in the absence of any experiment of that kind anywhere in the world showing that that is the public response to it. I think putting it quite simply, that my councillors would laugh at me if I were to propose such a proposition.

D.A.   How many of your councillors have to get about without cars?

J.G.   Quite a number.

Inspector   They are not alone. I would like to catch the 5.30 train back to London if possible. I wonder therefore if we might adjourn for today, and reconvene on Monday. Is that all right with you, Miss Grimsdyke?

J.G.   Certainly.

Inspector   And you, Mr Arkwright?

D.A.   Of course.

Postscript

The Inquiry went on for several more weeks. Six months after it ended the Inspector submitted his report to the Secretary of State for the Environment. He recommended that the bypass should be built. Public expenditure cuts since then have meant however that its construction has been delayed and it looks now as if it may never be built.

(In preparing this case study the author would like to acknowledge the help received from planning officers in several counties most notably those of Cambridgeshire, Herefordshire and Worcestershire, Hertfordshire, Leicestershire and East Sussex. He would like especially to thank Tony Duc of East Sussex C.C. for advice on the detailed planning and technical points involved.)

II ISSUES

II Issues

'Issues' seemed the most appropriate term to cover some of the knotty problems and dilemmas that occur one way or another in most organizations, and to which there are no easy or complete solutions. Often the more lurid examples of organizational failure seized on by the popular press arise from attempts at handling such dilemmas that are not so different from what commonly happens elsewhere but with less unfortunate results. Problems cannot always be avoided and a deeper understanding is needed than the language of neglect and 'incompetence' provides. The selection covers a range of problem-areas and the different ways of coping with them. The intention was to help those who work in organizations to see their own efforts and experience in a wider context, and realize they are not alone in finding that certain matters are seldom very satisfactorily resolved. Some of these issues are perennials, endemic in organizations — like the satisfactions and dissatisfactions of work, and the problems of 'misunderstandings' — while the others are more topical. But in each case, whether we are managers or managed, most of us will meet these issues in some form, and have to find ways of making the best of them.

The following extracts have been taken from a book which consists of verbatim records of ordinary people talking about their work. They present many issues as starkly as any organizational theorist could.

One of the themes of the book from which these extracts have been taken is that very few people find satisfaction in their work. Even fewer regard their work relationships as a source of satisfaction. There are clues about what the individuals want from work in most of the extracts, as well as some accounts of special moments that make all the rest seem worth while . . .

Working

S. Terkel

Introduction

This book, being about work, is, by its very nature, about violence — to the spirit as well as to the body. It is about ulcers as well as accidents, about shouting matches as well as fistfights, about nervous breakdowns as well as kicking the dog around. It is, above all (or beneath all), about daily humiliations. To survive the day is triumph enough for the walking wounded among the great many of us.

The scars, psychic as well as physical, brought home to the supper table and the TV set, may have touched, malignantly, the soul of our society. More or less. ('More or less', that most ambiguous of phrases, pervades many of the conversations that comprise this book, reflecting, perhaps, an ambiguity of attitude toward The Job. Something more than Orwellian acceptance, something less than Luddite sabotage. Often the two impulses are fused in the same person.)

It is about a search, too, for daily meaning as well as daily bread, for recognition as well as cash, for astonishment rather than torpor; in short, for a sort of life rather than a Monday through Friday sort of dying. Perhaps immortality, too, is part of the quest. To be remembered was the wish, spoken and unspoken, of the heroes and heroines of this book.

There are, of course, the happy few who find a savor in their daily job: the Indiana stonemason, who looks upon his work and sees that it is good; the Chicago piano tuner, who seeks and finds the sound that delights; the bookbinder, who saves a piece of history; the Brooklyn fireman, who saves a piece of life . . . But don't these satisfactions, like Jude's hunger for knowledge, tell us more about the person than about his task? Perhaps. Nonetheless, there is a common attribute here: a meaning to their work well over and beyond the reward of the paycheck.

Babe Secoli

She's a checker at a supermarket. She's been at it for almost thirty years. 'I started at twelve — a little, privately owned grocery store across the street from the house. They didn't have no cash registers. I used to mark the prices down on a paper bag.

'When I got out of high school, I didn't want no secretary job. I wanted the grocery job. It was so interesting for a young girl. I just fell into it. I don't know no other work but this. It's hard work, but I like it. This is my life.'

We sell everything here, millions of items. From potato chips and pop — we even have a genuine pearl in a can of oysters. It sells for two somethin'. Snails with the shells that you put on the table, fanciness. There are items I never heard of we have here. I know the price of every one. Sometimes the boss asks me and I get a kick out of it. There isn't a thing you don't want that isn't in this store.

You sort of memorize the prices. It just comes to you. I know half a gallon of milk is sixty-four cents; a gallon, $1.10. You look at the labels. A small can of peas, Raggedy Ann. Green Giant, that's a few pennies more. I know Green Giant's eighteen and I know Raggedy Ann is fourteen. I know Del Monte is twenty-two. But lately the prices jack up from one day to another. Margarine two days ago was forty-three cents. Today it's forty-nine. Now when I see Imperial comin' though, I know it's forty-nine cents. You just memorize. On the register is a list of some prices, that's for the part-time girls. I never look at it.

I don't have to look at the keys on my register. I'm like the

From *Working: People Talk About What They Do All Day and How They Feel About What They Do*, © 1972, 1974 by Studs Terkel. Reprinted by permission of Pantheon Books, a Division of Random House Inc., and Wildwood House Ltd., London.

secretary that knows her typewriter. The touch. My hand fits. The number nine is my big middle finger. The thumb is number one, two and three and up. The side of my hand uses the bar for the total and all that.

I use my three fingers — my thumb, my index finger, and my middle finger. The right hand. And my left hand is on the groceries. They put down their groceries. I got my hips pushin' on the button and it rolls around on the counter. When I feel I have enough groceries in front of me, I let go of my hip. I'm just movin' — the hips, the hand, and the register, the hips, the hand, and the register . . . (As she demonstrates, her hands and hips move in the manner of an Oriental dancer.) You just keep goin', one, two, one, two. If you've got that rhythm, you're a fast checker. Your feet are flat on the floor and you're turning your head back and forth.

Somebody talks to you. If you take your hand off the item, you're gonna forget what you were ringin'. It's the feel. When I'm pushin' the items through I'm always having my hand on the items. If somebody interrupts to ask me the price, I'll answer while I'm movin'. Like playin' a piano.

I'm eight hours a day on my feet. It's just a physical tire of standing up. When I get home I get my second wind. As far as standin' there, I'm not tired. It's when I'm roamin' around tryin' to catch a shoplifter. There's a lot of shoplifters in here. When I see one, I'm ready to run for them.

When my boss asks me how I know, I just know by the movements of their hands. And with their purses and their shopping bags and their clothing rearranged. You can just tell what they're doin' and I'm never wrong so far.

It's meats. Some of these women have big purses. I caught one here last week. She had two big packages of sirloin strips in her purse. That amounted to ten dollars. When she came up to the register, I very politely said, 'Would you like to pay for anything else, without me embarrassing you?' My boss is standing right there. I called him over. She looked at me sort of on the cocky side. I said, 'I know you have meat in your purse. Before your neighbors see you, you either pay for it or take it out.' She got very snippy. That's where my boss stepped in. 'Why'd you take the meat?' She paid for it.

Nobody knows it. I talk very politely. My boss doesn't do anything drastic. If they get rowdy, he'll raise his voice to embarrass 'em. He tells them not to come back in the store again.

Years ago it was more friendlier, more sweeter. Now there's like tension in the air. A tension in the store. The minute you walk in you feel it. Everybody is fightin' with each other. They're pushin', pushin' — 'I was first.' Now it's an effort to say, 'Hello, how are you?' It must be the way of people livin' today. Everything is so rush, rush, rush, and shovin'. Nobody's goin' anywhere. I think they're pushin' themselves right to a grave, some of these people.

A lot of traffic here. There's bumpin' into each other with shoppin' carts. Some of 'em just do it intentionally. When I'm shoppin', they just jam you with the carts. That hits your ankle and you have a nice big bruise there. You know who does this the most? These old men that shop. These *men*. They're terrible and just *jam* you. Sometimes I go over and tap them on the shoulder: 'Now why did you do this?' They look at you and they

just start *laughin'*. It's just hatred in them, they're bitter. They hate themselves, maybe they don't feel good that day. They gotta take their anger out on somethin', so they just *jam* you. It's just ridiculous.

I wouldn't know how to go in a factory. I'd be like in a prison. Like this, I can look outside, see what the weather is like. I want a little fresh air, I walk out the front door, take a few sniffs of air, and come back in. I'm here forty-five minutes early every morning. I've never been late except for that big snowstorm. I never thought of any other work.

I'm a couple of days away, I'm very lonesome for this place. When I'm on a vacation, I can't wait to go, but two or three days away, I start to get fidgety. I can't stand around and do nothin'. I have to be busy at all times. I look forward to comin' to work. It's a great feelin'. I enjoy it somethin' terrible.

Phil Stallings

He is a spot-welder at the Ford assembly plant on the far South Side of Chicago. He is twenty-seven years old; recently married. He works the third shift: 3.30 p.m. to midnight.

'*I start the automobile, the first welds. From there it goes to another line, where the floor's put on, the roof, the trunk hood, the doors. Then it's put on a frame. There is hundreds of lines.*

'*The welding gun's got a square handle, with a button on the top for high voltage and a button on the bottom for low. The first is to clamp the metal together. The second is to fuse it.*

'*The gun hangs from a ceiling, over tables that ride on a track. It travels in a circle, oblong, like an egg. You stand on a cement platform, maybe six inches from the ground.*'

I stand in one spot, about two- or three-feet area, all night. The only time a person stops is when the line stops. We do about thirty-two jobs per car, per unit. Forty-eight units an hour, eight hours a day. Thirty-two times forty-eight times eight. Figure it out. That's how many times I push that button.

The noise, oh it's tremendous. You open your mouth and you're liable to get a mouthful of sparks. (Shows his arms.) That's a burn, these are burns. You don't compete against the noise. You go to yell and at the same time you're straining to manoeuvre the gun to where you have to weld.

You got some guys that are uptight, and they're not sociable. It's too rough. You pretty much stay to yourself. You get involved with yourself. You dream, you think of things you've done. I drift back continuously to when I was a kid and what me and my brothers did. The things you love most are the things you drift back into.

Lots of times I worked from the time I started to the time of the break and I never realized I had even worked. When you dream, you reduce the chances of friction with the foreman or with the next guy.

It don't stop. It just goes and goes and goes. I bet there's men who have lived and died out there, never seen the end of that line. And they never will — because it's endless. It's like a serpent. It's just all body, no tail. It can do things to you . . . (Laughs.)

Repetition is such that if you were to think about the job itself, you'd slowly go out of your mind. You'd let your problems build up, you'd get to a point where you'd be at the fellow next to you — his throat. Every time the foreman came by and looked at you, you'd have something to say. You just strike out at anything you can. So if you involve yourself by yourself, you overcome this.

I don't like the pressure, the intimidation. How would you like to go up to someone and say, 'I would like to go to the bathroom?' If the foreman doesn't like you, he'll make you hold it, just ignore you. Should I leave this job to go to the bathroom I risk being fired. The line moves all the time.

I know I could find better places to work. But where could I get the money I'm making? Let's face it, $4.32 an hour. That's real good money now. Funny thing is, I don't mind working at body construction. To a great degree, I enjoy it. I love using my hands — more than I do my mind. I love to be able to put things together and see something in the long run. I'll be the first to admit I've got the easiest job on the line. But I'm against this thing where I'm being held back. I'll work like a dog until I get what I want. The job I really want is utility.

It's where I can stand and say I can do any job in this department, and nobody has to worry about me. As it is now, out of say, sixty jobs, I can do almost half of 'em. I want to get away from standing in one spot. Utility can do a different job every day. Instead of working right there for eight hours I could work over there for eight, I could work the other place for eight. Every day it would change. I would be around more people. I go out on my lunch break and work on the fork truck for a half-hour — to get the experience. As soon as I got it down pretty good, the foreman in charge says he'll take me. I don't want the other guys to see me. When I hit that fork lift, you just stop your thinking and you concentrate. Something right there in front of you, not in the past, not in the future. This is real healthy.

I don't eat lunch at work. I may grab a candy bar, that's enough. I wouldn't be able to hold it down. The tension your body is put under by the speed of the line . . . When you hit them brakes, you just can't stop. There's a certain momentum that carries you forward. I could hold the food, but it wouldn't set right.

Proud of my work? How can I feel pride in a job where I call a foreman's attention to a mistake, a bad piece of equipment, and he'll ignore it. Pretty soon you get the idea they don't care. You keep doing this and finally you're titled a troublemaker. So you just go about your work. You *have* to have pride. So you throw it off to something else. And that's my stamp collection.

It's gonna change. There's a trend. We're getting younger and younger men. We got this new Thirty and Out. Thirty years seniority and out. The whole idea is to give a man more time, more time to slow down and live. While he's still in his fifties, he can settle down in a camper and go out and fish. I've sat down and thought about it. I've got twenty-seven years to go. (Laughs.) That's why I don't go around causin' trouble or lookin' for a cause.

The only time I get involved is when it affects me or it affects a man on the line in a condition that could be me. I don't believe in lost causes, but when it all happened . . . (He pauses, appears bewildered.)

The foreman was riding the guy. The guy either told him to go away or pushed him, grabbed him . . . You can't blame the guy — Jim Grayson. I don't want nobody stickin' their finger in my face. I'd've probably hit him beside the head. The whole thing was: Damn it, it's about time we took a stand. Let's stick up for the guy. We stopped the line. (He pauses, grins.) Ford lost about twenty units. I'd figure about five grand a unit — whattaya got? (Laughs.)

I said, 'Let's all go home.' When the line's down like that, you can go up to one man and say, 'You gonna work?' If he says no, they can fire him. See what I mean? But if nobody was there, who the hell were they gonna walk up to and say, 'Are you gonna work?' Man, there woulda been nobody there! If it were up to me, we'd gone home.

Jim Grayson, the guy I work next to, he's colored. Absolutely. That's the first time I've seen unity on that line. Now it's happened once, it'll happen again. Because everybody just sat down. Believe you me. (Laughs.) It stopped at eight and it didn't start till twenty after eight. Everybody and his brother were down there. It was really nice to see, it really was.

Gary Bryner

He's twenty-nine, going on thirty. He is president of Local 1112, UAW. Its members are employed at the General Motors assembly plant in Lordstown, Ohio. 'It's the most automated, fastest line in the world.' A strike had recently been settled 'for a time'.

The almighty dollar is not the only thing in my estimation. There's more to it — how I'm treated. What I have to say about what I do, how I do it. It's more important than the almighty dollar. The reason might be that the dollar's here now. It wasn't in my father's young days. I can concentrate on the social aspects, my rights. And I feel good all around when I'm able to stand up and speak up for another guy's rights. That's how I got involved in this whole stinkin' mess. Fighting every day of my life. And I enjoy it.

Guys in plants nowadays, their incentive is not to work harder. It's to stop the job to the point where they can have lax time. Maybe to think. We got guys now that open a paper, maybe read a paragraph, do his job, come back, and do something else. Keeping himself occupied other than being just that robot that they've scheduled him to be.

When General Motors Assembly Division came to Lordstown, you might not believe it, but they tried to take the newspapers off the line. The GMAD controls about seventy-five percent of the assembly of cars produced for the corporation. There's eighteen assembly plants. We're the newest. Their idea is to cut costs, be more efficient, take the waste out of working, and all that kind of jazz. To make another dollar. That's why the guys labeled GMAD: Gotta Make Another Dollar. (Laughs.)

In '70 came the Vega. They were fighting foreign imports. They were going to make a small compact that gets good mileage. In the B body you had a much roomier car to work on. Guys could get in and out of it easily. Some guys could almost stand inside, stoop. With the Vega, a much smaller car, they were going from sixty an hour to a hundred an hour. They picked up an additional two thousand people.

When they started up with Vega, we had what we call Paragraph 78 disputes. Management says, that on every job you should do this much. And the guy and the union say, that's too much work for me in that amount of time. Finally, we establish work standards. Prior to October, when GMAD came down, we had established an agreement: the guy who was on the job had something to say. When GMAD came in, they said, he's long overdue for extra work. He's featherbedding.

Instead of having the guy bend over to pick something up, it's right at his waist level. This is something Ford did in the thirties. Try to take every movement out of the guy's day, so he could conserve seconds in time, to make him more efficient, more productive, like a robot. Save a second on every guy's effort, they would, over a year, make a million dollars.

They use time, stopwatches. They say, it takes so many seconds or hundreds of seconds to walk from here to there. We know it takes so many seconds to shoot a screw. We know the gun turns so fast, the screw's so long, the hole's so deep. Our argument has always been: that's mechanical; that's not human.

The workers said, we perspire, we sweat, we have hangovers, we have upset stomachs, we have feelings and emotions, and we're not about to be placed in a category of a machine. When you talk about that watch, you talk about it for a minute. We talk about a lifetime. We're gonna do what's normal and we're gonna tell you what's normal. We'll negotiate from there. We're not gonna start on a watch-time basis that has no feelings.

When they took the unimates on, we were building sixty an hour. When we came back to work, with the unimates, we were building a hundred cars an hour. A unimate is a welding robot. It looks just like a praying mantis. It goes from spot to spot to spot. It releases that thing and it jumps back into position, ready for the next car. They go by them about 110 an hour. They never tire, they never sweat, they never complain, they never miss work. Of course, they don't buy cars. I guess General Motors doesn't understand that argument.

There's twenty-two, eleven on each side of the line. They do the work of about two hundred men — so there was a reduction of men. Those people were absorbed into other departments. There's some places they can't use 'em. There's some thinking about assembling cars. There still has to be human beings.

If the guys didn't stand up and fight, they'd become robots too. They're interested in being able to smoke a cigarette, bullshit a little bit with the guy next to 'em, open a book, look at something, just daydream if nothing else. You can't do that if you become a machine.

Thirty-five, thirty-six seconds to do your job — that includes the walking, the picking up of the parts, the assembly. Go to the next job, with never a letup, never a second to stand and think. The guys at our plant fought like hell to keep that right.

There was a strike. It came after about four or five months of agitation by management. When GMAD took over the plant, we had about a hundred grievances. They moved in, and where we had settled a grievance, they violated 'em. They took and laid off people. They said they didn't need 'em. We had over fourteen hundred grievances under procedure prior to the strike. It's a two-shift operation, same job, so you're talking about twenty-eight hundred people with fourteen hundred grievances. What happened was, the guys — as the cars came by 'em — did what's normal, what they had agreed to prior to GMAD. I don't think GM visualized this kind of a rebellion.

The strike issue? We demanded the reinstitution of our work pace as it was prior to the onslaught by General Motors Assembly Division. The only way they could do it was to replace the people laid off.

Assembly workers are the lowest on the totem pole when it comes to job fulfillment. They don't think they have any skill. Some corporate guy said, 'A monkey could do the job.' They have no enthusiasm about pride in workmanship. They could care less if the screw goes in the wrong place. Sometimes it helps break the monotony if the screw strips. The corporation could set up ways to check it so when the product goes to the consumer it should be whole, clean and right. But they've laid off inspectors. 'Cause they could give a shit less. Inspectors are like parasites — they don't produce, they don't add something. They only find error. That error costs money to fix, so . . . they laid off, I don't know how many inspectors per shift. They want quantity.

The guys are not happy here. They don't come home thinking, boy, I did a great job today and I can't wait to get back tomorrow. That's not the feeling at all. I don't think he thinks a blasted thing about the plant until he comes back. He's not concerned at all if the product's good, bad, or indifferent.

Their idea is not to run the plant. I don't think they'd know what to do with it. They don't want to tell the company what to do, but simply have something to say about what *they're* going to do. They just want to be treated with dignity. That's not asking a hell of a lot.

I weave in on both sides of the assembly line. From the right side, the passenger's side, to the driver's side. Talking to guys. You get into a little conversation. You watch the guy, 'cause you don't want to get in his way, 'cause he'll ruin a job. Occasionally he'll say, 'Aw, fuck it. It's only a car.' It's more important to just stand there and rap. I don't mean for car after car. He'd be in a hell of a lot of trouble with his foreman. But occasionally, he'll let a car go by. If something's loose or didn't get installed, somebody'll catch it, somebody'll repair it, hopefully. At that point, he made a decision: It was just a little more important to say what he had on his mind. The unimate doesn't stand there and talk, doesn't argue, doesn't think. With us, it becomes a human thing. It's the most enjoyable part of my job, that moment. I love it!

Tom Brand

He is plant manager at the Ford Assembly Division in Chicago. He has been with the company thirty years. [. . .]

There's a plaque on the desk: Ford, Limited Edition. 'That was our five millionth car. There are about forty-five hundred people working here. That's about 3,998 hourly and about 468 salaried.'

Management and office employees are salaried.

You're responsible to make sure the car is built and built correctly. I rely on my quality control manager. Any defects, anything's wrong, we make sure it's repaired before it leaves the plant. Production manager takes care of the men on the line, makes sure they're doing their job, have the proper tools and the space and time to do it in. But the quality control manager is really our policeman. Quality control doesn't look at every item on the car. Some by surveillance. You take a sample of five an hour. Some, we look in every car. They make sure we're doing what we say we're doing.

Okay, we've got to build forty-seven an hour. Vega, down in Lordstown, had a hundred an hour. They got trapped with too much automation. If you're going to automate, you always leave yourself a loophole. I haven't seen their picture. I want to show it to all my managers. Okay, we build 760 big Fords a day.[. . .]

Three years ago, I had plenty of grievances. We had a lot of turnover, a lot of new employees. As many as 125 people would be replaced each week. Now with the economic situation, our last raises, and the seven days' holiday between Christmas and New Year's, this just changed the whole attitude. They found out it's a real good place to work. They're getting top dollar. Twelve paid vacation days a year, and they like the atmosphere. There was a lot of fellas would go in the construction industry about this time of the year. Less now.

I've had fellas come in to me and say, 'I'm not satisfied. Can I talk to you about it?' I say, 'Sure, come on in.' You can't run a business sitting in the office, 'cause you get divorced too much from the people. The people are the key to the whole thing. If you aren't in touch with the people they think, He's too far aloof, he's distant. It doesn't work. If I walk down the line, there'll be a guy fifty feet away from me. I'd wave, he'd wave back. Many of 'em I know by name. I don't know everyone by name, but I know their faces. If I'm in the area, I'll know who's strange. I'll kid with one of 'em. [. . .]

I don't think I'll retire at fifty. I'm not the type to sit around. Maybe if my health is good I'll go to fifty-seven, fifty-nine. I enjoy this work very much. You're with people. I like people. Guys who really do the job can spot a phony. When I walk out there and say good morning, you watch the fellas. There's a world of difference if they really know you mean it.

Doing my job is part salesmanship. I guess you can term it human engineering. My boss, so many years past, used to be a real bull of the woods. Tough guy. I don't believe in that. I never was raised that way. I never met a guy you couldn't talk to. I never met a man who didn't put his pants on the same way I do it in the morning. I met an awful lot of 'em that think they do. It doesn't work. The old days of hit 'em with a baseball bat to get their attention — they're gone.

If I could get everybody at the plant to look at everything through my eyeballs, we'd have a lot of the problems licked. If we have one standard to go by, it's easy to swing it around because then you've got everybody thinking the same way. This is the biggest problem of people — communication.

It's a tough situation because everybody doesn't feel the same every day. Some mornings somebody wakes up with a hangover, stayed up late, watched a late, late movie, missed the ride, and they're mad when they get to work. It's just human nature. If we could get everybody to feel great. [. . .]

Larry Ross

The corporation is a jungle. It's exciting. You're thrown in on your own and you're constantly battling to survive. When you learn to survive, the game is to become the conqueror, the leader.

'I've been called a business consultant. Some say I'm a business psychiatrist. You can describe me as an advisor to top management in a corporation.' He's been at it since 1968.

I started in the corporate world, oh gosh — '42. After kicking around in the Depression, having all kinds of jobs and no formal education, I wasn't equipped to become an engineer, a lawyer, or a doctor. I gravitated to selling. Now they call it marketing. I grew up in various corporations. I became the executive vice president of a large corporation and then of an even larger one. Before I quit I became president and chief executive officer of another. All nationally known companies.

Sixty-eight, we sold out our corporation. There was enough money in the transaction where I didn't have to go back in business. I decided that I wasn't going to get involved in the corporate battle any more. It lost its excitement, its appeal. People often ask me, 'Why weren't you in your own business? You'd probably have made a lot of money.' I often ask it myself, I can't explain it, except. . . .

Most corporations I've been in, they were on the New York Stock Exchange with thousands and thousands of stockholders. The last one — whereas, I was the president and chief executive, I was always subject to the board of directors, who had pressure from the stockholders. I owned a portion of the business, but I wasn't in control. I don't know of any situation in the corporate world where an executive is completely free and sure of his job from moment to moment.

Corporations always have to be right. That's their face to the public. When things go bad, they have to protect themselves and fire somebody. 'We had nothing to do with it. We had an executive that just screwed everything up.' He's never really ever been his own boss.

The danger starts as soon as you become a district manager. You have men working for you and you have a boss above. You're caught in a squeeze. The squeeze progresses from station to station. I'll tell you what a squeeze is. You have the guys working for you that are shooting for your job. The guy you're working for is scared stiff you're gonna shove him out of his job. Everybody goes around and says, 'The test of the true executive is that you have men working for you that can replace you, so you can move up.' That's a lot of boloney. The manager is afraid of the bright young guy coming up.

Fear is always prevalent in the corporate structure. Even if you're a top man, even if you're hard, even if you do your job — by the slight flick of a finger, your boss can fire you. There's always the insecurity. You bungle a job. You're fearful of losing a big customer. You're fearful so many things will appear on your record, stand against you. You're always fearful of the big mistake. You've got to be careful when you go to corporation parties. Your wife, your children have to behave properly. You've got to fit in the mold. You've got to be on guard.

When I was president of this big corporation, we lived in a small Ohio town, where the main plant was located. The corporation specified who you could socialize with, and on what level. (His wife interjects: 'Who were the wives you could play bridge with.') The president's wife could do what she wants, as long as it's with dignity and grace. In a small town they didn't have to keep check on you. Everybody knew. There are certain sets of rules. [. . .]

When the individual reaches the vice presidency or he's general manager, you know he's an ambitious, dedicated guy who wants to get to the top. He isn't one of the gray people. He's one of the black-and-white vicious people — the leaders, the ones who stick out in the crowd.

As he struggles in this jungle, every position he's in, he's terribly lonely. He can't confide and talk with the guy working under him. He can't confide and talk to the man he's working for. To give vent to his feelings, his fears, and his insecurities, he'd expose himself. This goes all the way up the line until he gets to be president. The president *really* doesn't have anybody to talk to, because the vice presidents are waiting for him to die or make a mistake and get knocked off so they can get his job.

He can't talk to the board of directors, because to them he has to appear as a tower of strength, knowledge, and wisdom, and have the ability to walk on water. The board of directors, they're cold, they're hard. They don't have any direct-line responsibilities. They sit in a staff capacity and they really play God. They're interested in profits. They're interested in progress. They're interested in keeping a good face in the community — if it's profitable. You have the tremendous infighting of man against man for survival and clawing to the top. Progress. [. . .]

To the board of directors, the dollars are as important as human lives. There's only yourself sitting there making the decison, and you hope it's right. You're always on guard. Did you ever see a jungle animal that wasn't on guard? You're always looking over your shoulder. You don't know who's following you. [. . .]

You have a nice, plush lovely office to go to. You have a private secretary. You walk down the corridor and everybody bows and says, 'Good morning, Mr Ross. How are you today?' As you go up the line, the executives will say, 'How is Mrs Ross?' Until you get to the higher executives. They'll say, 'How is Nancy?' Here you socialize, you know each other. Everybody plays the game.

A man wants to get to the top of the corporation, not for the money involved. After a certain point, how much more money can you make? In my climb, I'll be honest, money was secondary. Unless you have tremendous demands, yachts, private airplanes — you get to a certain point, money isn't that important. It's the power, the status, the prestige. Frankly, it's delightful to be on top and have everybody calling you Mr Ross and have a plane at your disposal and a car and a driver at your disposal. When you come to town, there's people to take care of

you. When you walk into a board meeting, everybody gets up and says hello. I don't think there's any human being that doesn't love that. It's a nice feeling. But the ultimate power is in the board of directors. I don't know anybody who's free. You read in the paper about stockholders' meetings, the annual report. It all sounds so glowing. But behind the scenes, a jungle.

Diane Wilson

She works for the OEO. 'This is a section called PM & S. I can't for the life of me ever remember what it means. Sometimes they change it. They reorganize and you get another initial. (Laughs.)

'I'm a processing clerk. There are three of us in this one department. We send grants to grantees after field reps have been out to see these poverty-stricken people. The grantees are organizations of the poor. Maybe the Mobilization Centre in Gary, where I live — Grand Rapids Poverty Center, something for senior citizens, a day care center. They give 'em all names.

'We mail 'em out forms to sign so they can get the money from Washington. When they return the forms to us there's another process we go through. We have a governor's letter and a package in an orange folder that we send out to him. He has to give his consent. We have a little telegram we type up. He approves it or he doesn't. We send it on. That makes it official. There's a thirty-day waiting period. After that time we send out the package to Washington. . . .

You wish there was a better system. A lot of money is held up and the grantees who want to know why they can't get it. Sometimes they call and get the run-around on the phone. I never do that. I tell the truth. If they don't have any money left, they don't have it. No, I'm not disturbed any more. If I was just starting on this job, I probably would. But the older I get, I realize it's a farce. You just get used to it. It's a job. I get my pay-check — that's it. It's all political anyway.

A lot of times the grantee comes down to our audit department for aid. They're not treated as human beings. Sometimes they have to wait, wait, wait — for no reason. The grantee doesn't know it's for no reason. He thinks he's getting somewhere and he really isn't.

They send him from floor to floor and from person to person, it's just around and around he goes. Sometimes he leaves, he hasn't accomplished anything. I don't know why this is so. You can see 'em waiting — so long. [. . .]

Life is a funny thing. We had this boss come in from Internal Revenue. He wanted to be very, very strict. He used to have meetings every Friday — about people comin' in late, people leavin' early, people abusin' lunch time. Everyone was used to this relaxed attitude. You kind of went overtime. No one bothered you. The old boss went along. You did your work.

Every Friday, everyone would sit there and listen to this man. And we'd all go out and do the same thing again. Next Friday he'd have another meeting and he would tell us the same thing. (Laughs.) We'd all go out and do the same thing again. (Laughs.) He would try to talk to one and see what they'd say about the other. But we'd been working all together for quite a while. You know how the game is played. Tomorrow you might need a favour. So nobody would say anything. If he'd want to find out what time someone came in, who's gonna tell 'em? He'd want to find out where someone was, we'd always say, 'They're at the Xerox.' Just anywhere. He couldn't get through. Now, lo and behold! We can't find *him* anywhere. He's got into this nice, relaxed atmosphere. . . . (Laughs.) He leaves early, he takes long lunch hours. We've converted him. (Laughs.)

After my grievances and my fighting, I'm a processing clerk. Never a typist no more or anything like that. (Laughs.) I started working here in 1969. There was an emergency and they all wanted to work overtime. So I made arrangements at home, 'cause I have to catch a later train. Our supervisor's black. All of us are black. We'll help her get it out so there won't be any back drag on this. Okay, so we all worked overtime and made a good showing.

Then they just didn't want to give us the promotion which was due us anyhow. They just don't want to give you anything. The personnel man, all of them, they show you why you don't deserve a promotion. The boss, the one we converted — he came on board, as they call it, after we sweated to meet the deadline. So he didn't know what we did. But he told us we didn't deserve it. That stayed with me forever. I won't be bothered with him ever again.

But our grievance man was very good. He stayed right on the case. We filed a civil rights complaint. Otherwise we woulda never got the promotion. They don't want anybody coming in investigating for race. They said, 'Oh, it's not that.' But you sit around and see white women do nothin' and get promotions. Here we're working and they say you don't deserve it. The black men are just as hard on us as the white man. Harder. They get angry with you because you started a lot of trouble. The way I feel about it, I'm gonna give 'em all the trouble I can.

Our boss is black, the one that told us we didn't deserve it. (Laughs.) And our union man fighting for us, sittin' there, punchin' away, is white. (Laughs.) We finally got up to the deputy director and he was the one — the white man — that finally went ahead and gave us the promotion. (Laughs.) So we went from grade 4 clerk-typist to grade 5 processing clerk.

We had another boss, he would walk around and he wouldn't want to see you idle at all. Sometimes you're gonna have a lag in your work, you're all caught up. This had gotten on his nerves. We got our promotion and we weren't continually busy. Any time they see black women idle, that irks 'em. I'm talkin' about black men as well as whites. They want you to work continuously. [. . .]

Oh, we love it when the bosses go to those long meetings, those important conferences. (Laughs.) We just leave in a group and go for a show. We don't care. When we get back, they roll their eyes. They know they better not say anything, 'cause they've done nothing when we've been gone anyhow. We do the work that we have to do. The old timekeeper, she sits and knits all that time, always busy.

6 Skilling and Deskilling

Like the rest of us, those engineers who design the equipment that other people use in their work, have developed particular beliefs concerning how to go about their job and what constitutes an effective outcome. And those beliefs work well for them. The snag — and it has been obvious for years — is that very often a new generation of equipment drastically reduces the skills required among those who will use it. The following article looks at some ways that modern technology gives new twists to this old dilemma — and argues that deskilling is not inevitable.

Engineers and the Work that People Do

H.H. Rosenbrock

1. Introduction

The phenomenon which I wish to discuss in this paper can be illustrated by a plant which was making electric light bulbs in 1979. Production was 800 bulbs an hour, of the type having a metallized reflector and the components of the glass envelope were made elsewhere. They travelled on a chain conveyor around the plant, which occupied an area about 30 feet by 10 feet and was quite new. It was noisy, and the large room which housed it was drab, but conditions were not unpleasant.

The plant was almost completely automatic. Parts of the glass envelope, for example, were sealed together without any human intervention. Here and there, however, were tasks which the designer had failed to automate, and workers were employed, mostly women and mostly middle-aged. One picked up each glass envelope as it arrived, inspected it for flaws, and replaced it if it was satisfactory: once every $4\frac{1}{2}$ seconds. Another picked out a short length of aluminium wire from a box with tweezers, holding it by one end. Then she inserted it delicately inside a coil which would vaporize it to produce the reflector: repeating this again every $4\frac{1}{2}$ seconds. Because of the noise, and the isolation of the work places, and the concentration demanded by some of them, conversation was hardly possible.

This picture could be matched by countless other examples, taken from any of the industrialized countries. Beyond the comment that the jobs were obviously bad ones, and that something should have been done about them, we are not likely to be surprised or to feel that the situation was unusual. Yet, as I shall hope to show, what has been described is decidedly odd.

2. A design exercise

To prepare the way, let us take one of the jobs, say the second one, and suppose that in a first year engineering degree course it was proposed, as a design exercise, to automate it. Picking up bits of wire out of a box is obviously too difficult, but we can easily avoid it. Let the wire be taken off a reel by pinch rollers and fed through a narrow tube. At the end of the tube, let it pass through holes in two hardened steel blocks. Then we can accurately feed out the right length, and by displacing one of the steel blocks we can shear it off. If this is all made small enough, it can enter the coil, so that when the wire is cut off it falls in the right place.

So far, so good, but the coil may perhaps not be positioned quite accurately. Then, if we cannot improve the accuracy, we shall have to sense its position and move the wire feeder to suit. Perhaps we could do this by using a conical, spring-loaded plunger, which could be pushed forward by a cam and enter the end of the coil. Having found its position in this way, we could lock a floating carriage on which the plunger and wire feeding mechanism were mounted, withdraw the plunger, and advance the wire feeder.

There would be scope here for a good deal of mechanical ingenuity, but of a kind which might not appeal to all of the students. 'Why not,' one of them might ask, 'why not use a small robot with optical sensing? The wire feeder could be mounted on the robot arm, and then sensing the position of the coil and moving the arm appropriately would be a simple matter of programming.'

An experienced engineer would probably not find much merit in this proposal. It would seem extravagant, using a complicated device to meet a simple need. It would offend what

Reprinted with permission from *IEEE Control Systems Magazine* vol 1 No. 3 pp4-8 September 1981.

Veblen[1] calls the 'instinct of workmanship', the sense of economy and fitness for purpose. Yet the student might not be discouraged. 'All that is true,' he might say, 'but the robot is still economically sound. Only a small number of these plants will be made, and they will have to bear the development costs of any special device we design. Robots are complicated, but because they are made in large numbers they are cheap, while the development costs will be much less.'

After a little investigation, and some calculation, it might perhaps turn out that the student was right. A plant might even be built using a robot for this purpose. What I would like to suggest, however, is that this would not be a stable solution. It would still offend our instinct of workmanship. The robot has much greater abilities than this application demands. We should feel, like the robot specialist[2], that 'To bring in a universal robot would mean using a machine with many abilities to do a single job that may require only one ability.'

As opportunity served we might pursue one of two possibilities. We might in the first place seek to find some simpler and cheaper device which would replace the robot. Alternatively, having a robot in place with capacities which had been paid for but were not being used, we might attempt to create for it a task which more nearly suited its abilities. It might, for example, be able to take over some other task on a neighbouring part of the line. Or we might be able to rearrange the line to bring some other suitable task within the reach of the robot. At all events, as engineers we should not rest happy with the design while a gross mismatch existed between the means we were employing and the tasks on which they were employed.

3.   The application

The drift of this fable will become clear. For robot, substitute man or woman, and then compare our attitudes. This I will do shortly, but first let me extend the quotation which was given above[2]: 'However, it is less obvious that robots will be needed to take the place of human beings in most everyday jobs in industry . . . To bring in a universal robot would mean using a machine with many abilities to do a single job that may require only one ability.' There is a curious discrepancy here between the apparent attitudes to robots and to people, and it is this which I wish to explore.

It will be readily granted that the woman whose working life was spent in picking up a piece of aluminium wire every $4\frac{1}{2}$ seconds had many abilities, and was doing a job which required only one ability. By analogy with the robot one would expect to find two kinds of reaction, one seeking to do the job with a 'simpler device', and the other seeking to make better use of human ability. Both kinds of reaction do exist, though as will be seen, with a curious gap.

First, one cannot read the literature in this field without stumbling continually against one suggestion: that many jobs are more fitted for the mentally handicapped, and can be better done by them. The following are some examples.

'Slight mental retardation . . . often enables a person to do tedious work which would handicap a "normal" worker because of the monotony.'[3]

'The U.S. Rubber Company has even pushed experimentation so far as to employ young girls deficient in intelligence who, in the framework of "scientific management" applied to this business, have given excellent results.'[4]

'The tasks assigned to workers were limited and sterile . . . the worker was made to operate in an adult's body on a job that required the mentality and motivation of a child. Argyris demonstrated this by bringing in mental patients to do an extremely routine job in a factory setting. He was rewarded by the patients' increasing the production by 400 per cent.'[5]

'Mike Bayless, 28 years old with a maximum intelligence level of a 12-year-old, has become the company's NC-machining-centre operator because his limitations afford him the level of patience and persistence to carefully watch his machine and the work that it produces.'[6]

Swain[7] remarks that 'The methodological difficulties of using this . . . approach to the dehumanised job problem cannot be glossed over,' the meaning of which, one hopes, is that society would utterly reject it. Nevertheless, the quotations should alert our instinct of workmanship to the gross misalignment between human abilities and the demands of some jobs. A much more respectable response to this misalignment is the one which appeals to many technologists and engineers — that is, to carry the process of automation to the point where human labour is eliminated.

This becomes easier in manual work as the robot becomes cheaper and more highly developed. So, for example, in the manufacture of automobile bodies spot-welding is now regularly done by robots, and spray-painting will also soon cease to be a human occupation. Similar possibilities for eliminating human labour in clerical work are opened up by the microprocessor.

When it is applied to jobs which are already far below any reasonable estimate of human ability, there can be no objection on our present grounds to this development. Difficulties begin when we consider jobs that demand skill and the full use of human ability. To automate these out of existence in one step is never possible. They have to go first through a long process of fragmentation and simplification, during which they become unsuitable for human performance.

The mismatch between jobs and human abilities has also been approached from the opposite side by social scientists. Seeing the under-use of human ability, they have developed their techniques[8] of job enlargement, job enrichment, and of autonomous groups. These take existing jobs, and redesign them in a way which makes more use of the human abilities of judgement and adaptability. For example, in an autonomous group the allocation of tasks among its members is not imposed from outside but is left to the group itself to decide. The jobs that result can be better matched to human abilities, within the usually severe constraints of the technology. As Kelly[9] has noted, the opening which is given for the exercise of judgment and adaptability within the group may account for some of the increased productivity that has been observed.

These, then, are the techniques available to us for eliminating the mismatch between jobs and human abilities. There are two which reduce the abilities deployed, one of them inadmissible and the other stemming from engineering. There is a group of techniques which seek to use the abilities of people more fully, and these stem from the social sciences. So far as I know there are no others of significance; and what is remarkable is that engineers and technologists have not produced any methodology for using to the full the abilities and skills of human beings.

The designer of the lamp plant, for example, had made its operation automatic wherever he could do so conveniently. Where he could not, he had used human beings. He might perhaps have used robots, and if so he would have been concerned to use them economically and to make full use of their abilities. He felt, it appears, no similar concern for the full use of human abilities. We may say, paradoxically, that if he had been able to consider people as though they were robots, he would have tried to provide them with less trivial and more human work.

4.   A paradigm

The conclusion we have reached discloses the oddity which was mentioned at the beginning of this paper. It is one that becomes more strange the more one considers it, and we are bound to ask how it arises.

The question has two parts: how do individual engineers come to adopt the view we have described, and how did this originate and become established in the engineering profession? As to the individual, engineers in my experience are never taught a set of rules or attitudes which would lead to this kind of view, nor do they base their actions on a set of explicit principles incorporating it. Instead, we have to imagine something like a 'paradigm' discussed by Thomas Kuhn.[10] This is the name he gives, in the sciences, to a matrix of shared attitudes and assumptions and beliefs within a profession.

The paradigm is transmitted from one generation to another, not by explicit teaching but by shared problem-solving. Young engineers take part in design exercises, and later in real design projects as members of the team. In doing so, they learn to see the world in a special way: the way in fact which makes it amenable to the professional techniques which they have available. Paradigms differ from one specialization to another within engineering, so that a control engineer and a thermodynamicist, for example, will see a gas turbine in slightly different ways. Effective collaboration between them will then demand a process of mutual re-education, as many will have discovered from this or other kinds of collaboration.

Seen in this way, as a paradigm which has been absorbed without ever being made fully explicit, the behaviour of the lamp-plant designer becomes understandable. We still have to ask how this paradigm arose. This is a question which deserves a more extended historical study than any I have seen. Tentatively, however, I suggest the following explanation, which has been given elsewhere[11] in somewhat greater detail.

Looking back at the early stages of the industrial revolution we tend to see the early machines as part of one single evolution. Examples of the machines themselves can be found in museums, and in looking at them we see the family resemblance which they all bear, deriving from the materials that were used

and the means by which they were fashioned. They were made of leather and wood, and of wrought and cast iron, and in all of them these materials were fashioned in similar ways.

What I wish to suggest is that there were in fact two quite different kinds of machine, similar only in their materials and their construction, but with opposed relationships to human abilities. One of them can be typified by Hargreaves's spinning-jenny, which he invented for his own or his family's use. It is a hand-operated machine, deriving from the spinning wheel, but allowing many threads to be spun at the same time. To use it demands a skill, which is a natural development from the skill needed to use the spinning wheel. This skill in the user is rewarded by a great increase in his productivity. Samuel Crompton's spinning-mule was a similar kind of machine, and even when it was driven mechanically it needed the skilled cooperation of the spinner.

The other type of machine can be typified by the self-acting mule which was invented by Richard Roberts in 1830. What Roberts set out to do was not, like Hargreaves or Crompton, to make skill more productive. Rather he set out to eliminate skill so that the spinner was no longer needed except to supervise a set of machines. Fragments of his job remained, such as mending broken threads or removing threads which had been spun. These jobs were given largely to children, and they began to resemble the jobs around the lamp-making plant.

For reasons which were valid enough in the early nineteenth century, and which are well documented by Ure[12] and Babbage[13], the second course proved more profitable for the inventor and the manufacturer than the first. When the engineering profession arose later in the century it therefore inherited only one attitude to the relation between machines and human skill, which is essentially the one described above.

Whether this attitude is appropriate at the present time is something which I should question. In a broad economic sense, the under-use of human ability is clearly a loss. Some of the reasons which made it nevertheless profitable for an early manufacturer no longer apply with the same force. Unskilled labour is still cheaper than skilled,[13] but much less so than it was at an earlier period. Once only skilled workers could strike effectively, [12] but the less-skilled now, by their numbers, may have even greater industrial strength.

Under present conditions, the motivation of workers may be a major preoccupation of managers. By 'quality circles' or other means they may strive to engage the abilities of the workers outside their jobs. By the social scientists' techniques of job-redesign they may seek to make the jobs themselves less repugnant to human ability. For engineers to spend effort and money at the same time on fragmenting jobs and reducing their content seems neither rational nor efficient, if there is any alternative.

5.   An alternative paradigm

If Hargreaves and Crompton could develop machines which collaborated with the skills of workers in the eighteenth century can we not do the same in the twentieth century, using the incomparable power and flexibility of new technology? A major difficulty is that the problem is not generally posed as a choice between two alternative routes along which technology could develop. The engineering paradigm is not explicit, and it prevails not by a conscious choice, but by suppressing the ability to see an alternative. It is therefore useful to construct an example to show how a valid choice could indeed be made. This is not easy. At least 150 years of engineering effort have been given to one alternative, while the other has been ignored. One path is therefore broad, smooth and easy, the other narrow, difficult and rough. The example, however, need not be taken from engineering. What has been said applies equally to all technology, and will take on a new force as the advance of the microprocessor affects newer and wider areas.

What proves easiest is to choose as example an area where high skill exists, and where the encroachment of technology upon skill has hardly yet begun. In this way, both possible routes which technological development could follow are placed upon an equal basis. Following an earlier account,[11] the example of medical diagnosis will be used.

Feigenbaum[14] has recently described a computer system called PUFF for the diagnosis of lung diseases. It uses information about patients obtained from an instrument and from their past history. The information is matched against a set of 'rules' which have been developed by computer scientists in collaboration with medical specialists. In the rules is captured the knowledge of the physician, part of which he was explicitly aware of knowing. Another part was knowledge which he used unconsciously and which only became explicit as he compared his own response with that of the computer.

Though still in an early stage of development, the system gave agreement of 90 to 100 per cent with the physician, according to the tests which were used. There is no difficulty in supposing that this and similar systems can be improved until they are at least as good as the unaided physician.

One way in which they might be used is to make the skill in diagnosis of the physician redundant. The computer system could be operated by staff who had not received a full medical training, but only a short and intensive course in the computer system and its area of application. There might then be no difficulty in showing that the quality of diagnoses was as good as before, and possibly even better. The cost would be reduced, and a better service could be offered to the patient.

Alternatively, diagnosis might still be carried out by the physician, but he could be given a computer system to assist him in his work. Much that he had carried in his mind before would now be in the computer, and he would not need to concern himself with it. The computer would aid him by relieving him of this burden, and would allow him to carry on his work more effectively.

Under this second system, the physician would usually agree with the computer's diagnosis, but he would be at liberty to reject it. He might do so if, for example, some implicit rule which he used had not yet found its way into the computer system; or if he began to suspect a side effect from some new drug. Using the computer in this way, the physician would gradually develop a new skill, based on his previous skill but differing from it. Most of this new skill would reside in the area

where he disagreed with the computer, and from time to time more of it might be captured in new rules. Yet there is no reason why the physician's skill in using the computer as a tool should not continually develop.

This is all speculation, but I believe not unreasonable speculation. Which of these two possible routes would be the better? The first leads, step by step, towards the situation typified by the lamp plant. The operators, having no extensive training, can never disagree with the computer, and become its servants. In time, the computer might be given more and more control over their work, requesting information, demanding replies, timing responses and reporting productivity. A mismatch would again arise between the abilities of the operators, and the trivialized tasks they were asked to perform. Social scientists might then be invited to study their jobs, and to suggest some scheme of redesign which would alleviate the monotony or the pressure of the work.

The second path allows human skills to survive and evolve into something new. It cooperates with this new skill and makes it more productive, just as Hargreaves's spinning-jenny allowed the spinner's skill to evolve and become more productive. There seems no reason to believe that this second path would be less economically effective than the first.

The example can be readily transposed into engineering terms. It applies with little change to the future development of computer-aided design. It suggests also that if we re-thought the problem, the operator's job on an NC machine tool need not be fragmented and trivialized, to the point where 'slight mental retardation' becomes an advantage. The task of making a part, from the description produced by a CAD system, could be kept entire, and could become the basis of a developing skill in the operator.

As I have said elsewhere,[15] the task of developing a technology which is well matched to human ability, and which fosters skill and makes it more productive, seems to me the most important and stimulating challenge which faces engineers today. If they are held back from this task, it will not be so much by its difficulty, as by the need for a new vision of the relation between engineering and the use of human skill. That I should pose such a problem to engineers will indicate, I hope, the very high position which I give to the role of engineering.

6.   Postscript

My paper could end at that point, but some readers may (and I hope will) feel a sense of unease. The argument which is developed above is in essence a broadly economic one. The skills and abilities of people are a precious resource which we are misusing, and a sense of economy and fitness for purpose, upon which we justly pride ourselves as engineers, should drive us to find a better relation between technology and human ability.

Yet economic waste is not the truest or deepest reason which makes the lamp plant repugnant to us. It offends against strong feelings about the value of human life, and the argument surely should be on this basis.

I wish that it could be, but my belief at present is that it cannot, for the following reasons. To develop such an argument we need a set of shared beliefs upon which to build the intellectual structure. Medieval Christianity, with its superstructure of scholastic philosophy, would once have provided the framework within which a rational argument could have been developed. By the time of the Industrial Revolution, this had long decayed, and nineteenth century Christianity did not unequivocally condemn the developments I have described.

Marxism provides an alternative set of beliefs, and a philosophical superstructure, and it utterly condemns the misuse of human ability: but only when it is carried on under a capitalist system. If it is carried on under socialism then Marxism seems not to condemn it unequivocally, and those are the conditions under which Marxism can have the greatest influence. In support, it is only necessary to say that the lamp plant was in a socialist state, and is in no way anomalous there.[16]

Humanism might serve as another possible basis, with its demand[17] 'that man make use of all the potentialities he holds within him, his creative powers and the life of the reason, and labour to make the powers of the physical world the instruments of his freedom'. This indeed underlies much of the thought in the social sciences, yet again it seems that no conclusive argument can be based on it.

The difficulties are twofold. First, no system of beliefs is as widely disseminated as industrial society. Therefore if a conclusive argument could be based on one system of beliefs, it would have only a limited regional force. Secondly, and almost axiomatically, if there is a system of beliefs from which some of the prevalent features of industrial society can be decisively condemned, it will not be found as the dominant set of beliefs in an industrialized country.

My own conclusion is that rejection of trivialized and dehumanized work precedes any possible rationalization. Tom Bell[18] tells the following story of his mate who, day after day, sharpened needles in Singer's Clydebank works. 'Every morning there were millions of these needles on the table. As fast as he reduced the mountain of needles, a fresh load was dumped. Day in, day out, it never grew less. One morning he came in and found the table empty. He couldn't understand it. He began telling everyone excitedly that there were no needles on the table. It suddenly flashed on him how absurdly stupid it was to be spending his life like this. Without taking his jacket off, he turned on his heel and went out, to go for a ramble over the hills to Balloch'.

No very large part of the population so far has turned on its heel and gone for a ramble over the hills, though a mood akin to that does exist. If industrial society ever comes to be decisively rejected, it seems to me that it will be in this way and for these reasons, rather than as the result of a logically argued critique. The thought, if valid, takes on a special significance at the present time, when we are engaged in determining the kind of work which men and women will do in the era of the microprocessor.

References

1. Veblen, T. (1898) 'The instinct of workmanship and the irksomeness of labor', *American Jour. of Sociology,* **4**, 2, pp. 187-201.
2. George, F.H. and Humphries, J.D. (eds) (1974) *The Robots are Coming,* NCC Publications, p.164.
3. Swain, A.D. (1977) (quoting Tinkham, M.L. (1971)) 'Design of industrial jobs a worker can do', in Brown, S.C. and Martin, J.N.T. (eds) *Human Aspects of Man-Made Systems,* Open University Press, p.192.
4. Freidmann, G. (1955) *Industrial Society,* Free Press of Glencoe, p.216.
5. Herzberg, F. (1966) *Work and the Nature of Man,* World Publishing, p.39.
6. *American Machinist* (1979), **123**, 7, July, p.58.
7. Swain, A.D., loc. cit.
8. Drake, R.I. and Smith, P.J. (1973) *Behavioural Science in Industry,* McGraw-Hill.
9. Kelly, J.E. (1978) 'A reappraisal of sociotechnical system theory', *Human Relations,* **31**, pp.1069-1099.
10. Kuhn, T.S. (1970) *The Structure of Scientific Revolutions,* Univ. Chicago Press, *passim* but especially pp.181-187.
11. *New Technology: Society, Employment and Skill* (1981), Council for Science and Society.
12. Ure, A. (1835) *The Philosophy of Manufactures,* Charles Knight, London. Also *The Cotton Manufacture of Great Britain* (1836), Charles Knight, London.
13. Babbage, C. (1832) *On the Economy of Machinery and Manufactures,* reprinted 1963, Kelley, New York.
14. Feigenbaum, E.A. (1979) 'Themes and case studies of knowledge engineering', in Michie, D. (ed) *Expert Systems in the Micro-electronic Age,* Edinburgh Univ. Press, pp.3-25.
15. Rosenbrock, H.H. (1977) 'The future of control', *Automatica,* **13**, Pergamon, pp.389-392.
16. Haraszty, M. (1977) *A Worker in a Worker's State,* Penguin Books.
17. Maritain, J. (1977) *True Humanism,* Geoffrey Bles, Centenary Press, p.xii.
18. Meacham, S. (1977) *A Life Apart,* Thames and Hudson, p.137, quoting Tom Bell.

7   Misunderstandings

If one had to choose a single problem that people in organizations bemoan more often than any others it would surely be the 'poor communication' and 'misunderstandings' that are pretty well endemic in all but the smallest and most stable organizations. But in referring to such occasions managers and administrators often imply that they result from no more than carelessness — and that in a well-run, professionally managed organization such events would not occur. In fact, the issue runs far deeper than this as the following piece makes very plain. It is a slightly condensed compilation of the first two chapters of a recent and valuable book that deals with these difficulties and goes on in later chapters to describe some novel ways of tackling them in the particular context of consultancy relationships. But it is obvious that much of what they say about the relation between clients and 'helpers' applies equally well to other organizational relationships, especially between staff or service personnel, and line managers.

Understanding Problems and the Problem of Understanding

C. Eden, S. Jones and D. Sims

Consider the following account.

John Smith is a marketing manager in a division of a large manufacturing company, Ian Brown the division's newly appointed marketing director. John Smith had just been to a meeting of the marketing department, the first with its new director. The appointment had not been a great surprise. Most people had assumed that Ian would get the job after his predecessor Brian Jones had been promoted to Head Office. In the three years since he had joined the division, Ian's area had been particularly successful, with two major and successful new product launches. He also had exactly the right kind of personality, John mused, aggressive, dynamic, self-confident. Personally John did not like him and thought he could be an 'absolute bastard' at times, but John had to admit that he was good at his job. Furthermore, with the successor to Ian's old job still undecided it would be stupid to 'get on the wrong side' of the man, even if his own chances of getting the job were, at this stage, remote. Anyway, he thought, the meeting had not been the exciting event everyone had been expecting, although the fact that no announcements had been made about the successor would be bound to get everybody talking. In the meeting Ian had just gone over the future plans and there was nothing new, the usual policy statements about the fact that the division was strong in some markets, weak in others and efforts to find new products would continue to have a high priority.

Peter Williams, responsible for the industrial products section, had put forward his usual argument that the problems in his area had little to do with the division's (i.e. his) efforts and much more to do with overall adverse market conditions. There was no doubt that he was probably right and Ian had not openly disagreed, though he had cut Peter short in the middle of his 'spiel'. (Peter did tend to go on a bit.)

As John walked down the corridor Martin Evans, the promotions co-ordinator, came up to him. 'What did you think of that, then?' he asked. 'O.K.', John grunted, guardedly, turning into his office. Martin was one of those people he disliked and distrusted. His efforts to impress Ian in the meeting had been so obvious as to be almost amusing John thought.

As John sat down Alan Dixon came in. Alan was the new-products manager and a good friend both in and outside work. He was looking anxious. 'Didn't like the sound of all that' he said. 'I reckon we are all going to be under the microscope now. Did you notice how he looked at me when he said we should pay more attention to exploiting existing names in development? (John hadn't.) You know how much trouble I had convincing Brian that we should keep separate identities for products in different market segments. I thought I had won that one. Now it

Eden, Jones and Sims. *Messing About with Problems*, 1983, Pergamon Press, Oxford.

looks as if I'll have to go through it all over again. I tell you, if he starts trying to change things radically in my area, it will be a disaster. And what about the way he was getting at Peter. I think he is definitely going to try to give Peter the push . . .'

Although this scene is an imagined one, we hope that what it describes believably captures some of the flavour of organizational life as most of us experience it.

We left John and his friend Alan in the middle of discussing what had 'gone on' in the meeting they had both just attended. It is clear that Alan had placed an interpretation upon the events occurring in that meeting, in terms of potential significance for him, quite different from that belonging to John. His interpretation had led him to feel distinctly anxious about the future behaviour of the new marketing director. John, on the other hand, had found the meeting rather uneventful. We may even suppose that he had been disappointed that it had not been more exciting. Are we 'rigging' the story? Of course. Yet we would ask you to consider how often when 'comparing notes' with colleagues after a meeting you find that each person will recall different aspects of the meeting, place different emphases on different aspects, or interpret the implications of the meeting in different ways, Sometimes the differences can be so significant that it hardly seems that the same meeting is being discussed.

The point that we wish to make here is so obvious that it appears almost trivial. Different people interpret situations in different ways. We have much in common with others in our social worlds — language, shared beliefs about the nature of things and relationships between them, and shared norms about what we should or should not do. Many of these come to have a meaning so institutionalized that they are taken to be 'matters of fact'.[1] Nevertheless our individual histories are unique to each of us. Different people interpret situations in different ways because they bring to a situation their own particular mental 'framework' of personal beliefs, attitudes, hypotheses, prejudices, expectations, personal values and objectives, with which they can make sense of (place an interpretation upon) the situation.[2] Thus they pay attention to certain things, ignore others, and regard some as having a particular significance for themselves in the future.

Returning to our example, this perspective would lead us to suggest that different recollections of a meeting by different individuals, have less to do with one person having a 'better' memory than another than with how those individuals differently made sense of the meeting in terms of their particular mental frameworks. That is to say, individuals' recollections of a meeting and interpretations of what was significant within it come from their own beliefs and expectations — for example, about the world of things and people in general, about meetings in their organization, about the people there and their intentions — and from the future implications they see in the meeting for themselves in terms of their values and objectives. [. . .]

An organization of human beings

Much of a person's hypothesizing about his world will be about the other human beings that make up that world. He will be concerned to understand what makes other people 'tick' as much as is enough for him to manage his interactions with them to his own satisfaction.

In the scenario described earlier we learned that John, the main protagonist, disliked his new boss but respected him for his competence, disliked and distrusted one of his colleagues and therefore avoided discussing his feelings about the meeting with him, but was involved in a close and friendly relationship with another who had dropped in immediately after the meeting for a 'post-mortem' on it. The point we wish to draw out here is that individuals in organizations are involved, as elsewhere, in complicated social relationships where they dislike, like, care about, find boring, are rude to, dismiss, fear, even fall in and out of love with, other members of the organizations. Much of their energy is spent in handling these relationships and in developing some understanding of those others in order to do so (and a large proportion of time is spent in, and enjoyment derived from, gossiping about other people).

So-called 'irrationalities' of personal evaluations of other people as those who 'get up my nose' or 'bore the pants off me' have a great deal more influence on decisions which involve those people than perhaps we would care to admit. Thus, for example, we know that being liked by the boss is at least as important as being seen by him as competent, in terms of what we might be able to persuade him to do.[3] Most of the time our own behaviour and that of others is not reflected upon or managed in a particularly self-conscious way. We are usually as human beings extremely competent in dealing with all the nuances, variations, surprising twists and turns of interactions with other people. Brief discontinuities, moments of uncomfortableness in an otherwise satisfactory or, to us, unimportant relationship rarely represent serious problems for us.

However, there clearly are times when we see events in relationships with others as having significant implications that we do not like. Indeed there is a large body of professional practice concerned with teaching about, or intervening in, 'interpersonal' problems in organizations. Often it is assumed that there is some relatively straightforward demarcation between such 'interpersonal' problems and other kinds of problems. That such a demarcation is rarely, if ever, clear cut is one of the points we hope our example illustrates.

Political concerns

John and his friend Alan had been ruminating about what Ian Brown, the new director, being the sort of man they believed him to be, and in the light of the things he had said in the meeting, might do in the future which would have implications for their life in the organization. In his new role Ian had suddenly become someone of much greater significance than in the past. The meeting had left Alan feeling anxious and we can readily imagine him spending no small amount of mental energy on attempting to predict exactly what Ian's future actions might be with respect to himself. He will probably attempt to 'suss' out the opinions and feelings of various colleagues. He will probably consider what strategies he might use to prevent Ian from interfering in ways that he does not like, and so on. We are touching here upon that category of activities in which individuals engage with respect to one another known as organizational politics. Specifically, self-consciously and according to some strategic sense of a desired end to be served, they seek to gain other people's support for, or prevent them from hindering, certain states of affairs relating to those ends.

To do this, individuals will seek to ensure that other people hold the definition of a situation that they want them to hold. They can do this in several ways. For example they will sometimes attempt to persuade through the power of 'rational' argument, or through the self-evident merit of their image of desired ends or means, or by appeal to their own 'superior' expertise. Sometimes they will lie, cheat and attempt to manipulate. In either case they will be selective about what information they reveal and order its presentation in particular ways according to their own understanding of what is likely to be most persuasive to the particular people concerned. They will usually present their argument as reflecting a concern for the 'good' of the organization, or at least of those particular people. Often they will believe this to be so, sometimes they will not, but to admit otherwise would be to break one of the cardinal rules of the organizational political game — that of admitting to 'selfish' motives. The essence of this rule is not that people actually believe others to be unselfish, indeed usually quite the opposite. Simply that there appears to be an almost 'fact of the matter' norm among members of most organizations that it is illegitimate to admit to personal ends.

Because individuals with distinct perspectives and political concerns rarely reach complete agreement about ends and means, compromise outcomes are often negotiated or bargains struck about favours to be exchanged at different times.[4] Alliances will be formed, some relatively stable and enduring, others relatively short term. The energetic will spend considerable effort and time in finding out what others do want and think on a particular issue. (Often this involves a game-like process in which both parties know what is going on, are ready to be involved in what is going on, but do not acknowledge openly that they are participating in a lobbying process.) They will 'chat up' those they regard as powerful, not for any particular purpose but still with some strategic conception that such activities will bear fruit later in some particular context.[5] And they will do these things because they seek, as reasonable men and women, to pursue what they regard as right and best. It is important to be clear that organizational politics is not the sole territory of self-interested manipulators, megalomaniacs or charlatans. [. . .]

To take this perspective seriously means that it is impossible to assume, self-evidently and non-problematically, that the way other people interpret a situation, is the same as, or even similar to, the way we interpret that 'same' situation. An event which you or I might see as a major crisis for a particular reason may be seen as a major crisis by someone else for completely different reasons, by another person as a minor difficulty, and yet other people may not even have noticed it at all. No situation is inherently, 'objectively' a problem. A problem belongs to a person; it is an often complicated, and always personal (albeit in some part shared with some others) construction that an individual places on events. [. . .]

The experience of problems

We can usually give some sort of an answer to the question 'What is the problem?', but it may not be an answer that convinces us, and we often feel we have only been able to give a rather limited description. So it is quite common that the only descriptions we can find for problems are, without in any way being intended to be lies, not descriptions that we feel contain the most important truths about our problems.

Now this is a common feature of the experience of many people, that the step between feeling some sort of discomfort or dissatisfaction, feeling that there is some problem somewhere, and being able to say 'The problem is such-and-such' is a very big step. In fact quite often we find that if we can say what the problem is we have gone a long way towards solving it. This seems to be true with any kind of problem, whether it be some technically oriented work problem, a relationship problem at home, or anything in between.

One of the properties of problems with which helpers have found it quite hard to grapple is the extent to which all problems are personal; different persons see different problems in what other people would take to be the same situation. This is an important point in our argument, and it is fairly well accepted in everyday 'common sense'. This point does not seem to raise much disagreement when it is expressed theoretically, but it is often rather more difficult to bear it in mind and act upon it in practice. For this reason, we shall give three examples of what different people seeing different problems may look like.

Suppose that a student reported himself as feeling tired and listless, generally not very well, and that he did not feel he could be bothered to do anything. A students' union officer might conclude that the student's problem was depression, and might probe to find out more about the depression by asking the student how long it had been going on. The doctor at the University medical centre might say that the problem was a cold, that there were a lot of them about and that she had just had one herself. The student's academic tutor might think that the student was not absorbing himself sufficiently in his work, and that a bit more application and hard work would make still more application and hard work easier. The campus radical might think that the problem was classical anomie and alienation, brought on by the death throes of the capitalist system, and the student counsellor might start from the belief that the problem must lie with the student's sex life. Each of these people finds a different problem in the situation, at least in part because they are each inclined to attribute different causes to events.

For another example, think of a board of directors in a medium-sized manufacturing firm, confronted with a set of figures which show that they 'have a problem of' their market share declining. In this case, the people involved might agree this label for their problem, but might have quite different interpretations of that agreed problem label. The production director may think that the problem is a hopeless advertising campaign that the marketing department have bought, the marketing director may think that the problem is the inflexibility of the production department, which prevents them from being able to offer customers the delivery dates and special options that competitors can achieve. The finance director may think that the problem is excessive conservatism on the part of both the marketing and the production directors in continuing with rigid quality control even though it means that their product is a little more expensive than others on the market.

It is by no means always the case that people assume that problems stem from others rather than themselves. For example, on a magazine, it would be quite possible for an editor to think that they are losing readers because the features editor has become fascinated by some subject which bores most of their readers, while the advertisement controller may attribute loss of readers to a decrease in the number of advertising pages. Both people might believe that it is really their contribution that the magazine depends on, and so any serious problems must stem from their own function.

When we talk about problems, we are not necessarily thinking of problems in the negative sense — our definition was that a problem was a situation where someone wanted something to be different from how it was and was not quite sure how to go about making it so. Thus opportunities for building on strengths and making positive improvements, openings that you feel are there to be exploited but you cannot quite see how at the moment, are also counted as problems for our purpose. The same point about how different people see different problems still applies. The editor and the advertisement controller of a successful magazine may well see different problems in the sense of different opportunities for their magazine, where the editor may think that there is an opportunity to expand the editorial content by a few pages, and thus bring in large numbers of extra readers, ensuring the health, future and profitability of the magazine. The advertisement controller may at the same time see an opportunity to tie the editorial matter more closely to the advertising material, and increase the number of pages of prestige advertising, thus enabling them to increase the rate per page for advertising there, and so ensuring the health, future and profitability of the magazine!

So different people see different problems, and in this sense problems are made and not born. To some extent we believe we can generalize about the kinds of problems that people of different roles, personalities and cultures define for themselves. For example, there is a frequent generalization in the Health Service that, while physicians see everything (not just patients) as complicated and needing a lot of thought, surgeons see all problems as much more cut and dried. Some personalities seem to find the running of a large business to be something which they just get on with and which they do not see as problematic, while others find it a very difficult problem to decide what to eat for lunch. In some cultures, possession of a certain kind of problem seems to be very important to people. For some people in British engineering companies, for example, to have no problem of stress and over-working suggests to them that they are slacking, or unimportant, or in some other way deficient. With some people it seems that if they are short of problems at work they manage to devise themselves the most amazingly complicated problems to do with how they go on holiday.

All these differences in the kinds of problem that different people see do not necessarily imply that any of them are wrong, or that they are deceiving themselves, but rather that almost any situation that a person might be dissatisfied with can be seen as having multiple causes, and any one of those causes may be taken as the central point to hang a problem around. If a person is dissatisfied with the amount of money they have, they may say that the problem is too much taxation, or that their company pays them too little, or that their financial aspirations are too high, or any of a huge number of possible tags could be used to describe the problem that they are experiencing. They may say all of these things, and mean them, which means that it is very important not to take the first verbal tag offered as being 'the problem', but only as an initial indicator that there may be a complicated interlocking mess of problems there to be investigated.[7]

When we are in a situation which is complex and worrying, we are usually too busy and too anxious and too involved with that situation to perceive such choices of what we might see the problem as being; they are often visible only from the outside.

The helper and problems

Problems, then, are very individual things in the sense that different persons might see quite different problems in the same situation. The individual may find it helpful to remember that another person might construct a quite different problem, or even no problem at all, if they were in the same situation; this fact may be of some help in letting a person think more laterally about their problems.

The argument becomes much more significant, however, when we think about problems with which several persons are concerned, because in that case those persons might have quite different views of the problem, both because they have different ways of understanding what is going on around them, and also possibly because they have different interests, responsibilities, duties, and relationships, which lead them to quite different concerns. [. . .]

It would not be untypical in an organization for a person to feel unease or disquiet about something, and for them then to need the agreement of their colleagues and their boss before they can talk to a helper about it. When they talk to their colleagues and boss, they will almost certainly have to answer questions from them about 'What is the problem?' They will need to give them some answer to that question, which shows that the problem is of a type that they need help with, but which also does not suggest that they need help because they are incompetent (presuming they do not want to be thought incompetent), and also probably which suggests to them that it is in their interests too to have help with this problem; so the person might well choose to state their problem in a way that implies that a solution to it might also solve problems that they suspect some of their colleagues have. They will also almost invariably feel the need to talk about this problem in terms of not being satisfied over the things that are publicly regarded in their organization as legitimate values; this means that a lot of problems which might initially have had nothing to do with such concepts end up being talked about in the teams of the persons who have them in terms of profit, efficiency, ensuring future markets and so on. Even within a team of managers who get on reasonably well and trust each other, it would be unusual for a problem to be phrased in more personal and less legitimate terms such as promotion, making life easier for oneself, or gaining some advantage over another department in the organization.

Not only will the person who introduces the problem produce a carefully doctored version in this way, but also the other members of the team will want to have their say, and so produce further and possibly drastic changes, as the problem is discussed and negotiated within the team. Once again, the points they make are edited by them in line with years of hard-earned and successful experience in that organization, as to what sort of things they need to say in order to get what they want and maintain a favourable image with one another. The skills which all of us who work in organizations develop mean that, without anyone being in the least untruthful or deliberately deceitful, the discussion is almost bound to be quite some way removed from a frank and open discussion of what it is that is eating us. [. . .]

All this, it should be noted, presumes good will and no intention to mislead on the part of anybody. We are for the moment ignoring such situations as when a person presents a problem which they intend to lead to the downfall and removal of one of their colleagues, or where someone lays claim to a problem which they do not actually feel, but they think will impress their colleagues, or where a helper is brought in to talk about a problem in the hope that they will fail, so that the problem concerned can be shown to be of huge proportions and unassailable. A current favourite is to put a problem to a helper in such a way that you get a report back from him which can then be argued as a case for making people redundant; 'we deeply regret this, but the study that has been carried out by independent consultants has shown that . . .', and the helper, by being set a carefully selected problem, has produced a predictable answer which can then be used by the clients as a pseudo-objective justification for the action they were going to take anyhow.

For another example, two departments in an oil company both retained Operational Research consultants to look at the question of how much storage tankage should be built at a particular refinery. Both groups set out to produce profit-maximizing answers to the question. Each group was given the context of the issue by its employing department, and both groups came up with answers which were in the interests of their department; the two answers conflicted sharply. Even in this case, it seems unlikely that the persons concerned thought they were distorting anything. Much more likely is that they thought they were giving the 'right' description of the problem.

So how does a helper begin to be helpful in such a complicated situation?

The first answer to this question that we have found useful is to find ways to help clients to talk as directly as they can about what it is that is concerning them. If the helper is labelled as an Operational Researcher, clients may feel that they should quantify as much as they can of what they say to him. Nothing wrong with that, of course, if they were already thinking of it all quantitatively, but quite often they may not have been doing so, the quantities they give may be an afterthought; they do not feel very confident in the quantification, and therefore however good the rest of the helper-client interaction, they will not feel very confident in the outcome of whatever work the helper does. They know that it was all based on doubtful data in the first place. So it is important that the client should feel able to talk about things in non-quantitative ways.

Similarly, a lot of factors that are significant in many of the more important organizational decisions are not seen by the decision maker as being definite points, but rather are feelings, or hunches, or theories. When talking to helpers they are quite likely to feel that they should not spend their time telling a 'management scientist' about feelings and theories, but should rather stick to the 'facts'. It is our experience that the things that are seen as objective, hard 'facts' around problems that are really concerning people are often fairly trivial compared with the subjective, soft 'feelings' or 'theories' that they see as central to it. This is scarcely surprising, because people who are dealing with complicated and large issues will have built up a body of experience and wisdom over time which probably incorporates more different things than they would know how to separate out or talk about; their 'feelings' are actually based on a huge number of 'facts', but because they cannot remember and describe those facts individually, they may not regard the resulting feeling as a worthy topic to talk about in front of a helper. Helpers who let such an inhibition persist will be deprived of most of their clients' important thinking about their situations. [. . .]

Thereby the helper does not find out what is really bothering his clients. They work together on a problem which either neither of them, or just the helper 'owns'. In these circumstances often neither of them feels satisfied with the outcome, as for example, when a helper works, with the best of intentions and effort on a problem he thought his client had only to find out afterwards that his recommendations have been quietly ignored and the client is acting in ways that make no sense with respect to the problem the helper heard about; while the client, while acknowledging that the helper has done his best, is confirmed in his belief that the helper can only provide assistance with particular, and limited, aspects of problems.

Footnotes

[1] For a detailed and important analysis of the relationship between 'subjective' and 'objective' realities and knowledge see Berger, P.L. and Luckmann, T. (1966) *The Social Construction of Reality*, New York, Doubleday. Another useful but difficult book in this context is by Silverman, D. (1970) *Theory of Organizations*, who describes and evaluates several different perspectives for understanding organizations, including his own orientation to the nature of actions as arising from the meaning individuals ascribe to events (see particularly Chapter 6).

[2] For a discussion of the nature of beliefs and values see Chapter 3 in Eden, C., Jones, S. and Sims, D. (1979) *Thinking in Organizations*, London, Macmillan. See also Young, M. (1977) *Society, State and Schooling*, and Rokeach, M. (1973) *Nature of Human Values*.

[3] For a discussion of the significance of personal relationships and what he terms 'particularism' in organizational decision making see Perrow, C. (1972) *Complex Organizations*.

[4] For an interesting analysis of the difficulty in distinguishing between means and ends in the pursual of goals and objectives see Ackoff, R.L. (1979) 'The Future of Operations Research is Past', *Journal of the Operations Research Society*, **30**, 93-104.

[5] For a book which describes in detail the internal political aspects of organizational decision making using the case study of the purchase of a computer see Pettigrew (1973) *Politics of Organizational Decision Making*. Another fascinating case is described, almost in the form of a novel, by Jones, R. and Lakin, C. (1978) *The Carpet Makers*, Maidenhead, McGraw-Hill.

[6] For further discussion of this question see: Eden, C. and Sims, D. (1979) 'On the nature of problems in consulting practice', *Omega*, **7**, 2, pp.119-127; Sims, D. (1978) 'Problem construction in teams', Ph.D. Thesis, University of Bath; and Sims, D. (1979) 'A framework for understanding the definition and formulation of problems in teams', *Human Relations*, **32**, 11, pp.909-921.

[7] The idea of problems being found in 'messes' comes from Ackoff, R.L. (1974) *Redesigning the Future*, who describes a mess as a 'system of problems'. Kepner, C.H. and Tregoe, B.B. (1965) *The Rational Manager*, New York, McGraw-Hill, use on page 63 a different definition of mess, very similar to our definition of 'problem'.

The benefits of information technology are something of a 'promised land': you have to endure a veritable wilderness of sensitive, ferociously complicated, and far-reaching decision-making in order to get there, not to mention some large expenditures; and still it doesn't work as you hoped. Indeed, for every major blessing it brings, as likely as not there will be a clutch of nasty little curses. If the new system is infuriating when it doesn't do what it's supposed to, it may be even more infuriating when it does. The following article provides a clear account of these increasingly familiar problems; it argues the case for an evolutionary and participative approach to system design as a way to overcoming them; but it is commendably frank about the difficulties of such an approach. As usual, there are no easy answers . . .

The Process of Introducing Information Technology

K.D. Eason

1   The age of information technology

We are constantly being bombarded with the news that we are entering a new information technology era which will revolutionize the office, bring robots to our production lines, change the face of our high streets and bring information services of all kinds into our own homes (Evans 1979, Forester 1979, Toffler 1980). We are also forcefully told of the threat this revolution poses for employment (Jenkins and Sherman 1979) but nevertheless we are exhorted to embrace the technology speedily because unless we do our companies will lose their competitiveness.

Close behind the reports of the wonders of the new technology are reports of the slow rate at which companies are responding to the challenge. Zermeno *et al* (1979) for example, documents the slow march of robots into British manufacturing industry whilst Mackintosh (1981) reports a survey of top U.K. industrial managers which shows that they know something is going on but are 'either incapable or unwilling to learn about its strategic implications for their own organizations'.

Why are we being slow to adopt information technology? Many reasons can and have been advanced. One argument is that we are in a recession and when the main preoccupation is survival there is no point in making long term plans to introduce new technology. A second argument is that within organizations, and especially within management, there is a deep-rooted ignorance of this technology and its significance. This argument leads to efforts to increase the computer literacy of

management and to schemes such as the regional centres of the National Computing Centre in the U.K. which will provide advice to local businessmen.

A third argument is that, whilst information technology may have many potential benefits, it is not easy to realize these benefits. Most reasonably sized organizations have made some use of computers and found it very difficult to achieve the promised results. Some systems were never implemented; others that were implemented became sources of inertia and inflexibility within their organizations. In a recent study (Lyne and Davis 1981) we found that management were very suspicious of the claims of computer salesmen and were being very cautious with their money. There is also a widespread recognition that introducing information technology creates human, social, political and organizational problems which have to be solved before implementation can be successful. The increasing awareness of trade unions of these implications serves to make management more wary. If they are unsure of the benefits claimed and are aware of the potential problems, it is small wonder managers are slow to venture into the information technology revolution.

Of these arguments the one that is receiving most attention at the moment is the need to improve the level of computer literacy: to show people the technology and help them to understand it. I believe this to be a necessary but not sufficient condition for the successful implementation of information technology. It leaves potential users with a wide variety of problems concerning the choice of a system which will meet their specific

Behaviour and Information Technology Vol. 1, No. 2, April-June 1982.

needs and how to implement the system with the minimum of negative ramifications within their organization. In this paper my intention is twofold; to consider in more detail the nature of the problems to be overcome and then to consider how best organizations may be assisted to cope with these problems.

2   The impact of computerization

We can conveniently divide these issues into two groups:
(1) Issues concerning the functions to be performed by the technology.
(2) Consequential effects of implementing the system within the organization.

2.1 The functions of information technology

Computer-based technology is potentially very flexible. However before it can be used by the non-specialist it has to be programmed to perform very specific activities. If these activities are what is required by the organization, all may be well. If the activities performed by the system differ even slightly from what is needed major problems can develop; either the system is rejected or perhaps is only partly used (where the 'fit' is best) or the organization modifies what is required (the 'tool' defines the 'task') (Eason *et al.* 1974). The experience of the latter is of a system rigidly shaping how activities are undertaken; representatives of the organization and their customers find their freedom to behave appropriately to their task constrained by 'what the computer will allow'. Over time, as the task of the organization changes a badly fitting and rigid system can become a major obstacle to the organization's ability to respond adaptively. Far from becoming a major vehicle to facilitate change, the system can become a major source of inertia.

These problems point to many issues which concern the would-be user of information technology. What are his needs and how unique are they? Can he get a good fit from a package or does he need special purpose software? How flexible is the software and how readily can it be modified as organizational needs change? To answer these questions the user must obviously understand the potential of the technology but he must also and pre-eminently be able to assess his own needs.

Even if a system has the potential to serve a user's needs, the potential may not be realized. The user may find the system difficult to use, difficult to understand, takes too much of his time or involves unacceptable and unnatural behaviour from him. These issues make up the problem of 'usability' or 'user acceptance' and Eason (1981a) has described how the strategies users adopt when confronted by these problems can mean that a new system remains unused. When introducing a new system, therefore, it is necessary to consider not only the user's needs but also the forms of answering these needs which will be acceptable to him.

2.2   Consequences of implementing information technology

In some ways the information flows in an organization can be compared with the nervous system in a body. To install a new means of processing information is rather like providing the body with a major transplant. We know that an organ transplant in the body may be unsuccessful in two ways; it may be rejected as foreign tissue or it may lead to severe complications because of the adaptations it necessitates in interdependent systems. The body is a collection of systems which need to work in some degree of harmony. Similarly an organization is a collection of systems which have to achieve a degree of harmony if useful work is to be produced. The insertion of a computer system in the role of purveyor of information between systems can disrupt the harmony. The result may be a rejection of the system or serious negative complications elsewhere in the organization which effectively dissipate the gains made by introducing the system.

Figure 8.1 presents a sociotechnical systems view of an organization showing the many different subsystems which have to operate within it, any of which may be disrupted by the injection of a computer system into a central information processing role. A considerable volume of research has been conducted to show where and in what form the knock-on effects of computer technology are likely to show themselves. The following is a brief summary of the major effects that can occur in the social systems identified in Figure 8.1.

2.2.1 Job numbers. There is frequently a change in the number of jobs required within the organization. Perhaps the largest perceived threat of computer technology is that it will lead to a massive loss of jobs. This is sometimes the case but there are also many examples of increases in job numbers. However, it is often the case that the new jobs will require different skills from the old ones and many people may be displaced because they are deemed unsuitable for the new jobs (Gotlieb and Borodin 1973).

2.2.2 Job content. Contrary to many popular views, people are still needed when computers are in use. What they do will almost certainly change. One view has man freed of dull routine and able to become the creative problem solver of the organization. Another view has man in dull repetitive jobs serving the computer by providing input for it. In practice both kinds of jobs have been created and there is often considerable potential for designing appropriate kinds of jobs (Eason and Sell 1981).

2.2.3 Health issues. There is growing awareness that the use of visual display units might be a health hazard. The evidence for serious impairments is by no means conclusive and appears to relate primarily to full-time users engaged in routine work. There is plenty of evidence for more transitory health problems e.g. visual fatigue and postural problems, such as backache (Pearce 1980a, b, 1981).

2.2.4 Skills and training. Changing jobs means changing skills and therefore new training programmes. Obviously this will mean the development of keyboard skills or learning the procedures of the computer systems but in practice it often goes much further than this and affects the way people perceive their jobs and they way they learn to exploit the facilities of the computer system to perform the job differently.

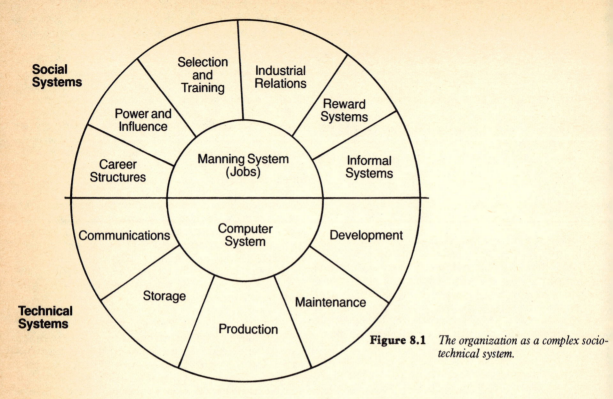

Figure 8.1 *The organization as a complex socio-technical system.*

2.2.5 Formality. Perhaps the most commonly found consequence of computerization is an increase in the formality of organizational procedures. The functioning of a computer depends upon formal programs and their use demands a degree of formality. As a result formality and discipline spread into the organizational procedures which surround the system. Whether this becomes a useful source of order and efficiency or an inhibiting source of rigidity and inflexibility depends upon how the organization manages this effect (Bjorn-Andersen and Eason 1980).

2.2.6 Power and influence. Information often leads to power, influence and status. There has long been an argument that computerization will lead to a further centralization of power, as senior managers with better sources of information are better able to control their organizations. However, the evidence from empirical studies, whilst showing this as a prevalent trend, also shows decentralization and lateral transfers of power and influence (Bjorn-Andersen and Rasmussen 1980).

2.2.7 Personnel policies and industrial relations. Changes in job content and skills have knock-on effects for other personnel policies. Payment systems have to be rethought, grading systems for new and changed jobs evaluated and career patterns replanned. The industrial relations practices of the organizations may suddenly need amendment; for example demarcation agreements may be rendered irrelevant. The attitude and actions of trade unions to these changes may be vital to the success of technological change.

2.3   Consequences for systems design

Other ramifications, particularly for interdependent technical systems, have not been listed. Suffice it to say that any change in the ground rules by which an organization operates will have many effects. The purpose of cataloguing these effects is to make four points:

(1) Whilst it is necessary to understand the new technology there are a host of other issues which must also be understood before technical change can be successful.

(2) Whilst there are many ramifications, there is very little that is unidirectional or inevitable about them. Jobs may be lost but jobs may also be gained, poor jobs or good jobs may be created, etc. *The choice of system and the choice of the way it is integrated into the organization will determine the kinds of effects that are found.*

(3) If systems selection and design is conducted largely on technical and economic criteria (as has tended to be the case) without explicit recognition of these organizational issues, the process will be one of fighting many fires as they become apparent. It will also be one in which the sociotechnical system created has not been designed but has arisen in an *ad hoc* way. It may in fact lead to a form of organization ineffective for organizational purposes and unwanted by the

personnel of the organization.

(4) There is a wide choice of systems and ways in which they may be implemented and therefore, to a large extent, the effects can be controlled and guided. We need forms of systems design which explicitly tackle these issues if we are not to be surprised by the obstructions to technological progress and unhappy with the results.

3 Strategies for considering organizational consequences in systems design

As a member of the HUSAT Research Group at Loughborough University of Technology I have been working on the human and organizational ramifications of computer systems for over a decade. This group has contributed to research on the effects of systems but much of our work has also been to help organizations confront these ramifications and plan for them during systems design. Initially we worked within the normal systems design framework and found it difficult to ensure appropriate attention to human and organizational issues. Gradually we have evolved a different approach which is now becoming popular in the organizations with whom we have worked. In the sections that follow I trace the changes in approach we have found necessary and document the strategies we are now following.

3.1 Stage 1: human factors in a traditional systems design process

In the early stages of our efforts to help organizations consider the human ramifications of systems during the design process we found ourselves operating within what might be considered a traditional design process and this is probably still the dominant approach in use today. The major elements of this approach are presented in Figure 8.2. In this approach the dominant theme is putting together a working technical system.

The system is usually created by a design team consisting of technical experts with senior management in a steering role concerning themselves with cost-benefit aspects of the system. The design process usually consists of some kind of feasibility study followed by a phase in which equipment is purchased and software purchased and/or designed. Finally the working and tested system is implemented.

Our role is primarily to help the organization and its employees learn about the system and its consequences and to take appropriate action to achieve the benefits and avoid or minimize the negative effects. This proved to be a quite difficult feat. Under the technology-led approach the end users of the system did not become involved until the system was implemented. The end users are the people best able to predict the consequences of a specific system because (a) they have an intimate knowledge of the nature of the work and (b) they understand the workings of the many related systems that may be affected. An outsider can point to where effects may occur but it takes a detailed knowledge of the specific organizational fabric to judge what form they will take.

Our work in this kind of systems design process was therefore confined to helping people appreciate the issues of a system that had already been designed. Their new learning could not be used to develop a system with different effects: it could only be used to ameliorate the effects by accommodating them within other organizational systems and by adaptation of the users themselves. The situation is summarized in Figure 8.3.

We can look upon the design process as one of progressive 'firming up'. Initially the technology can in theory do everything but in practice can do nothing. By a succession of design decisions a system is gradually developed which can achieve something specific but at the same time it loses the rest of its potential. In this systems design process the design of the technical systems is virtually frozen before users become sufficiently aware of the ramifications of the system to take action. They can then only take action within the interrelated systems of the organization or can reject the system or minimize its use.

Design process	Phased (feasibility-design-implementation)
Design mechanisms	Technical design team with management steering group
Organizational learning and adaptation processes	From implementation onwards and non-design oriented

Figure 8.2   *The design elements in technology-led systems design.*

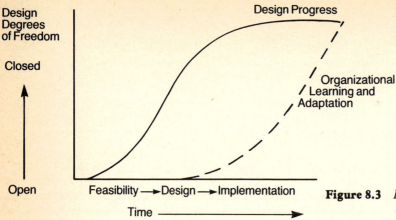

Figure 8.3   *Design closure and organizational learning in technology-led systems design.*

3.2 Stage 2: user involvement in systems design

During the 1970s it became apparent to many people that the traditional systems design process was not an adequate vehicle for taking full account of the organizational issues surrounding the implementation of new technology. There was a movement, particularly strong to Scandinavia (see, for example, Bjorn-Andersen 1980) towards involving users much earlier in the design process in order that they could affect the design of the systems they were to use. In the Scandinavian countries these moves have been given the backing of a legal framework. In the U.K., we promoted similar approaches as did many others, notably Enid Mumford (Mumford and Henshall 1979).

The general change in approach is summarized in Figure 8.4. The major change is that the mechanisms by which the system is created are expanded to include end users at both the steering level and at the detailed design level. There are many ways of accomplishing this ranging from co-opted user representatives in the technical design team to 'user design' in which users effectively develop their own system (a classification of alternative forms of user involvement is given by Damodaran and Eason (1981)). The overall aim of such schemes is always, however, to encourage users to participate in the creation of the system throughout the design process.

There has now been considerable experience of user-involvement schemes and one general point emerges; it is an essential feature for many reasons but it is exceptionally difficult to manage effectively. The main problems encountered are as follows.

3.2.1 Influence and control. There is always the question of how much of a voice users have in design decisions. If they find they can have little influence and are there merely because a gesture towards consultation was supposed to smooth implementation, they can become disenchanted and resistant. On the other hand if they have a major voice, the technologists or management may feel they have been robbed of their prerogatives and may become resistant to user involvement.

3.2.2 Understanding systems terminology. The nature of the technology and the terminology of systems design is initially a mystery to most users. It is especially difficult in the early stages of design when there is only an abstract version of the system available. It is very difficult for users to comment meaningfully on a flow-chart or a system specification. They need time and help before they can make their contribution. It is much easier to comment when a working system becomes available but by then it is too late to make changes.

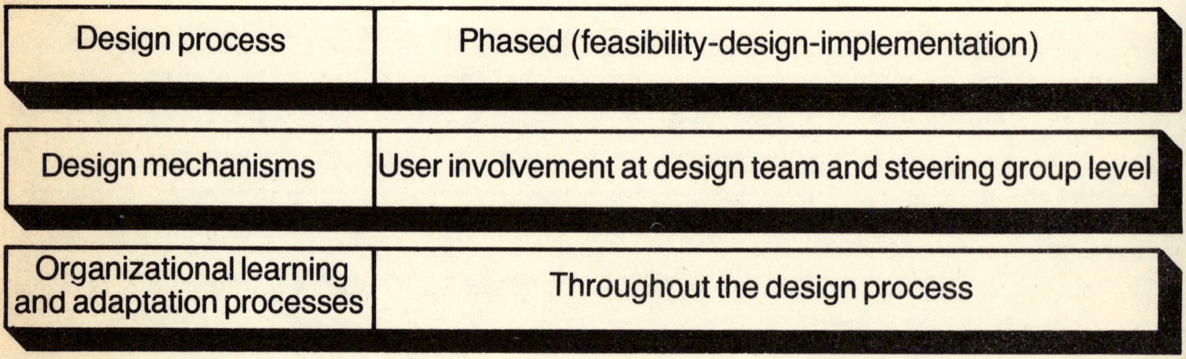

Design process	Phased (feasibility-design-implementation)
Design mechanisms	User involvement at design team and steering group level
Organizational learning and adaptation processes	Throughout the design process

Figure 8.4   *The design elements in systems design with user involvement.*

3.2.3 Stepping out of day-to-day work. Regular work may mean the user has the necessary experience to judge the ramifications of system proposals, but he often needs help to go from an action role to a reflective and predictive role in which he can summarize his experience in useful ways. Again time and help are needed.

3.2.4 Choosing between alternatives. There are many options in the way a system is designed and how it is implemented. Choosing between them means deciding what is desirable and what is undesirable, trading-off different criteria and predicting what will be necessary and worth while in the future. The users may be the best placed to make these decisions but it is not a familiar exercise and they frequently need help to make explicit the aspirations of themselves and their organizational units.

3.2.5 Conflict management. There will inevitably be conflicts of interest and disagreement about what is needed and how it should be implemented. Some conflicts are obvious and there will probably be institutional ways of dealing with them, e.g. industrial relations procedures for dealing with redundancies. There are, however, also likely to be many conflicts between different groups of users about the services provided by the system, the siting of terminals, who shall have access to information, etc., and such conflicts must be resolved during the design process.

3.2.6 Taking technical decisions during user involvement. It will be apparent that users come ill-equipped to contribute to systems design and they need time and help before their experience is available in a usable form. In the meantime technical designers are trying to establish a hardware specification and make decisions about software, etc. If users are to influence systems design, the output from users must be available before the design is frozen. Unfortunately the length of time it takes for users to learn and adapt and for conflicts to be resolved often

exceeds design deadlines which either means delays in schedules or decisions taken without the full contribution of the users. It is frequently the case that, in practice, user involvement makes little contribution to systems design but helps to ameliorate the effects of the system elsewhere as users see the ramifications and help plan for them.

The situation is summarized graphically in Figure 8.5. As a result of user involvement, the influence of users has moved to an earlier phase of the design process. However, because of the problems listed above, they inevitably need time before they are capable of making an effective contribution. During this time the design of the system is gradually being frozen and there is only a limited 'window' during which users can influence design decisions. In many situations it is a time when the users are still ill-equipped to make their contribution. As a result the process remains largely technology-led although the impact of user involvement has helped to predict and plan for the organizational ramifications.

3.3   Stage 3: evolutionary design for organizational learning

User involvement has made it possible for us to plan for the organizational ramifications of new technology. We are still however a long way from the ideal situation in which the members of an organization are able to proceed through the following three steps:

(1) Determine the future opportunities and/or demands on their organization.
(2) Establish the most desirable way in which they should be organized for their future tasks.
(3) Select appropriate forms of technology to support the chosen form of organization.

At present decisions made upon technical criteria tend to make this process operate in reverse. It is of course possible for technologists to determine the appropriate form of organization and to select technological systems that support it but (*a*) they

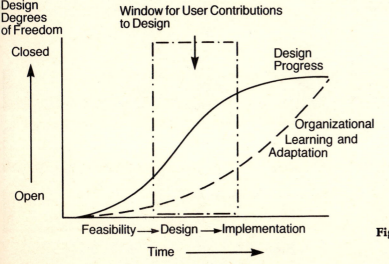

Figure 8.5 *Design closure and organizational learning in user involvement.*

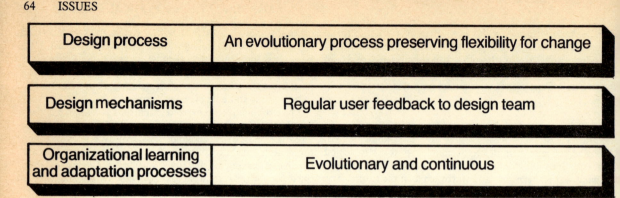

Design process	An evolutionary process preserving flexibility for change
Design mechanisms	Regular user feedback to design team
Organizational learning and adaptation processes	Evolutionary and continuous

Figure 8.6   *Design elements in evolutionary design.*

have a more limited understanding of the organization than those who run it and work in it and (*b*) they will not have to live with the consequences of the decision.

In our view we need systems design methods which enable potential users to work through this process to ensure that the technology chosen supports the kind of organization they conclude they need. We have been working on various schemes to facilitate user and organization learning so that they are better able to contribute to design decisions but inevitably it takes time. This technique can never be wholly successful if we are always faced with a limited period before the degrees of freedom in design are lost. We have therefore turned our attention to design methods in which this does not happen; to evolutionary design.

In this approach a system is gradually put together from small beginnings always with the possibility that parts of it may be modified, withdrawn or elaborated. Rather than being an entity which is conceived and built at one time and implemented to remain that way for its operational life, the system is now conceived as something that will grow and change over time as the needs of the organization change. This is a very different concept and fortunately there have been develop-

ments in the technology which make it an increasingly practical proposition. The advent of microelectronics means hardware is cheap and portable and that a small stand-alone system can be implemented quickly, the facilities of which can be added to later with the possibility of linking it to other systems. Similarly developments in software mean that the service the user receives can be changed with relative ease. Indeed it is quite possible for the interface to be 'personalized' so that the same system provides tailor-made services to a variety of users.

These changes mean that we can rewrite the way many systems are developed in order to give users a much greater say in what is being created in their name. In Figures 8.6 and 8.7 this approach to design is summarized and its implications highlighted.

Figure 8.6 identifies the main features we require in an evolutionary design process. We need a form of technology which will permit growth and change and design mechanisms in which there is a regular transmission of information about needs and problems from users to design staff. In order that this flow of information can be valid and relevant, we also need to facilitate an evolution of learning by the users about system facilities and how they may be exploited.

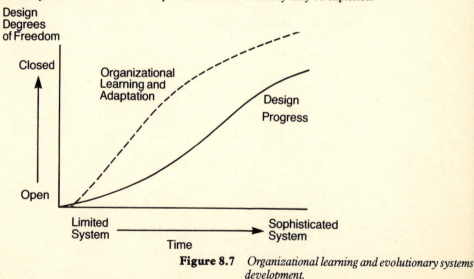

Figure 8.7   *Organizational learning and evolutionary systems development.*

Figure 8.7 expresses what we might hope to achieve if we seek the goals expressed in Figure 8.6. Recognizing that organizational learning about technology and adaptation must begin slowly and progressively evolve, we can hope to ensure that systems development follows a similar pattern so that organizational learning can inform systems development. It is also important that systems development never reaches complete closure, that there is always potential for change, because the organizational learning and change process will never end.

We have been working with a number of organizations to implement design processes with these features. We cannot claim to have developed a complete methodology but many elements of the strategy are emerging and are described in the next section.

4 Methods of promoting participative and evolutionary systems development

The strategy we have evolved identifies three strands to the systems development process:
(1) A technical system undergoing development and evolution.
(2) System usage which is also growing with time.
(3) Forms of user involvement which serve the dual functions of enabling the users to participate in design activities and to be supported in system usage.

In our view these three strands are mutually dependent. For example, users need experience of a real system before they can participate fully and effectively and systems evolution depends upon continued input from users about their emerging needs. . . . some of the major activities . . . in the systems development process are . . . described below.

4.1 Involvement

If there is to be effective user involvement, mechanisms need to be established which will provide for involvement. This may mean the establishment of working parties with briefs for different facets of the development, the selection of user representatives, etc. There can be no single answer to the form these structures could take because each organization will have a unique array of user groups, a culture which creates certain expectations about participation, a set of industrial relations procedures, etc., and these will shape the structures that are appropriate to carry user involvement. The general rules should be (*a*) to ensure all 'stakeholders' (i.e. everyone who will be affected by the system) are involved in some capacity, (*b*) to ensure representatives maintain good contact with those they represent and (*c*) to arrange that users are involved in those aspects of design upon which they have expertise and about which they have a keen interest. This means that some users may be involved in broad strategic discussions about the kind of system to be developed whilst the involvement of others may concern questions of office layout.

4.2 Pilot systems

The people working within the user-involvement structures need real experience of relevant systems before they can take informed decisions. The existence of cheap and easily implemented small-scale systems based on minis and micros means that it is possible for organizations to implement systems for experimental and learning purposes. The system should be either a package which provides a relevant service to an important function in the organization or should be a 'prototyping' system, i.e. a flexible system which can be rapidly shaped to provide a relevant service. The objective of these systems is *not* to test and prove the service so that it might be more widely implemented. The objective is to provide users with an experience which will enable them to delineate the service they require. It is important therefore to dispel any expectations that the initial system will be permanent in the form it is first implemented.

4.3 Trials and experiments

Pilot systems provide the vehicle for the user-involvement structures to consider many different design issues as well as for users to become familiar with system usage. Figure 8.8. lists some of the possibilities.

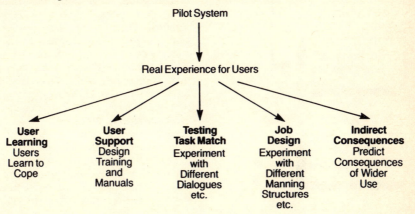

Figure 8.8 *Trials for user learning and design.*

In an environment where their manifest purpose is to examine the system to determine their needs of such a system, users can learn to cope with the system without the anxieties which usually accompany the learning of a system they have to master to retain their jobs. The learning process can also be used to catalogue the issues and problems which will have to be covered by user-support structures, e.g. manuals, in-system aids, training schemes, etc. More centrally to design issues the pilot system can be used to test task matches with tasks of the organization. Users may be encouraged to 'stress test' the service of the system by examining how well it would support the variety of forms their tasks take, i.e. the normal and the abnormal. If the system is of the prototyping form it should be possible to change the form of the interactive dialogues, the data-base structures, the forms of output, etc., to examine how well alternatives can meet user needs.

In addition to examining the form the technical system might take, it is also possible to use the pilot system to examine alternative forms that might be taken by the organization. The users might, for example, examine different forms of job design, i.e. different ways of manning the system and allocating responsibilities. They might, for example, create a specialist job of terminal operation or share terminal operations across all users (Eason 1981b). The system may also provide a basis for thinking through the wider consequences of system usage for skills, job number, job grades, careers, payment systems and the relations between sections of the organization. In one organization, for example, staff within three branches used a pilot system to examine the implications of co-ordinated action through the systems upon their individual autonomy.

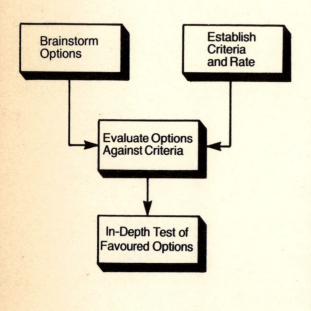

Figure 8.9 *Structured design exercises for users.*

4.4 *Structured design exercises*

Trials with pilot systems can provide relevant user experience upon which decisions can be based but we have found it necessary to structure the process by which this experience is used to take decisions. The reason for this is that it is very easy for the user experience to become unrelated to the decision process; it may not, for example, be fed to those taking the decisions, or the people concerned may not be able to make the jump from specific experience to general requirement. We therefore use the four-stage design exercise procedure depicted in Figure 8.9 as a means of focusing user experience on design decisions. This procedure is in a general form which can be used to debate the wide variety of decisions which concern users; from alternative systems the organization might employ to alternative sites for a VDU in an office. The initial stage is to elicit alternative solutions. This can be a problem because people tend to be limited by the current position or by the organization of the pilot system. If it has been possible to examine a variety of options in the pilot these barriers may already have been removed. If not it may be necessary for external agents to identify other options and to encourage users to contribute other ideas. It is often appropriate to treat the generation of alternatives as a brain-storming exercise in which anything goes, i.e. not to permit criticism of any idea that is advanced. This is especially important in circumstances where the users may be anxious about the presence of more senior staff or clever systems staff who might reveal their ideas to be nonsense.

A parallel activity to the generation of options is the generation of criteria which will be used to evaluate options. This is again a sensitive procedure because different groups may put priority on quite different criteria, e.g. for one group the important issue may be the recency of information, for another it may be the computational facilities, for another it may be security and privacy of the data base. The eliciting of criteria and their placement in rank order can be a very revealing process for all concerned and can reveal deep splits in the demands being made on the system. It is important that these splits come to light before design rather than being revealed afterwards when some users find their requirements have been disregarded. Where there are major differences of objectives, the help of experts in group dynamics may be necessary to seek effective ways of meeting the conflicting demands.

The next stage is to relate the option to the leading criteria that have been identified and to judge how each option will perform. This is a stage when the experience of the users in the pilot study and more generally in their task environment can be very useful in judging the viability of an option. It may also be possible to try out some of the options if the design issue is, for example, concerned with dialogues or the siting of terminals.

The final phase is to elaborate and test favoured options. In our work we have found that our detailed knowledge of the human implications of many systems can be fed into all the stages of this procedure without prejudicing the rights of users and systems designers to take their own decisions. It is possible, for example, to suggest options, to identify criteria others have found relevant, to show how others have sought to resolve conflicts, to help identify areas where options may have implications and to identify ways of detailing and testing favoured options.

The objective of this procedure is to offer a sequence of activities within which those involved in taking design decisions can make the best use of their knowledge and the knowledge available from other sources in order to make the best decisions for their circumstances.

4.5   Progressive implementation of facilities

From the viewpoint of the user, a computer system consists of a set of facilities which he gradually comes to understand, to master and to exploit. A pilot system will usually have a limited array of facilities and there are difficult questions about how to move from this stage to a more permanent, operational system. One possibility is to progressively replace pilot system facilities with improved facilities and to elaborate the system by adding further facilities as it becomes apparent they are needed. The learning that comes from the trials and experiments and the structured design exercises can provide the evidence for the facilities that are required. Similarly the output from the user evaluation studies and from user support (see below) provides continuing evidence for changes in required facilities. The provision of facilities is therefore a continuing process if the system is to evolve as the users' learning and, therefore, their definition of their needs, evolves. Establishing a technical system which can be continually amended and elaborated poses many difficult questions beyond the scope of this paper. They are being debated elsewhere and some of the issues are, for example, examined by Edmonds (1981).

It might be assumed that the process of making more or different facilities available to users of necessity means progressively adding more hardware and software to an initially small system. This is not inevitably the case. An alternative is to employ a large-scale system which is sufficiently flexible to permit the tailoring of facilities to users' needs as they become apparent and to permit users progressively greater access to facilities as they become more experienced with the system.

4.6   User evaluation studies

The principle of evolutionary systems design is that the system will continue to be modified and elaborated in accordance with emergent user needs. An essential ingredient is a feedback loop from the users to system managers and designers (see Figure 8.10) and we have found remarkably few systems where this is a regular, institutionalized procedure. In a number of the organizations with whom we have worked we have organized evaluation studies in which we have conducted semi-structured interviews with users to explore their experiences of systems. The interviews make assessments on a series of system acceptability measures (Damodaran 1981) which range from assessments of the quality of the information service (task fit), through evaluations of ease of use and the effectiveness of user support, to assessments of the effects upon job content and other indirect consequences. A relatively formal evaluating procedure of this kind is necessary to ensure that the organization learns from pilot schemes but it is also needed during the subsequent life of the system if there is to be informational feedback to show how the system should evolve.

4.7   User support and organizational learning

It might be thought that once a user understands the procedures of a computer system, he has mastered it. However, real mastery comes when the user begins to perceive how the system can and could be used by him and by his organization to perform organizational tasks in different and more effective ways. This kind of learning tends to come a considerable while after the system is first implemented and sometimes never occurs because the conditions do not exist to promote such continuous development. To promote these developments the technical system needs to be complemented by a social system dedicated to its use and its development. This social system consists in part of user support staff (liaison staff, training staff, etc.) whose function is to help users find new ways of exploiting the system (in effect, to promote continuous user learning) and to carry information about system inadequacies and the need for system development back to system designers. Another part of the social system consists of those system designers whose function is to maintain and develop the system. In the traditional systems-design process the assumption is that the design team breaks up when the system is implemented leaving only a skeletal team to operate and maintain it. An evolutionary concept requires that a design capability is retained through the life of the system.

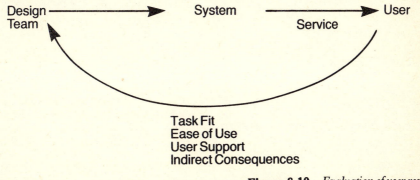

Figure 8.10   *Evaluation of user responses to systems.*

As Figure 8.11 illustrates, this support structure is a vehicle for providing evaluative feedback and for providing user support. In its support role, not only does it provide staff who can give support but it is responsible for the provision of other support methods (training, in-system aids and manuals). The support can be considered to be of two types: compensatory and developmental. It is normal for there to be provision of compensatory support, e.g. what do I do when the system goes down? I do not understand a command, I've got an error message I do not understand, etc. What is often missing is a forum in which the user can discuss a new need and be helped to see how the system could be used to meet it or indeed the system can be revised to meet it.

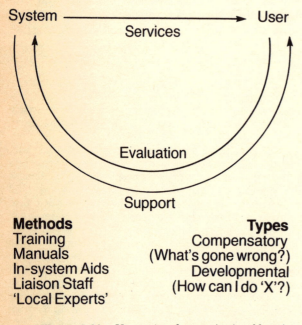

Figure 8.11 *User support for organizational learning.*

5   Conclusions

If one examines closely the radical and far-reaching consequences of introducing information technology, it is small wonder that organizations are slow to embrace the new technology. Our traditional systems-design methods tend to be technology led and often lead to implementation problems. In trying to help organizations plan systems design we have found it difficult to obtain adequate attention for human factors issues in this traditional approach. The move to user involvement in systems design provides the potential for fuller consideration of organizational ramifications. However, users confronted by the need to make a contribution need time and opportunities to learn about the intended system and its effects. Frequently they are only able to see the ramifications clearly when it is too late to change the system. Their contribution therefore becomes confined to amelioration of the system's negative effects.

In our view if we are to achieve the desirable goal of permitting organizational needs to define the nature of the technology, we need to change the way we approach systems design. In our work with organizations we have been moving away from 'one-shot implementation' towards a more evolutionary way of introducing a system, which is never regarded as finished. The nature of modern computer technology means this approach is now a practicable proposition and it means users have the time and opportunity to gather experience before they have to specify the systems they regard as desirable. In working with organizations we have tried to promote learning for design decisions by creating temporary design bodies, implementing pilot studies specifically for learning purposes, developing user design exercises, instituting regular evaluation procedures and creating social structures for user support and system evolution. It is our view that only by adopting such practices within organizations can we give members of the organization the confidence and knowledge to take on new technology and exploit it to the full.

Acknowledgements

The concepts reported in this paper have been developed as a result of working with Professor Brian Shackel, Leela Damodaran, Susan Pomfrett and other colleagues in the HUSAT Research Group. I am happy to acknowledge their contribution to the development of the strategy for introducing new technology which is outlined in this paper. The strategy has emerged as a result of our close collaboration with a number of organizations and I also acknowledge the pioneering spirit of the staff of these organizations without which our ideas could not be tested.

References

Bjorn-Andersen, N. (ed) (1980) *The Human Side of Information Processing*, North-Holland, Amsterdam.

Bjorn-Andersen, N. and Eason, K.D. (1980) 'Myths and realities of information systems contributing to organisational rationality', in Mowshowitz, A. (ed) *Human Choice and Computers Vol 2*, North-Holland, Amsterdam, pp.97-100.

Bjorn-Andersen, N., and Rasmussen, L.B. (1980) 'Sociological implications of computer systems', in Smith, H.T. and Green, T.R.G. (eds) *Human Interaction with Computers*, Academic Press, London.

Damodaran, L. (1981) 'Measures of user acceptability', in Pearce, B.G. (ed) *Health Hazards of VDUs? Vol 3*, Loughborough University of Technology, Loughborough, pp.61-70.

Damodaran, L. and Eason, K.D. (1981) 'Design procedures for user involvement and user support', in Coombs, M. and Alty, J. (eds) *Computer Skills and the User Interface*, Academic Press, London.

Eason, K.D. (1981a) *Manager-computer interaction. A study of a task-tool relationship.* Ph.D. Thesis, Loughborough University of Technology.

Eason, K.D. (1981b) 'Job design and VDU operation', in Pearce, B.G. (ed) *Health Hazards of VDUs? Vol 3*, Loughborough University of Technology, Loughborough, pp.71-88.

Eason, K.D., Damodaran, L. and Stewart, T.F.M. (1974) A survey of man-computer interaction in commercial applications, LUTERG No. 144, Loughborough University of Technology.

Eason, K.D. and Sell, R.G. (1981) 'Case studies in job design for information processing tasks', in Corlett, E.N. and Richardson, J. (eds) *Stress, Work Design and Productivity*, Wiley, Chichester.

Edmonds, E.A. (1981) 'Adaptive man-computer interfaces' in Coombs, M. and Alty, J. (eds) *Computer Skills and the User Interface*, Academic Press, London.

Evans, C.R. (1977) *The Mighty Micro*, Hodder & Stoughton, Sevenoaks.

Forester, T. (ed) (1979) *The Micro-electronics Revolution*, Blackwell, Oxford.

Gotleib, C.C. and Borodin, A. (1973) *Social Issues of Computing*, Academic Press, New York.

Jenkins, C. and Sherman, B. (1979) *The Collapse of Work*, Eyre Methuen, London.

Lyne, M. and Davis, R. (1981) 'A Microprocessor in Lincoln' *National Electronics Review 1980/1*, pp.55-59.

Macintosh, I.M. (1981) Letter to the *Guardian*, 10 April.

Mumford, E. and Henshall, D. (1979) *A Participative Approach to Computer System Design*, Associated Business Press, London.

Pearce, B.G. (ed) (1980a) *Health Hazards of VDUs? Vol 1*, Loughborough University of Technology, Loughborough.

Pearce, B.G. (ed) (1980b) *Health Hazards of VDUs? Vol 2*, Loughborough University of Technology, Loughborough.

Pearce, B.G. (ed) (1981) *Health Hazards of VDUs? Vol 3*, Loughborough University of Technology, Loughborough.

Toffler, A. (1980) *The Third Wave*, Collins, London.

Zermeno, R., Moseley, R. and Braun, E. (1979) 'The robots are coming — slowly', in Forester, T. (ed) *The Micro-electronics Revolution*, Blackwell, Oxford, pp.184-197.

9   The Problems of Planning

Planning is an issue because although nearly everyone now agrees it is needed, there is virtually no agreement on how it should be done. In considering the difficulties it's important to remember that planning poses both organizational and intellectual problems. Of the two readings that follow the first is more concerned with the organizational aspects, and makes very clear why planning is not something one can simply leave to 'the planners'.

The second piece was created by savagely editing a long, comprehensive, and in places somewhat technical, review of the literature relevant to forecasting and planning (which cited no less than 175 references). The original paper surveyed a considerable body of psychological literature concerning human biases in information-handling and decision-making, as well as reviewing the various studies that have attempted to evaluate forecasting and planning. What follows presents some of the principal findings and conclusions but scarcely does justice to a paper that anyone closely involved in planning should have at their bed-side.

9(a)   The Challenge of Corporate Planning

D.E. Hussey

[. . .] While most organizations purport to practise corporate planning and it is possible to find planners in most large companies, there is considerable research evidence, supported by the opinions of informed observers, that very few companies obtain optimum benefit from their planning efforts. Many plan very badly. The pitfalls in planning are well documented, but despite this many companies approach planning from somewhere deep down in the elephant trap.

[. . .] The building of corporate planning is made difficult by the nature of the job. Planning is not a profession, such as accountancy or chartered secretaryship. Although it has an able association in the Society for Long Range Planning, it does not have examinations or professional qualifications. It does not generally offer a career in itself, but positions in a total general management career. It attracts good people, most of whom get promoted very quickly to other jobs. The result is breadth rather than depth of experience: several people in an organization with some planning knowledge, but too few with very much. [. . .]

The 10 Major Traps in Corporate Planning

1. *Top management's assumption that it can delegate the planning function to a planner.*

2. *Top management becomes so engrossed in current problems that it spends insufficient time on long-range planning, and the process becomes discredited among other managers and staff.*

3. *Failure to develop company goals suitable as a basis for formulating long-range plans.*

4. *Failure to obtain the necessary involvement in the planning process of major line personnel.*

5. *Failure to use the plan as standards for measuring managerial performance.*

6. *Failure to create a climate in the company which is congenial and not resistant to planning.*

7. *Assuming that corporate comprehensive planning is something separate from the entire management process.*

8. *Injecting so much formality into the system that it lacks flexibility, looseness, and simplicity and restrains creativity.*

9. *Failure of top management to review with departmental and divisional heads the long-range plans which they have developed.*

10. *Top management's consistently rejecting the formal planning mechanism by making intuitive decisions which conflict with formal plans.*

(Adapted from a study of 215 companies by George Steiner: published as Pitfalls in Comprehensive Long Range Planning, Planning Executives Institute, *1972.)*

This chapter consists of extracts from 'The Challenge of Corporate Planning' in *Professional Administration*, April 1979, which also appears in Taylor, B. and Hussey, D.E. (1982) *The Realities of Planning,* and 'The Evolution of Planning Approaches', Oxford, Pergamon Press.

Figure 9.1 tracks the evolution of planning concepts, and at once illustrates some of the problems of improving planning in the UK. Each of the forms of planning illustrated is still practised by some organizations even though the process of development has moved on. Many of the organizations which claim to practise corporate planning are in fact using what are outdated concepts, some of which no longer fit the social environment in which we operate. They may still benefit the organization, but at a sub-optimal level.

The figure of course simplifies. There are variations within each of the labelled boxes, and some overlapping of concepts. Also the evolution is of planning thinking, not a process through which every organization must pass. Most join at a particular point on the evolutionary tree. It must also be stressed that success may result from any of the stages: the argument of this article is that the aim should be to do even better, rather than being satisfied with current levels of success. The right approach to corporate planning can bring the additional degree of success.

Let me explain the stages in Figure 9.1.

1. Informal planning

This is the state known to everybody, where top management keeps its plan in its heads, and does not attempt to make a formal plan for the organization. It works, often very well, for the autocratic, opportunistic entrepreneur with flair. Unfortunately many who approach their planning by this method, also lack flair. It is an approach which becomes increasingly untenable under modern pressures for more participation.

2. Extended budgeting

Hesitating steps were taken on the road to corporate planning when organizations began to extrapolate the annual budget into the future. Usually an accounting exercise, it represented an attempt to see the logical future consequences of the chosen course of action. It fails because it is unresponsive to environmental changes, carries an implicit and incorrect assumption that present policies will continue into the future, and has a tendency to become a mere figures exercise. Few organizations practise it in its extreme form, although it has not become extinct.

3. Top-down planning

Here we begin to follow the first of two forks, which might loosely be termed 'analytical' and 'behavioural'. Top-down

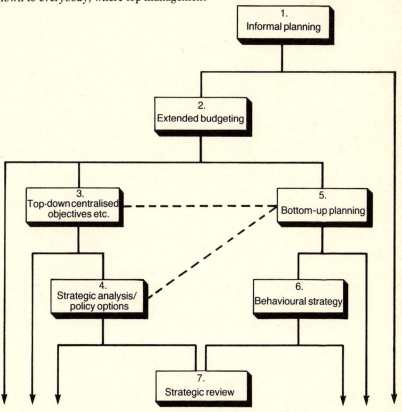

Figure 9.1   *Evolution of planning approaches.*

planning involves only a few at the top of the organization, sets objectives without the involvement of those who have to attain them, and is frequently dominated by O.R. approaches and corporate models (not that these are bad in themselves).

Three forms might be typified: 'ivory tower', where a planner remote from the organization prepares the plans, 'tablets from the mountain' where objectives and guide lines are produced on the assumption that all wisdom is concentrated in head-office, and 'boffin' where the corporate model produces all the answers, but only the expert can operate the model. These types of planning are still widespread, despite the fact that lack of involvement ensures that plans are rarely implemented.

4.   Strategic analysis / Policy options

The analytical branch evolves into a more rational approach at strategic thinking, moving to a planning role of presenting management with policy options, rather than one-solution plans. It uses very worthwhile techniques like portfolio analysis, and is responsive to environmental changes. Many organizations would benefit by getting this far along the evolutionary tree: comparatively few have. Its main danger is under-rating the significance of human behaviour.

5.   Bottom-up planning

The rationale for this style of planning is to involve those who are concerned with implementing the plans. A very common sub form is the 'church collection method'. It works like this. Everyone in the organization is asked to write a plan for his own area. His contribution is dropped into the corporate hat. Someone adds it all up, rejecting a few obvious faked coins, but usually accepting with gratitude what is donated. This becomes the plan.

It fails because the board room ignores it and carries on with strategies which are outside of the plan, and because the involvement is a sham: it is too narrow to be real. Another version attempts to combine top-down with bottom-up by issuing objectives as edicts and inviting managers to say in detail how they will attain them. Variations of bottom-up planning are very common.

6.   Behavioural strategy

This attempts to broaden the degree of involvement of managers in planning. There are various approaches. One is a form of planning conference where all managers identify and work through the issues facing the company, aiming to produce an outline plan as its end product. Another is a carefully structured organizational development approach to strategy, which encourages individual creativity and wide involvement.

Philips Eindhoven have been leading exponents of an O.D. approach. The weaknesses of the behavioural approach are the difficulties of reconciling the actions from the initiative with the top management strategy, the problem of quick response to changing circumstances, and the fact that measures such as this tend to become less effective as they are repeated in successive years.

7.   Strategic review

Finally we have the latest stage in the evolution, a deliberate attempt to take what is best from each branch and blend analysis with behavioural in a structured way. Typically the approach defines objectives and strategic guidelines in a participative way, but ensures that the decisions taken are founded on sound analysis. Those who are interested can find a case study of the approach in *Corporate Planning at Rolls-Royce Motors Ltd.* by R. Young and D.E. Hussey, *Long Range Planning*, April 1977.

Government could take a lead in improving the quality of corporate planning in the UK. So far its approach has been largely through the planning agreements initiative. One of the biggest difficulties this faces is the practical one. Many organizations either do not have corporate plans and therefore have nothing which they can agree with government, or they produce plans in which top management has little confidence. To have a planning agreement one presumably needs a plan.

My feeling is that government has gone down the wrong road. What it should be doing is getting the process of planning more widely discussed and practised. One way of doing this is by an enquiry into corporate planning, to do for planning what the Sandiland's Committee did for inflation accounting.

The purpose of such a study might be to examine the research evidence on good and bad planning, to study alternative approaches, to examine how corporate planning can be made more participative, to see what the business schools and professional bodies are teaching in this area, and to establish the things that should be done to help the entire country improve its corporate planning efforts.

Something needs to be done.

9(b)   Forecasting and Planning: an Evaluation

R.M. Hogarth and S. Makridakis

Intuitive forecasting and planning are not new phenomena. On the other hand *formal* Forecasting and Planning (F & P) activities have risen to prominence in business, nonprofit, and public organizations within only a few decades. Furthermore, annual expenditure related to F & P now involves billions of dollars.

The utility of these activities has, however, been questioned (e.g.(7), (33)). The purpose of this paper, therefore, is to assess forecasting accuracy and planning effectiveness in organizations and to provide guidelines to calibrate expectations. [. . .]

Forecasting and planning: empirical evidence

[. . .] *Long-range forecasting and planning.* Long-range forecasting (two years or longer) is notoriously inaccurate. Ascher

Management Science Vol.27 No.2 February 1981. Copyright © 1981 The Institute of Management Sciences. Reprinted with the author's permission.

(4) has examined the predictive accuracy of forecasting (and indirectly, planning) in the fields of population, economics, energy, transportation, and technology. His conclusions are pessimistic. Ascher found errors varying from a few to a few hundred percentage points, as well as systematic biases. He also stated that one could not specify beforehand which forecasting approach, or forecaster, would have been right or wrong. Furthermore, because policymakers are supplied with so many, varying forecasts, the problem of 'choosing' a forecast can be as difficult as making one's own. Parenthetically, it should be noted that the fields examined by Ascher are characterized by much experience and expertise in making forecasts as well as readily available data. One can therefore imagine the situation in other fields with data less 'suitable' for forecasting (i.e. with less aggregation and greater fluctuations).

Ascher's conclusions are echoed by opinions expressed in the long-term forecasting literature (e.g. (8)). It is difficult to assess the size of forecasting errors; unforeseen changes in trends can occur; discontinuities are possible; and new events or conditions emerge. Moreover, past data can provide contradictory clues to future trends (6). For instance, while growth of some products in an industry can occur in one way, others follow different patterns (5).

[. . .] Despite many fervent proponents, there is concurrently much disappointment in long-range planning as presently practised (6) (7) (11) (26) (31) (33). Long range planning, it is claimed, has fallen short of its promises and fundamental changes are necessary both in conception and execution. This has given rise to 'strategic planning' (see (2), (10)). In practice, however, 'many managers use the phrases strategic planning and long-range planning interchangeably' (10 p.24). Long-range planning, it should be noted, grew and flourished in the sixties (21), a period characterized by relative stability and high growth rates. Furthermore, forecasting errors tended to be positive (i.e. actual values exceeded forecasts). Thus, even if plans proved to be 'wrong', few complained of the direction of the errors. However, this did not occur in the seventies when forecasting was on occasion grossly in error in the opposite direction.

Medium-term forecasting and planning. Medium-term plans (three months to two years) are theoretically derived from long-term plans and incorporate medium-term forecasts, estimates of available resources, constraints and competitive considerations. The most common forms are operational budgets which also serve the important function of control mechanisms.

Considerable misconceptions exist concerning the ability of economists and business forecasters to predict important changes either in the general level of economic activity or for a given industry, firm or product. Cyclical turning points, in particular, are notoriously difficult to forecast (22), (23). The problem faced by economists and planners is two-fold: first, unanticipated recessions occur: second, predicted recessions fail to materialize. Furthermore, the timing of economic recessions and accelerations is frequently missed. Finally, as with long-term forecasts, there are many different forecasts available from which people can choose those that best fit their preconceptions. [. . .]

Forecasters and planners have shown systematic deficiencies in their predictions and plans for the future; furthermore, in a majority of cases their estimates are less accurate than those of simple quantitative models (however, for exceptions see the finance literature, e.g. (5)). [. . .]

Short-term forecasting and planning. There is considerable inertia in most economic and natural phenomena. Thus the present states of many variables are predictive of the short-term future (i.e. three months or less). Rather simple, mechanistic methods such as those used in time series forecasting can often make accurate short-term forecasts and even outperform more theoretically elegant and elaborate approaches used in economic forecasting (3) (22).

Short-term planning is characterized by several operations essential to basic business functions, e.g., establishment of schedules for production, distribution and employment, cash management, etc. It is the only form of F & P for which forecasts can be reasonably accurate and where real gains can be made consistently. However, it typically receives less attention than it merits.

The comparative studies indicate both systematic biases and large errors; quantitative models outperform judgemental forecasts; in addition, simpler models are often at least as accurate as sophisticated ones; even random walk models sometimes outpredict the alternative formulations. Moreover, simple decision rules can often be as effective as elaborate F & P procedures (see also below).

General examination of forecasting and planning. [. . .]

In an important study, Grinyer and Norburn (9) attempted to relate measures of corporate financial and management performance to planning activities. They examined 21 companies in a variety of industries. No significant relationship was found between extent of planning and financial and management measures. Indeed, the only significant relationship detected was 'between the number of items of information used in reaching decisions on appropriate action and financial performance.' Further studies have also indicated lack of relationships between planning and various measures of financial performance (17). On the other hand, studies by Karger and Malik (16) Herold (12), and Thune and House (32) concluded that formal planning was positively related to financial performance: in addition, a study by Ansoff *et al* (1) indicates that mergers were managed more effectively with explicit planning. The evidence is unclear and was recently well summarized by Wood and LaForce (34): 'The review of the available empirical studies disclosed conflicting findings in the planning evaluation area' (p.517). More studies are, therefore, urgently needed despite the inherent methodological problems of isolating the effects of formal planning systems from other variables. [. . .]

Forecasting and planning: implications and reconceptualization

[. . .] There is uncanny similarity between the history of F & P and experiments concerning the 'illusion of control' (18) (19). Observation of successes in predicting the outcomes of known random processes (e.g. coin tossing) can lead to unfounded beliefs of control in experimental situations. Similarly, the successes met by F & P in the sixties caused by under- as opposed to over-prediction seem to have led to analogous real-world illusions of control which have been shattered by subsequent events. Nonetheless, people have a tendency to attribute success to their own efforts and failure to external factors (14). Indeed, both animals and humans have sometimes been shown to develop more effective decisions if they do have 'illusions of control' — the illusion leads to more proactive and self-fulfilling behaviour (25). The issue that is not clear, however, is the extent to which such illusions are functional.

Linked to the illusion of control are tendencies to see patterns where none exist (29). These are further related to extensive findings indicating that intuitive notions of probabilistic concepts are deficient. Experiments show that people often lack the concepts of independence between random events and sampling variability (15): in addition, they frequently underestimate the uncertainty inherent in the environment (13) which leads, inter alia, to mistaken confidence in judgment (20). For F & P, the implications involve the all too frequent surprises by unforeseen events which, in turn, discredit F & P.

Paul Samuelson has probably best captured the inability of forecasters and planners to understand the full extent of uncertainty: 'I think that the greatest error in forecasting is not realizing how important are the probabilities of events other than those everyone is agreeing upon' (28, p.51).

A further important psychological finding is that although the availability of additional information increases confidence in judgment, it does not necessarily increase predictive accuracy (24) (30). This has serious implications for F & P given the tendency to consult and subscribe to many forecasting services, and to create huge data banks. Furthermore, since people have a tendency to retain information selectively in accord with their prejudices and to reject possible disconfirming evidence, the potential dysfunctional consequences of collecting data from many often differing sources is disturbing. As more information becomes available, it is increasingly easier to 'prove' what one wishes. Emshoff and Mitroff (7) emphasize this point in relation to problems engendered by large strategic MIS: 'Access to more information results in its selective use to support preconceived positions . . . They (managers) assume that the quality of decisions has improved because of the amount of information that support it' (p.50). [. . .]

We have already said much about human limitations. Of particular importance is the need to develop appropriate attitudes for facing the uncertainty inherent in the future. People should heed Russell's admonition to learn 'how to live without certainty, and yet without being paralysed by hesitation' (27, p.14). Forecasting must therefore be used to identify sources of uncertainty in the environment. Planning should concern itself with developing policies which acknowledge the uncertainties and are on the efficient frontier. Planning cannot assume forecast accuracy.

Some argue that executives and policymakers do admit the inherent deficiencies of planning but recognize functional side-effects such as improvements in communication and co-ordination, educating people to think explicitly about the future, and the use of planning as a mechanism for motivation and control. However, the question that should be raised is whether these side-effects could not be achieved more effectively through direct means.

The specificity of goals and forecasts should be linked to the time-frame. Long- and medium-term plans involve periods for which action-outcome-feedback loops are necessarily deficient and where learning is problematic. However, objectives that define direction are necessary. The precision with which such direction is specified should, we argue, be an inverse function of the length of the planning horizon. Whereas textbooks advocate precise goals, there are many advantages to deliberate ambiguity. [. . .]

Given the limitations of F & P, what should be done from a practical viewpoint? Would it be better, for example, to abandon formal F & P and rely solely on intuitive procedures? We do not think so.

First, intuitive procedures do not have an impressive record. Second, in the short-term, 'traditional' F & P are not only feasible but can be accurate. Indeed, we believe that few organizations avail themselves of the considerable benefits to be had in this domain. For instance, evidence has been cited that quantitative, and particularly simple models can outperform humans in a wide range of situations. Quite simple models can provide comparable, and often better results than more sophisticated models. Formal F & P can and should be used in 'traditional' mode for short-term situations. On the other hand, more careful analysis is needed concerning longer F & P horizons. [. . .]

Although it may be comforting to seek additional information to improve specific forecasts, the possibility of increasing forecast accuracy and the corresponding costs and benefits should be assessed. The *value of information* is, paradoxically, often overestimated by unaided intuition with the result that the search for additional information brings no more than false psychological comfort. For example, a recent case that came to our attention was the expenditure of $20 million to plan and forecast a $160 million investment. However, a detailed analysis of the situation and possible errors in forecasts indicated that even perfectly accurate forecasts would not be worth anything like $20 million. In some situations, even perfect knowledge of the future has relatively little value. [. . .]

One of our major arguments is for realism in F & P. Illusions and limitations need to be recognized; the use of F & P for control, motivation and communication accepted for what they are, and the extent of future uncertainties both appreciated and appropriately incorporated in plans. F & P can be useful, but current practices need to be changed. [. . .]

References

1. Ansoff, H., Avner, J., Brandenberg, R.G., Portner, F.E. and Radosevich, R. (1970) 'Does planning pay? The effect of planning on success of acquisition in American firms', *Long Range Planning*, **3**, 2, pp.2-7.
2. Ansoff, H., Avner, J., Brandenberg, R.G., Portner, F.E. and Radosevich, R. (1977) 'The state of practice in planning systems', *Sloan Management Rev.*, **18** Winter, pp.1-24.
3. Armstrong, J.S. (1978) 'Forecasting with econometric methods: folklore versus fact', *Jour. Business*, **51**, 4, pp.549-564.
4. Ascher, W. (1978) *Forecasting: An Appraisal for Policy Makers and Planners*, The Johns Hopkins University Press, Baltimore.
5. Brown, L.D. and Rozeff, M.S. (1978) 'The superiority of analyst forecasts as measures of expectations: evidence from earnings', *Jour. Finance*, **33**, 1, pp.1-16.
6. Dhalla, N.K. and Yuspeh, S. (1976) 'Forget the product life cycle concept', *Harvard Business Rev.*, **54**, 1, pp.102-112.
7. Emshoff, J.R. and Mitroff, I.I. (1978) 'Improving the effectiveness of corporate planning', *Business Horizons*, **21**, 5, pp.49-60.
8. Gold, B. (1976) 'The shaky foundations of capital budgeting', *California Management Rev.*, **19**, 2, Winter, pp.51-60.
9. Grinyer, P.H. and Norburn, D. (1975) 'Planning for existing markets: perceptions of executives and financial performance', *Jour. Roy. Statist. Soc. A*, **138**, Part 1, pp.70-98.
10. Guth, W.D. (1971) 'Formulating organizational objectives and strategy: a systematic approach', *Jour. Business Policy*, Fall, pp.24-31.
11. Hayashi, K.K. (1978) 'Corporate planning practices in Japanese multinationals', *Acad. Management Jour.*, **21**, 2, pp.211-226.
12. Herold, D.M. (1972) 'Long range planning and organizational performance', *Acad. Management Jour.*, **15**, 1, pp.91-102.
13. Hogarth, R.M. (1975) 'Cognitive processes and the assessment of subjective probability distributions', *Jour. Amer. Statist. Assoc.*, **70**, 350, pp.271-289.
14. Hogarth, R.M. and Makridakis, S. (1979) 'Decision making in a dynamic, competitive environment: random strategies and causal attributions'. Unpublished manuscript, University of Chicago, Graduate School of Business, Center for Decision Research.
15. Kahneman, D. and Tversky, A. (1972) 'Subjective probability: a judgment of representativeness', *Cognitive Psychology*, **3**, 3, pp.430-454.
16. Karger, D.W. and Malik, Z.A. (1975) 'Long range planning and organizational performance', *Long Range Planning*, **8**, 6, pp.60-64.
17. Kudla, R.J. (1980) 'The effects of strategic planning on common stock returns', *Acad. Management Jour.*, **23**, 1, pp.5-20.
18. Langer, E.J. (1975) 'The illusion of control', *Jour. Personality and Social Psychology*, **32**, 2, pp.311-328.
19. Langer, E.J. and Roth, J. (1975) 'The effect of sequence of outcomes in a chance task on the illusion of control', *Jour. Personality and Social Psychology*, **32**, 6, pp. 951-955.
20. Lichtenstein, S., Fischoff, B. and Phillips, L.D. (1977) 'Calibration of probabilities: the state of the art', in Jungermann, H. and de Zeeuw, G. (eds) *Decision Making and Change in Human Affairs*, Reidel, Dordrecht, Netherlands.
21. Lucado, W.E. (1974) 'Corporate planning — a current status report', *Management Planning*, Nov/Dec, pp.27-34.
22. Makridakis, S. and Hibon, M. (1979) 'Accuracy of forecasting: an empirical investigation', *Jour. Roy, Statist. Soc. A.*, **142**, Part 2, pp.97-125.
23. McNees, S.K. (1979) 'Forecasting performance in the 1970s', *TIMS Studies in Management Sci.*, **12**.
24. Oskamp, S. (1965) 'Overconfidence in case-study judgments', *Jour. Consulting Psychology*, **29**, 3, pp.261-265.
25. Perlmutter, L.C. and Monty, R.A. (1977) 'The importance of perceived control: fact or fantasy?', *Amer. Scientist*, **65** Nov/Dec, pp.759-765.
26. Ringbakk, K.A. (1969) 'Organised planning in major U.S. companies', *Long Range Planning*, **2**, 2, pp.46-57.
27. Russell, B. (1961) *History of Western Philosophy* (2nd edition), George Allen & Unwin, London.
28. Samuelson, P. (1974), quoted in *Business Week*, 21 Dec. p.51.
29. Simon, H.A., Newell, A. and Sumner, R.K. (1968) 'Patterns in music', in Kleinmuntz, B. (ed) *Formal Representation of Human Judgment*, Wiley, New York.
30. Slovic, P. (1980) 'Toward understanding and improving decisions', in Howell, W. (ed) *Human Performance and Productivity*, Erlbaum, Hillsdale, New Jersey.
31. Stonich, P.J. (1975) 'Formal planning pitfalls and how to avoid them', *Management Rev.*, **64**, 6, pp.4-11.
32. Thune, S.S. and House, R.J. (1970) 'Where long-range planning pays off', *Business Horizons*, **13**, 4, pp.81-87.
33. Wildavsky, A. (1973) 'If planning is everything, maybe it's nothing' *Policy Sci.*, **4**, 2, pp.127-153.
34. Wood, D.R. Jr. and LaForce, R.L. (1979) 'The impact of comprehensive planning on financial performance', *Acad. Management Jour.*, **22**, 3, pp. 516-526.

III CONCEPTS

III Concepts

'Concepts' can often mean jargon; clumsy and pretentious new words; elaborate and empty abstractions; obfuscations. But those that follow are of a different ilk: they are intended to be *practical* and *useful* tools for thought. This means, first, that they are not the tightly specified and fully operational terms beloved of social research; they are looser and more comfortable, meant to be used on a day-to-day basis, and relevant to more everyday concerns. Secondly, they actually help; they can make things easier — or, at least, clearer. Because concepts are for helping us think. They highlight distinctions, clarify what we were half aware of, encapsulate aspects or relationships that we might otherwise overlook. Concepts are the creations and the bearers of different ways of seeing and thinking; and by using them to make sense of our experience, we are learning those other ways of seeing and thinking.

It may help to distinguish roughly between two different sorts of concepts presented in the selections that follow. First there are *specific* concepts, those captured by a special term (or an ordinary term in a new use); these are usually distinctions, or some recurrent pattern, that is 'flagged' or captured by the term (Reading no. 11(a) provides a short, clear example of this sort of concept). Secondly, there are broader conceptual frameworks, or perspectives, that provide a particular way of looking at a subject, a distinctive 'angle' on it; such frameworks provide a set of related concepts, a sort of analytic tool-kit.

The notion of concepts being tools for thought is also useful if it suggests that, as with other tools, mastering their proper use may take time: *knowing about*, say, chisels, is very different from *knowing how* to use one. Or a better parallel may be with learning a foreign language: there is a great difference between someone who has recently learned the basic grammar and a limited vocabulary, and someone else who is a fluent speaker. The former thinks in his or her own native language, and laboriously works out the foreign equivalent. Conversations are so slow and difficult they are hardly worth the effort. The fluent speaker actually *thinks* in a foreign language — it's no effort at all (and there are any number of benefits to be gained). In learning concepts, there is a first, rather mechanical, stage of getting hold of the basic ideas: it may involve being able to remember definitions and recognize correct and incorrect uses of key terms. The second stage takes longer and is more problematic: it involves steadily greater familiarity with the ideas, being able to apply them more easily (and less self-consciously) to new situations and to everyday experience, until in due course they are taken for granted — part of the way one normally thinks about events of that sort.

The implications should be clear: if you find initially that some of the concepts introduced in the selections that follow are strange and difficult remember that until you have become fairly familiar with them, you can't really assess their worth. But also, if the concepts seem sensible and straightforward, don't imagine that that means they will automatically be incorporated into your thinking. Frequent use is the only way to ensure that.

Interpersonal work relationships display the complete spectrum of possibilities; cooperative and competitive, loving and hateful, trustful and suspicious and so on. Most individuals would like to be able to improve some of their work relationships so as to make their job easier or more rewarding or more effective. The problem is that even though we can all recognize relationships that aren't right, only a very few know how to improve them. Often attempts to improve relationships are based on analyses of what the other person is doing wrong. Such an approach never works and usually makes things worse.

There are three requirements to improving relationships. The first is to have a well-tried framework for thinking about and understanding what goes on in relationships — a theory. The second is to apply the theory to oneself so as to discover how one elicits the responses one gets and why these are unsatisfactory. The third is to use the theory and one's self-understanding to set about doing something different, i.e. relating to others in a different way. Experience in all sorts of management training, relating workshops, therapy groups, training groups and so on has demonstrated that such an approach can work; individuals who follow the above steps do find their relationships improving. One of the theoretical frameworks used in this sort of exercise is the 'Transactional and Structural Analysis' developed by Eric Berne. The following article describes its main features and gives some examples of how relationships can be improved.

Personality Dynamics and Transactional Analysis (TA)

J. Martin

There are many *very* different approaches that have been devised for looking at human personality, and you should remember that we are only looking at one of them — Eric Berne's *transactional and structural analysis*, usually abbreviated as *TA*.

The way you describe a personality depends on your objectives in doing so. In TA the objectives of the description are:

1   that it should allow people to describe and understand their own and other people's normal interactions in a simple, clear and explicit way;

2   that the understanding so gained should allow people to exert more control over, and take more responsibility for, their own interactions with others.

In other words, this is a description of personality intended to be used in a practical setting, rather than being an academic description for a detached observer. As Berne puts it, it is 'a theory of personality and social action'.

The boundary is usually set around a very small group of people, usually two or three, and the *transactions* between them.

A *transaction* in this sense is a single two-way communication exchange. If my dog puts her nose on my lap, and I push her away, that is a single transaction: dog to me, me back to dog.

The most basic transactions are those between infants and their parents; a simple touch or change of pressure responded to by another touch or change of pressure. Amongst animals and between people at their most intimate, these simple touch transactions remain very important throughout their lives; however, in most non-intimate adult human transactions touch is either formalized (shaking hands) or replaced completely by speech ('good morning!', 'what a beautiful design!') or reduced to gestures which can be as little as a momentary exchange of eye contact. Because touch is such a basic form of social exchange, Eric Berne talks of the two components of a basic two-way transaction as *strokes*. So if I walk into your room and say 'Isn't it a lovely day!' and you look up and grunt irritably at me, that is a two-stroke transaction: me to you, and you back to me.

It is quite possible that in a purely rational world inhabited solely by science fiction robots, transactions would occur only when communication was actually needed to carry out functionally necessary tasks (though even robots might find it necessary to inform one another of their presence and state of health!). Human transactions, particularly some verbal ones, do of course serve this rational function. But they also have other functions which have little to do with actual communication of practical information. Berne talks of *stimulus hunger* (the need for sensations of any sort) *recognition hunger* (the need for human, or at least animate, contact) and *structure hunger* (the need to have a framework that gives us something coherent to do). These are very powerful needs. Babies can quite literally die or suffer permanent psychological damage if these needs are not satisfied (and they can also be overwhelmed by inappropriate or excessive strokes), and solitary confinement has been a hated tool of punishment and torture for centuries.

This means that the simple *occurrence* of strokes of any kind can be almost as important as the practical information they carry. For instance, many of the transactions at a party are made purely for the pleasure of making them, rather than for the information they convey. In fact *even very unpleasant strokes are often much better than no strokes at all.* It may be much better to be kicked than to be ignored. In the words of the melancholy lyric to one of the songs by the rock group Cream:

'Born under a bad sign . . .
If it wasn't for bad luck
I wouldn't have no luck at all'

Clearly we can distinguish between:

1 Direct symbol-free stroking by physical contact.

2 Indirect or symbolic stroking that carries rather little additional information, including non-verbal gestures, eye-contact, voice inflexion, physical setting (such as a plushy restaurant), and the ritual statements such as 'hello'.

3 Indirect or symbolic stroking as a secondary function of speech whose primary function is to convey practically relevant information — such as in a committee that is trying to make an important decision.

As we grow and develop, the repertoire of strokes we can give and transactions we can take part in also develops. Obviously a new-born baby has a rather limited repertoire, but by the time a child is six or seven, and is very clearly a person in their own right, the major categories of transaction are largely developed, though they continue to evolve or change throughout life. It is often difficult for us to realize as adults just how much of our personality gets laid down in these very early years. Obviously we can change throughout our lives; for instance, we may well become richer or poorer, happier or sadder, more or less healthy, more or less successful, more or less entertaining or boring — there are always new possibilities that we can try out as we grow. But the deepest strategies we find ourselves adopting in our lives often go back a long way; for instance, how fundamentally private or sociable we are, or some of our deep-

est reactions to personal relationships and personal roles. It can be quite a thought-provoking experience to line up all the photos you can find of yourself at different ages, and see how early on you can begin to recognize the rudiments of some of your adult feelings and expressions. I can still identify quite closely with some aspects of an early photo of myself, aged three, even though some forty years have passed since then.

Adult, Parent and Child

The central figure of TA is the observation that there seem to be three major *ego-states*, or sub-personalities, that can be involved when you interact with someone else. Berne calls them the Adult, the Parent and the Child, represented diagrammatically in Figure 10.1.

Figure 10.1 *The personality subsystems of TA.*

The *Adult* is the computer-like part of your behaviour that is concerned with external reality, collecting information about your environment, solving problems, making estimates and plausible guesses, devising and changing appropriate strategies, and so on. Some of this is conscious and explicitly worked out. Some of it is barely conscious and more or less automatic. Some of it can be argued logically, and some of it relies on intuitive judgement and pre-logical thought processes. It can use both current information and remembered information. Even when one of the other subsystems is taking the limelight, the Adult is usually still lurking in the corner, and able to retake control if necessary. Everyone has an Adult, even a small child, but obviously the Adult skills vary with age. The Adult of a five-year old is struggling with problems such as how to get the crayons out of a box, while the Adult of a forty-year-old is working out how to pay the mortgage and also get the family to the Costa Brava for their holidays. The Adult is the part of you that 'grows up' as you get older, whereas in an important sense the Parent and Child do not — they develop very early on, and then stay with you largely unchanged.

The *Parent* is mainly laid down in the first three or four years of life, as a result of the young child copying the people in its environment that are most important to it — typically its parents. We may, of course continue throughout our lives to absorb cultural precepts by crude copying, but this early phase is the most important one because then we are at our most receptive, vulnerable, and uncritical, so that it establishes the basic foundations that tend to direct the growth of our later value systems. The Parent is an important mechanism for passing on the parent role and the general value system of a particular culture from one generation to the next. But it can just as easily transmit *undesirable* behaviour patterns from generation to generation; and in a rapidly changing society, the useful practices of one generation may become the problems of the next. Therefore being a good parent is often very different from behaving as directed by your Parent subsystem.

When a child is developing its Parent subsystem it often looks quite comic — long words, exaggerated social conventions copied from adults it knows, elaborate caring or controlling, all addressed to a doll or a pet. You can often see a clear continuity, with this behaviour leading to caring for or controlling younger children at home, then at school, and eventually in adult life, where it may become part of successful leadership or parenting, or, if it misfires, of overbearing, smothering or rigidly traditional behaviour.

The *Child* is the basic biologically-given subsystem and at birth it is the only subsystem operating. Do not be misled by its title into dismissing it as something you ought to grow out of. Not only does it stay with you all your life, but it is by far the most important subsystem, because it provides all the basic drives, emotions, feelings and energy.

It is the cause of all pleasure, sadness, excitement, destructiveness, curiosity and fun. The Child is very much the biological core of what you are, and the other two sub-personalities are merely its agents or tools — the Parent keeping it on the rails culturally, and the Adult trying to solve its problems and satisfy its needs.

The Child subsystem has virtually all its basic components at birth, though they do adjust and rearrange themselves under various pressures over the first few years. Like the Parent subsystem, a fairly stable configuration has usually emerged by the age of four or five, and the only further major event is the emergence of adult sexuality at puberty.

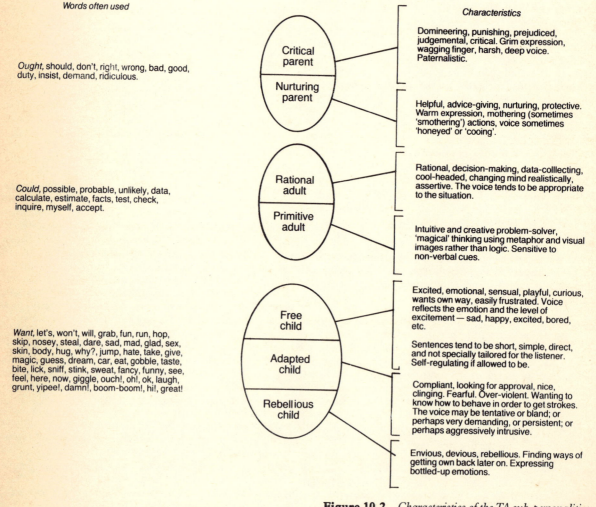

Figure 10.2   *Characteristics of the TA sub-personalities.*

One useful way of distinguishing these three subsystems is to remember that the key phrase of the Adult is 'I think I could do X', the key phrase of the Parent is 'I ought to do X', and the key phrase of the Child is 'I want X'.

Because the Parent and Child subsystems are both established so early, the transactional viewpoint is essentially to ask 'What would a one-, two-, or three-year old child do that would correspond to this grown-up's behaviour?'

Subdivisions within Parent, Adult and Child

While there are only three basic subsystems, it is possible to subdivide each in various ways, giving the elaborated structure shown in Figure 10.2. The Parent, for instance, could be divided up according to the different individuals the child did actually copy (typically its mother and its father). More usefully, it can be divided into the two main functions parents have to exercise — the *Nurturing Parent* who cuddles, supports and forgives, and the *Critical Parent* who makes demands, sets standards and gives reprimands.

The Adult is not usually subdivided in TA, but it will be useful to distinguish the two main types of computation that we seem to be capable of as the *Primitive Adult*, and the *Rational Adult*. The Primitive Adult tends to rely on complex imagery and on pre-logical or 'magical' relationships such as analogy and metaphor. It may use empathy and marked sensitivity to nonverbal cues as the basis for interacting with others. It may have great difficulty in explaining in words why particular activities seemed right. It is the most primitive form of problem-solving mechanism, quite close to the way an inarticulate animal solves problems. It is the most important part of the Adult in young children who have not yet developed their Rational Adults and is probably the basis for the uncanny ability children often show at picking up emotions that adults are trying to conceal. The Rational Adult evolves from the Primitive Adult as the child's linguistic and conceptual skills increase, and includes the logical, convergent, analytical behaviour we normally think of as problem-solving. In our culture it often tends to *replace* rather than *add onto* the Primitive Adult in adolescence. It can be very important in creative thought for this not to happen, and for the two to develop side by side.

The Child starts off at birth as the *Natural* or *Free Child*, expressing direct, uncomplicated and immediate needs that switch rapidly into frustration and anger if they are not met. Since simple self-regulation on this basis is rarely acceptable for long, it soon has to learn to compromise, accepting substitute or delayed satisfaction instead of its original demands. The Free Child therefore becomes overlaid by the *Adapted Child*, and its converse the *Rebellious Child*.

In children, the key characteristics of the Adapted Child/ Rebellious Child combination are that the behaviour always tends to be a bit 'too much', perhaps rather obviously good, or rather obviously bad, and it tends to be focused on the other people involved, usually adults, in a way that gets attention (strokes). For instance, children can get attention *passively* either by demure niceness or seductive prettiness, or they can get it *actively* by being over-supportively helpful or antagonistically naughty.

Parents will readily recognize many variants, and the concealed kickbacks they often contain; for instance, fear underlying dependence, bitchiness underlying niceness, jealousy underlying the need for approval, insecurity underlying aggressive naughtiness, and so on. These are all strategies that the child tries out in order to produce a workable compromise. A child may try out many different strategies, but one or two will tend to stick, surviving (sometimes much transformed) into adult life. In adults, the Adapted Child element is very evident in, say the ultra-dutiful employee, the adult 'daddy's girl' or 'mummy's boy', the 'nice' person who never seems to quite make it, the abrasive person who always seems to pick unnecessary fights, the alcoholic who drinks in order to get sympathy, and so on. We all show Adapted Child behaviour of one sort or another.

Simple transactions

A stroke always arises from one particular subsystem in you and is directed towards one particular subsystem in the other person. The reply likewise comes from one of the other person's subsystems, and is directed towards one or other of yours. Transactions should ideally be viewed holistically, with the particular words or gestures that make up the central parts of the strokes seen merely as the focal points of complete behavioural units involving context, posture, feelings and so on. In a text like this, all I can give you to practise on are transcripts of the verbal elements of the stroke, and that is obviously far from ideal.

Imagine that you have spent all morning at a difficult meeting in which plans for improving your section's output were discussed. The divisional manager, in collaboration with staff from Finance, want to restructure the way your section works. You have an alternative plan that you've worked out in conjunction with Charlie Barnes, the head of production. However Charlie didn't turn up at the meeting and you spent all your time trying to defend your plan and resist having the Finance plan imposed on you. You come back to your office where you meet Ken, who shares responsibility for part of the section.

You: 'I feel lousy. I have a terrible headache — *that meeting*, it went on all morning! I could kill Charlie — he never showed up!'

Here are seven replies that you might get from Ken:

A. I warned you to be better prepared for that meeting. You knew Charlie's unreliable, you should have arranged for someone else to support you. One of these days you'll learn.

B. You poor sod! You have had a rough time. Sit and read the paper while I get you a cup of coffee. I've got some aspirins for your headache if you want.

C. Yes, long meetings can be very stressful. If you want some peace and quiet I can make sure you're not disturbed for a while.

D. What's up? Sounds as if things went badly. Was it serious?

E. Didn't show up at all? Those meetings are such a pain. Hey,

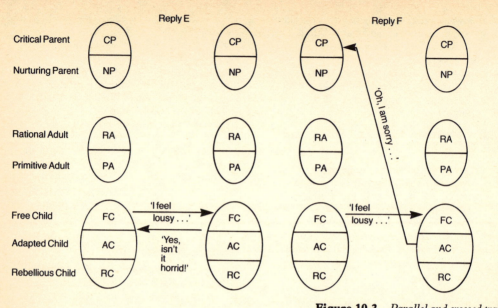

Figure 10.3   *Parallel and crossed transactions.*

come on! Let's go to the golf course this afternoon to get a breath of fresh air.

F. Oh I am sorry. Would you like a cup of tea or a drink? I had thought to talk to you about budgets this afternoon, but if you're not well I wouldn't dream of it. Shall I get you some aspirin, or would you prefer something else? Do you want to rest or go straight off to lunch?

G. Serves you right for being in such a bloody awful mood this morning. *You* can sort out the problem on the Nicoll's contract this afternoon, I'm going out.

Compare these seven replies with the sub-personalities and their components and see if you can work out which goes with which, and why. The next few sections look at some of the ways in which transactions can go wrong, leading to apparently irrational behaviour.

Crossed and complementary transactions

It looks from the replies above as if you were directing your comment at either the listener's Free Child or their Nurturing Parent, though it is hard to be sure without actually hearing and seeing you. Let us say you wanted a Free Child response. Then you will be happiest with reply E (Free Child). Replies B (Nurturing Parent), C (Rational Adult) or D (Primitive Adult) suggest that the other person is not going to match your mood, but is at least responding positively. If you get replies A (Critical Parent), F (Adapted Child) or G (Rebellious Child) something is obviously very wrong; clearly you're not seeing eye to eye! Figure 10.3 illustrates what happens for replies E and F.

If a transaction is to work, there must be agreement about which sub-personality is talking to which. If someone is feeling pathetic and inadequate, as in the example, they may want you

to be strong and supportive; that is, their Child is trying to talk to your Parent, and wants your Parent to talk back to their Child. If this works, you have a smoothly running *complementary* or *parallel* transaction in which each side plays its role 'correctly'.

However, if two people involved do *not* agree about the roles they are supposed to play, you get a *crossed transaction*. Perhaps I am feeling that I would like a nice, Parental, reassuring gossip about how much better things used to be in the old days, and yet you insist on replying with serious Adult statistics, comparing now and then objectively. Or I am trying to talk to you in an Adult way because I want us to work out how to make our money last till the end of the week, but you reply with some generalized Parental clichés about thrift and good management. In the example in Figure 10.3, the Adapted Child response (reply F) was a *crossed* transaction because it was treating you as a powerful Parent figure to be placated and asked to make decisions, when in fact you were not feeling remotely able to cope with the Parent role, and wanted to be Parented yourself. Crossed transactions do not always result in crossed lines on the diagram, but they often do.

In a smoothly running dialogue, a single crossed transaction may simply signal that one of the participants wishes to change role, starting a new sequence of parallel transactions of a different type — P-C, P-C, P-A, A-A, A-A, and so on, where P-A indicates the transition point. But when crossed transactions do not result in a smooth transition, the result is at very least a sense of embarrassment or irritation, which easily grows to frustration, anger, or a disturbing sense of being unable to make contact or see eye to eye. This is why crossed transactions are a major source of apparently irrational behaviour.

You can see that even if you only consider the three main personality subsystems, there are nine different complementary transactions: P-P, P-A, P-C, A-P, A-A, A-C, C-P, C-A and C-C. Berne argues that a stable, rich relationship between two people is often connected with the ability to relate well transactionally over most of the possible complementary combinations without generating many crossed transactions.

Double messages

As well as getting your messages crossed, you can also create confusion by giving double (or even treble) messages. Typically there is an explicit, spoken message forming one level of transaction, and a second tacit level communicated by non-verbal means, called the *ulterior* transaction.

For instance, suppose that as a junior member of your organization you are called into a senior manager's office. He asks you an Adult to Adult question, but his gestures and manner unconsciously convey an ulterior Parent to Child stroke as well because of the way he regards your junior status. If you reply at Adult level only, the Adult to Adult complementary transaction is satisfied, but the expected Child to Parent response to his stroke is not and he is going to feel uncomfortable. Since he is unaware of his ulterior stroke, he may interpret his discomfort as you being pushy or over-confident.

Sometimes, of course, we may be fully aware of both levels. The apparently Adult to Adult transaction 'Why not come and see my new flat?', 'Oh yes, I'd love to!' illustrated in Figure 10.4 may well have unmistakable Child to Child undertones that both people fully recognize!

Longer sequences: the structuring of time

As we saw earlier, one of the purposes of transactions is to structure time. Berne suggests that there are six levels of structuring activity that permit progressively richer and richer supplies of strokes, but also leave you more open and vulnerable. These are:

A   Periods of privacy or withdrawal with no strokes at all. You can have too many strokes, and everyone needs periods of privacy to recuperate.

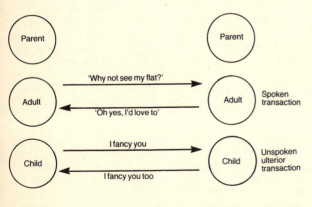

Figure 10.4   *Two-level transactions.*

B   Rituals. These are totally stereotyped conventional activities. Each side knows exactly what will happen. The commonest example is a greeting (smile, shake hands, 'Good morning', 'How are you?', 'Lovely day, isn't it?').

C   Pastimes. These form the superficial conversation that follows ritual greetings, before people have begun to relax. They tend to be a little like multiple-choice questions, with a very limited range of possible answers. They are a safe way of probing to see if it is worth going further.

D   Activity or work, including job, sports, hobbies, and so on. The practical requirements of the activity structure the way time is spent and generate strokes as a by-product.

E   Games. We all have our own special patterns of 'stroking' we need, often established back in childhood (for instance, as part of our Adapted Child). We therefore have to find a reliable and safe way of getting them. One solution is to develop a repertoire of situations we set up (often quite unconsciously) that allow us to manoeuvre someone else into providing the needed strokes. If the partner is compatible, they will get their secret supply of strokes out of it also. Some examples of games are given in the next section.

F   Intimacy or openness. This is the state in which all or most of the nine combinations of transactions can function easily and appropriately. Since the defensive barriers that normally restrict transactions are reduced in this state, intimacy provides the greatest potential for getting and giving positive strokes, since you can simply ask for them or offer them; but being open in this way also involves sensitivity to being rejected and hurt.

In addition to these relatively brief structures, Berne has also explored what he calls *scripts* — very long-term structures that may take a complete lifetime to work out. However, these are beyond the scope of this article.

Some examples of games

Two examples below are adapted from Berne's book *Games People Play*, which lists in detail some forty common games and mentions many others. In both cases the behaviour appears *irrational* if you set the boundary of analysis at the public, social, level. In *Why don't you . . . Yes, but . . .* White never gets a reasonable answer; in *Now I've got you, you son of a bitch* White's response is out of all proportion to the degree to which he is provoked. This behaviour becomes understandable when the boundary of analysis is extended to include the psychological level, with various *invisible* pay-offs arising from ulterior, private, and often unconscious, fears or needs in White.

Why don't you . . . Yes, but . . .

A typical exchange illustrating this game runs as follows.

Mr White enters the office of his boss, Mr Black, looking flustered and upset. Hardly waiting for Black to look up he starts . . .

White 'We have lost the file on the Noble contract. This is the third time this week a file has been lost. I'm fed up with wasting my time chasing lost files.'

Black 'Why don't you get the secretaries from next door to help?'

White 'Yes, but they're busy typing the Annual Report, it's got to go off tomorrow.'

Black 'How about Pam and Judy from downstairs?'

White 'Yes, but Pam's not in today and Judy can't leave the office unattended.'

Black 'Why don't you get security to chase it up?'

White 'Yes, but they get annoyed at chasing trivial things, after all it's not a confidential file — thank goodness.'

Black 'Why don't you find out who last had it?'

White 'Yes, but half the department are out today and none of the people in can remember using it.'

Such an exchange is typically followed by a silence.

Since the solutions are, with rare exceptions, rejected, it is apparent that this game must serve some ulterior purpose. It is not played for its ostensible purpose (an Adult quest for information or solutions), but to reassure and gratify the Child. A bare transcript may sound Adult, but in the living tissue it can be observed that White presents himself as a Child inadequate to meet the situation, whereupon Black becomes transformed into a sage Parent anxious to dispense his wisdom for White's benefit.

This is illustrated in Figure 10.5. The game can proceed because at the social level both stimulus and response are Adult to Adult, and at the psychological level they are also complementary, with Parent to Child stimulus ('Why don't you . . .') eliciting Child to Parent response ('Yes, but . . .'). The psycho-logical level is usually unconscious on both sides, but the shifts in ego state (Adult to 'inadequate' Child on White's part, Adult to 'wise' Parent by Black, can often be detected by an alert observer from changes in posture, muscular tone, voice and vocabulary. The basic principle is that no suggestion is ever accepted, the Parent is never successful. The motto of the game is 'Don't get panicky, the Parent never succeeds.'

In summary, then, while each move is amusing, so to speak, to White, and brings its own little pleasure in rejecting the suggestion, the real pay-off is the silence or masked silence which ensues when the other has racked his brains and grown tired of trying to think of acceptable solutions. This signifies to both that White has won by demonstrating it is Black who is inadequate. If the silence is not masked, it may persist for several minutes.

If the opening is of the form 'What do you do if . . .' (*WYDI*), a suggested response (to prevent the game) is: 'That is a difficult problem. What are you going to do about it?' If it is of the form '*X* didn't work out properly,' the response then should be 'That is too bad'. Both of these are polite enough to leave White at a loss, or at least to elicit a crossed transaction, so that his frustration becomes manifest and can then be explored.

Now I've got you, you son of a bitch

White needed some plumbing fixtures installed, and he reviewed the costs very carefully with the plumber before giving him a go-ahead. The price was set and it was agreed that there would be no extras. When the plumber submitted his bill, he included a few dollars extra for an unexpected valve that had to be installed — about four dollars on a four-hundred-dollar job. White became infuriated, called the plumber on the phone and demanded an explanation. The plumber would not back down. White wrote him a long letter criticizing his integrity and ethics and refused to pay the bill until the extra charge was withdrawn. The plumber finally gave in.

It soon became obvious that both White and the plumber were playing games. In the course of their negotiations, they had recognized each other's potentials. The plumber made his provocative move when he submitted his bill. Since White had the plumber's word, the plumber was clearly in the wrong. White now felt justified in venting almost unlimited rage against him. Instead of merely negotiating in a dignified way that befitted the Adult standards he set for himself, perhaps with a little innocent annoyance, White took the opportunity to make extensive criticisms of the plumber's whole way of living. On the surface their argument was Adult to Adult, a legitimate business dispute over a stated sum of money. At the psychological level it was Parent to Adult; White was exploiting his trivial but socially defensible objection to vent the pent-up furies of many years on his cozening opponent, just as his mother might have done in a similar situation. In discussing the incident later, he quickly recognized his underlying attitude and realized how secretly delighted he had been at the plumber's provocation. He then recalled that ever since early childhood he had looked for similar injustices, received them with delight and exploited them with the same vigour. In many

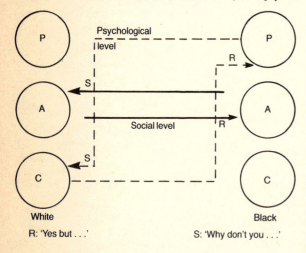

R: 'Yes but . . .'   S: 'Why don't you . . .'

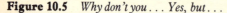

Figure 10.5   *Why don't you . . . Yes, but . . .*

of the cases he recounted, he had forgotten the actual provocation, but remembered in great detail the course of the ensuing battle.

The best antithesis is correct behaviour. The contractual structure of a relationship with a player of this game should be explicitly stated in detail at the first opportunity, and the rules strictly adhered to. In everyday life, business dealings with them are always calculated risks. The wife of such a person should be treated with polite correctness, and even the mildest flirtations, gallantries or slights should be avoided, especially if the husband himself seems to encourage them.

Clearly 'games' are recurring patterns of complex behaviour that do not seem to be wholly (or even partially) explainable in terms of some sort of externally visible objective, so that they appear irrational to the onlooker (though not usually to the participants).

The particular explanation given by Berne (derived from the types of explanation originally developed by Sigmund Freud) describes these activities as re-enactments of childhood patterns (often from the Adapted Child subsystem) in order to satisfy anxieties and needs that were real in childhood, but are now maintained only as powerful emotional memories. On this theory, the source of the game lies within the individuals, in the concealed childhood memory that continues to 'fuel' the game; if the force of this memory can be discharged in some way, the game should dissolve completely, since its concealed payoffs no longer function. Therefore for Berne the real key to change lies in recovering and disentangling the individual's memories. He does also recognize that you can intervene in the communications pattern if you want to avoid getting into someone else's game, in the ways he recommends in the two games quoted above. But he sees this purely as a temporary expedient, not a 'cure'.

Bateson, and the other writers who have explored the same idea, suggested that you can often reverse the emphasis characteristic of Berne and other post-Freudians. They argue that while there probably was some pattern of events in childhood that started it all going, it would be largely irrelevant for practical purposes if its effect had been maintained into adulthood not by *internal* memories but by *external* communication systems. In such cases the splits created around the original events have been exaggerated by positive feedback and then 'frozen' by very stable networks of feedback loops within the family system. In other words, we have a homeostatic system whose target state is suboptimal (and sometimes pathological) from the point of view of some or all of the people caught up in it.

On this type of theory, the best way to dissolve the game playing is not to poke around in early memories but to try to understand the current self-maintaining mechanisms. In this way you can work out how to block or modify some of the key feedback channels so as to break the homeostatic grip they hold over the system, so that it can re-establish a different target state that is less stressful to the individual system components.

This piece has necessarily been an introduction intended to convey the nature of the approach and provide some usable ideas; in no way is it a full exposition. Anyone interested in learning more about TA should consult one of the following books:

Novey, T.B. (1964) *T.A. for Management*, Jalmar Press, California.

Berne, E. (1964) *Games People Play*, Grove Press, New York.

Berne, E. (1963) *The structure and dynamics of organizations and groups*, Grove Press, New York.

11   Goals and Decision-Making

An enormous amount of management teaching proclaims the virtues of what is basically an engineering model of rational choice, for which clear and explicit goals used to evaluate rival options, are an essential prerequisite. But how much do the formal statements of organizational purpose actually tell us about what is going on? When organizational decision-making occurs in quite other ways (as it often does) is this necessarily inappropriate? And since there are other bases for rational choice perhaps greater clarity over goals is not always an unalloyed benefit for which organizations should be striving? These are the questions addressed by the three pieces in this section. The first draws a simple distinction that is as relevant today as when the famous article from which it was taken first appeared twenty-five years ago. Indeed, it attracts the ultimate accolade of being 'common sense' — but is overlooked easily enough. The second piece is a succinct summary of a very different but perfectly reasonable view of how decisions are made, and often should be made. Finally, the third piece is a masterful survey of different views of decision-making. The author starts with the rational view, considers the problems posed for it by uncertainty and ambiguity, and then discusses alternative conceptions of decision-making in terms of conflict, rules, disorder and symbolic action, pointing in each case to the implications of these views for a practical understanding of decision processes. These alternatives do not make the rational view irrelevant; but they do support a more sympathetic attitude to the common vagaries of decision-making. These views reveal how deviations from the rational model may yet be wise in their own way.

11(a)   The Analysis of Goals in Complex Organizations
C. Perrow

The over-rationalistic view

Most studies of the internal operation of complex organizations, if they mention goals at all, have taken official statements of goals at face value. This may be justified if only a limited problem is being investigated, but even then it contributes to the view that goals are not problematical. In this view, goals have no effect upon activities other than in the grossest terms; or it can be taken for granted that the only problem is to adjust means to given and stable ends. This reflects a distinctive 'model' of organizational behavior, which Gouldner has characterized as the rational model.[1] Its proponents see the managerial elite as using rational and logical means to pursue clear and discrete ends set forth in official statements of goals, while the worker is seen as governed by nonrationalistic, traditionalistic orientations. If goals are unambiguous and achievement evaluated by cost-accounting procedures, the only turmoil of organizational life lies below the surface with workers or, at best, with middle management maneuvering for status and power. Actually, however, nonrational orientations exist at all levels, including the elite who are responsible for setting goals[2] and assessing the degree to which they are achieved.

One reason for treating goals as static fixtures of organizational life is that goals have not been given adequate conceptualization, though the elements of this are in easy reach. If making a profit or serving customers is to be taken as a sufficient statement of goals, then all means to this end might appear to be based on rational decisions because the analyst is not alerted to the countless policy decisions involved. If goals are given a more elaborate conceptualization, we are forced to see many more things as problematic.

Official and operative goals

Two major categories of goals will be discussed here, official

American Sociological Review, Vol 26, December 1961, pp854-856. This material has been edited.

and 'operative' goals.[3] Official goals are the general purposes of the organization as put forth in the charter, annual reports, public statements by key executives and other authoritative pronouncements. For example, the goal of an employment agency may be to place job seekers in contact with firms seeking workers. The official goal of a hospital may be to promote the health of the community through curing the ill, and sometimes through preventing illness, teaching and conducting research. Similar organizations may emphasize different publicly acceptable goals. A business corporation, for example, may state that its goal is to make a profit or adequate return on investment, or provide a customer service, or produce goods.

This level of analysis is inadequate in itself for a full understanding of organizational behavior. Official goals are purposely vague and general and do not indicate two major factors which influence organizational behavior: the host of decisions that must be made among alternative ways of achieving official goals and the priority of multiple goals, and the many unofficial goals pursued by groups within the organization. The concept of 'operative goals'[4] will be used to cover these aspects. Operative goals designate the ends sought through the actual operating policies of the organization; they tell us what the organization actually is trying to do, regardless of what the official goals say are the aims.

Where operative goals provide the specific content of official goals they reflect choices among competing values. They may be justified on the basis of an official goal, even though they may subvert another official goal. In one sense they are means to official goals, but since the latter are vague or of high abstraction, the 'means' become ends in themselves when the organization is the object of analysis. For example, where profit-making is the announced goal, operative goals will specify whether quality or quantity is to be emphasized, whether profits are to be short run and risky or long run and stable, and will indicate the relative priority of diverse and somewhat conflicting ends of customer service, employee morale, competitive pricing, diversification, or liquidity. Decisions on all these factors influence the nature of the organization, and distinguish it from another with an identical official goal. An employment agency must decide whom to serve, what characteristics they favour among clients, and whether a high turnover of clients or a long run relationship is desired. In the voluntary general hospital, where the official goals are patient care, teaching, and research, the relative priority of these must be decided, as well as which group in the community is to be given priority in service, and are these services to emphasize, say, technical excellence or warmth and 'hand-holding.'

Unofficial operative goals, on the other hand, are tied more directly to group interests and while they may support, be irrelevant to, or subvert official goals, they bear no necessary connection with them. An interest in a major supplier may dictate the policies of a corporation executive. The prestige that attaches to utilizing elaborate high-speed computers may dictate the reorganization of inventory and accounting departments. Racial prejudice may influence the selection procedures of an employment agency. The personal ambition of a hospital administrator may lead to community alliances and activities which bind the organization without enhancing its goal achievement. On the other hand, while the use of interns and residents as 'cheap labor' may subvert the official goal of medical education, it may substantially further the official goal of providing a high quality of patient care.

The discernment of operative goals is, of course, difficult and subject to error. The researcher may have to determine from analysis of a series of apparently minor decisions regarding the lack of competitive bidding and quality control that an unofficial goal of a group of key executives is to maximize their individual investments in a major supplier. This unofficial goal may affect profits, quality, market position, and morale of key skill groups. The executive of a correctional institution may argue that the goal of the organization is treatment, and only the lack of resources creates an apparent emphasis upon custody or deprivation. The researcher may find, however, that decisions in many areas establish the priority of custody or punishment as a goal. For example, few efforts may be made to obtain more treatment personnel; those hired are misused and mistrusted; and clients are viewed as responding only to deprivations. The president of a junior college may deny the function of the institution is to deal with the latent terminal student, but careful analysis such as Clark has made of operating policies, personnel practices, recruitment procedures, organizational alliances and personal characteristics of elites will demonstrate this to be the operative goal.[5]

Footnotes

[1] Gouldner, A. (1959) 'Organizational analysis', in Merton, R., Broom, L. and Cottrell, L.S. Jnr. (eds) *Sociology Today*, Basic Books, New York, p.407.

[2] A strong argument for considering changes in goals is made by Thompson, J.D. and McEwen, W.J. (1958) 'Organizational goals and environments; goal-setting as an interaction process', *Amer. Sociological Rev.*, **23**, Feb. pp.23-31.

[3] A third may be distinguished: social system goals, which refer to those contributions an organization makes to the functioning of a social system in which it is nested. In Parsons' terminology, organizations may serve adaptive, integrative, or pattern-maintenance functions. See Parsons, T. (1956) 'Sociological approach to the theory of organizations', *Administrative Science Quarterly*, **1**, June-September, pp. 63-86, 225-240. This alone, however, will tell us little about individual organizations, although Scott, in a suggestive article applying this scheme to prisons and mental hospitals, implies that organizations serving integrative functions for society will place particular importance upon integrative functions within the organization. See Scott, F.G. (1959) 'Action theory and research in social organizations', *Amer. Jour. of Sociology*, **64**, January, pp.386-395. Parsons asserts that each of the four functions mentioned above also must

be performed within organizations if they are to survive. It is possible to see a parallel between these four functions and the four tasks discussed below, but his are, it is felt, too general and ambiguous to provide tools for analysis.

[4] The concept of 'operational goals' or 'sub-goals' put forth by March and Simon bears a resemblance to this but does not include certain complexities which we will discuss, nor is it defined systematically. See March, J.G. and Simon, H.A. (1958) *Organizations*, Wiley, New York, pp. 156-157.

[5] Clark, B. (1960) *The Open Door College*, McGraw-Hill, New York.

11(b)   Lindblom on Policy Making

A.O. Hirschman and C.E. Lindblom

Lindblom's point of departure is a denial of the general validity of two assumptions implicit in most of the literature on policy making. The first is that public policy problems can best be solved by attempting to understand them; the second is that there exists sufficient agreement to provide adequate criteria for choosing among possible alternative policies. Although the first is widely accepted — in many circles almost treated as a self-evident truth — it is often false. The second is more often questioned in contemporary social science; yet many of the most common prescriptions for rational problem solving follow only if it is true.

Conventional descriptions of rational decision making identify the following aspects: (a) clarification of objectives or values, (b) survey of alternative means of reaching objectives, (c) identification of consequences, including side effects or by-products, of each alternative means, and (d) evaluation of each set of consequences in light of the objectives. However, Lindblom notes, for a number of reasons such a *synoptic* or comprehensive attempt at problem solving is not possible to the degree that clarification of objectives founders on social conflict, that required information is either not available or available only at prohibitive cost, or that the problem is simply too complex for man's finite intellectual capacities. Its complexity may stem from an impossibly large number of alternative policies and their possible repercussions, from imponderables in the delineation of objectives even in the absence of social disagreement on them, from a supply of information too large to process in the mind, or from still other causes.

It does not logically follow, Lindblom argues, that when synoptic decision making is extremely difficult it should nevertheless be pursued as far as possible. And he consequently suggests that in many circumstances substantial departures from comprehensive understanding are both inevitable and on specific grounds desirable. For the most part, these departures are familiar; and his exposition of them serves therefore to formalize our perceptions of certain useful problem-solving strategies often mistakenly dismissed as aberrations in rational problem solving.

These strategies, which we shall call 'disjointed incrementalism', are the following:

1. Attempts at understanding are limited to policies that differ only incrementally from existing policy.

2. Instead of simply adjusting means to ends, ends are chosen that are appropriate to available or nearly available means.

3. A relatively small number of means (alternative possible policies) is considered, as follows from 1.

4. Instead of comparing alternative means or policies in the light of postulated ends or objectives, alternative ends or objectives are also compared in the light of postulated means or policies and their consequences.

5. Ends and means are chosen simultaneously; the choice of means does not follow the choice of ends.

6. Ends are indefinitely explored, reconsidered, discovered, rather than relatively fixed.

7. At any given analytical point ('point' refers to any one individual, group, agency, or institution), analysis and policy making are serial or successive; that is, problems are not 'solved' but are repeatedly attacked.

8. Analysis and policy making are remedial — they move *away* from ills rather than *toward* known objectives.

9. At any one analytical point, the analysis of consequences is quite incomplete.

10. Analysis and policy making are socially fragmented; they go on at a very large number of separate points simultaneously.

The most striking characteristic of disjointed incrementalism is (as indicated in 9) that no attempt at comprehensiveness is made; on the contrary, unquestionably important consequences of alternative policies are simply ignored at any given analytical or policy-making point. But Lindblom goes on to argue that through various specific types of partisan mutual adjustment among the large number of individuals and groups among which analysis and policy making is fragmented (see 10), what is ignored at one point in policy making becomes central at another point. Hence, it will often be possible to find a tolerable level of rationality in decision making when the process is viewed as a whole in its social or political context, even if at each individual policy-making point or center analysis remains incomplete. Similarly, errors that would attend over-ambitious attempts at comprehensive understanding are often avoided by the remedial and incremental character of problem solving. And those not avoided can be mopped up or attended to as they appear, because analysis and policy making are serial or successive (as in 7).

While we cannot here review the entire argument, Lindblom tries to show how the specific characteristics of disjointed incrementalism, taken in conjunction with mechanisms for partisan mutual adjustment, meet each of the characteristic difficulties that beset synoptic policy making: value conflicts, information inadequacies and general complexity beyond man's intellectual capacities. His line of argument shows the influence of pluralist thinkers on political theory, but he departs from their interest in the control of power and rather focuses on

Behavioral Science vol 7, 1962.

the level of rationality required or appropriate for decision making.

11(c) Theories of Choice and Making Decisions

J.G. March

Actual decision making, particularly in organizations, often contrasts with the visions of decision making implicit in theories of choice. Because our theoretical ideas about choice are partly inconsistent with what we know about human processes of decision, we sometimes fail to understand what is going on in decision making, and consequently sometimes offer less than perfect counsel to decision makers. Behavioral research on how decisions are made does not lead to precise prescriptions for the management of choice. It will not tell the president of the United States, the president of Mitsubishi, or the reigning mafioso how to make decisions. Nor will it tell a headmistress of a private academy what she should do as she decides what new programs to offer, whom to hire, what kinds of staff development to authorize, what uniforms to prescribe, what new rooms to build, what kinds of disciplinary procedures to implement, and what kinds of promises to make to what kinds of patrons. However, the research results may contain a few observations that might — when combined with a headmistress's own knowledge and imagination — provide clues of how to think about decision making. In that spirit, this article attempts to summarize some recent work on how decisions are made in organizations. It draws heavily on work I have done jointly with Michael Cohen, Martha Feldman, Johan Olsen, Guje Sevón, and Zur Shapira.

Rational choice

Standard theories of choice view decision making as intentional, consequential action based on four things:

- A knowledge of alternatives. Decision makers have a set of alternatives for action. These alternatives are defined by the situation and known unambiguously.
- A knowledge of consequences. Decision makers know the consequences of alternative actions, at least up to a probability distribution.
- A consistent preference ordering. Decision makers have objective functions by which alternative consequences of action can be compared in terms of their subjective value.
- A decision rule. Decision makers have rules by which to select a single alternative of action on the basis of its consequences for the preferences.

In the most familiar form of the model, we assume that all alternatives, the probability distribution of consequences conditional on each alternative, and the subjective value of each possible consequence are known, and we assume a choice is made by selecting the alternative with the highest expected value.

The durability of the structure has been impressive. It is also understandable. Simple choice models capture some truth. Demand curves for consumer products generally have negative slopes, and labor unions usually are more resistant to wage cuts than to wage increases. Moreover, the core ideas are flexible. When the model seems not to fit, it is often possible to re-interpret preferences or knowledge and preserve the axioms. Finally, choice is a faith as well as a theory; it is linked to the ideologies of the Enlightenment. The prevalence of willful choice models of behavior in economics, political science, psychology, sociology, linguistics, and anthropology attests to the attractiveness of choice as a vision of human behavior.

The attraction extends to ordinary discourse and journalism. A reading of the leading newspapers or journals of any Western country will show that the primary interpretive model used by individuals in these societies is one of willful choice. The standard explanation provided for the actions of individuals or institutions involves two assertions: Someone decided to have it happpen. They decided to have it happen because it was in their self-interest to do so. In cases involving multiple actors, a third assertion may be added. Different people, in their own self-interest, wanted different things and the people with power got what they wanted. Ideas of willful, rational choice are the standard terms of discourse for answering the generic questions: Why did it happen? Why did you do it?

The same basic structure underlies modern decision engineering. Operations analysis, management science, decision theory, and the various other analytical approaches to improving choices are variations on a theme of rational choice, as are standard ideas for determining the value of information and the design of information systems. These efforts at improving the decisions of individuals and organizations have been helpful. Systematic rational analyses of choice alternatives have improved the blending of aviation fuel, the location of warehouses, the choice of energy sources, and the arrangement of bank queues, as well as providing the solutions to many other decision problems. And although it is also possible to cite examples in which the consequences of decision analysis have been less benign, a balanced judgment must conclude that these modern technologies of choice have done more good than harm.

Within such a framework, the advice we give to a headmistress is straightforward: Determine precisely what your alternatives are. Define clearly what your preferences are. Estimate the possible consequences stemming from each alternative and the likelihood of occurrence. Select the alternative that will maximize the expected value.

This basic theory of choice has been considerably elaborated over the past thirty years with the discovery of computational procedures for solving problems and the development of various more specific models within the general frame. At the same time, empirical research on the ways in which decisions are actually made by individuals and organizations has identified some problems in fitting the standard theory of choice to observed decision behavior.

Uncertainty and ambiguity

Theories of choice presume two improbably precise guesses

Social Science and Modern Society, Vol. 20, No 1. 1982. © 1982 by Transaction Inc. This material has been edited.

about the future: a guess about the future consequences of current actions and a guess about future sentiments with respect to those consequences. Actual decision situations often seem to make both guesses problematic.

The first guess — about the uncertain future consequences of current action — has attracted attention from both students of decision making and choice theorists. In fact, some of the earliest efforts to relate studies of decision making and theories of choice raised questions about the informational assumptions of the theories. Even if decisions are made in a way generally consistent with choice theories — that is, that estimates of the consequences of alternative actions are formed and that action is *intendedly* rational — there are informational and computational limits on human choice. There are limits on the number of alternatives that can be considered, and limits on the amount and accuracy of information that is available. Such a set of ideas leads to the conception of limited rationality for which Herbert Simon received the Nobel Prize in 1978.

The core ideas are elementary and by now familiar. Rather than all alternatives or all information about consequences being known, information has to be discovered through search. Search is stimulated by a failure to achieve a goal, and continues until it reveals an alternative that is good enough to satisfy existing, evoked goals. New alternatives are sought in the neighbourhood of old ones. Failure focuses search on the problem of attaining goals that have been violated, success allows search resources to move to other domains. The key scarce resource is attention: and theories of limited rationality are, for the most part, theories of the allocation of attention.

They are also theories of slack — that is, unexploited opportunities, undiscovered economies, waste, etc. As long as performance exceeds the goal, search for new alternatives is modest, slack accumulates, and aspirations increase. When performance falls below the goal, search is stimulated, slack is decreased, and aspirations decrease. This classic control system does two things to keep performance and goals close. First, it adapts goals to performance; that is, decision makers learn what they should expect. At the same time, it adapts performance to goals by increasing search and decreasing slack in the face of failure, by decreasing search and increasing slack when faced with success. To the familiar pattern of fire alarm management are added the dynamics of changes in aspirations and slack buffers.

These ideas have been used to explore some features of adaptation to a changing environment. Decision makers appear often to be able to discover new efficiencies in their operations under conditions of adversity. If we assume that decision makers optimize, it is not immediately obvious why new economies can be discovered under conditions of adversity if they could not be discovered during good times. The explanation is natural in the slack version of adaptation. During favorable times, slack accumulates. Such slack becomes a reservoir of search opportunities during subsequent periods of trouble. As a result, environmental fluctuations are dampened by the decision process. Such a description seems to provide a partial understanding of the resilience of human institutions in the face of adversity.

Thus, in the case of our headmistress, we would expect that so long as the academy prospered, slack would accumulate. Control over the pursuit of private pleasures by staff members would be relaxed; search for improvements in existing programs would be lackadaisical; discipline would decline. If, on the other hand, a major patron were dissatisfied, or demand for the product weakened, or a loss in quality recorded, then discipline and control would be tightened and search for refinements in existing techniques would be stimulated. As a result, we would probably expect that refinements of existing techniques in the academy, or more energetic performances, would be more likely during times of adversity, but that, because of the extra slack, experiments with unusual new techniques would be more common during times of success.

Partly as a result of such observations by students of decision making, theories of choice have placed considerable emphasis on ideas of search, attention, and information costs in recent years, and these efforts in combination with concern for the problems of incomplete information and transaction costs have turned substantial parts of recent theories of choice into theories of information and attention — tributes to the proposition that information gathering, information processing, and decision making impose heavy demands on the finite capacity of the human organism. Aspiration levels, incrementalism, slack, and satisfaction have been described as sensible under fairly general circumstances.

The second guess — about the uncertain future preferences for the consequences of current actions — has been less considered, yet poses, if anything, greater difficulties. Consider the following properties of preferences as they appear in standard theories of choice:

■ Preferences are *absolute*. Theories of choice assume action in terms of preferences; but they recognize neither discriminations among alternative preferences, nor the possibility that a person reasonably might view his own preferences and action based on them as morally distressing.

■ Preferences are *stable*. In theories of choice, current action is taken in terms of current preferences. The implicit assumption is that preferences will be unchanged when the outcomes of current actions are realized.

■ Preferences are *consistent* and *precise*. Theories of choice allow inconsistency or ambiguity in preferences only insofar as they do not affect choice (i.e., only insofar as they are made irrelevant by scarcity or the specification of tradeoffs).

■ Preferences are *exogenous*. Theories of choice presume that preferences, by whatever process they may be created, are not themselves affected by the choices they control.

Each of these features of preference seems inconsistent with observations of choice behavior among individuals and social institutions: not always, but often enough to be troublesome. Individuals commonly find it possible to express both a preference for something and a recognition that the preference is repugnant to moral standards they accept. Choices are often made without much regard for preferences. Human decision makers routinely ignore their own, fully conscious preferences in making decisions. They follow rules, traditions, hunches, and the advice or actions of others. Preferences change over time in such a way that predicting future preferences is often difficult. Preferences are inconsistent. Individuals and organizations are aware of the extent to which some of their preferences conflict with others: yet they do little to resolve those inconsistencies. Many preferences are stated in forms that lack precision. And while preferences are used to choose among actions, it is also often true that actions and experience with their consequences affect preferences.

Such differences between preferences as they are portrayed in theories of choice and preferences as they appear in decision making can be interpreted as reflecting some ordinary behavioral wisdom that is not always well accommodated within the theory. Human beings seem to recognize in their behavior that there are limits to personal and institutional integration in tastes. As a result they engage in activities designed to manage preferences. These activities make little sense from the point of view of a theory that assumes decision makers know what they want and will want, or a theory that assumes wants are morally equivalent. But ordinary human actors sense that they might come to want something that they should not, or that they might make unwise choices under the influence of fleeting but powerful desires if they do not act to control the development of unfortunate preferences or to buffer actions from preferences. Like Ulysses, they know the advantages of having their hands tied.

Human beings seem to believe that the theory of choice considerably exaggerates the relative power of a choice based on two guesses compared with a choice that is itself a guess. As observers of the process by which their beliefs have been formed and are consulted, ordinary human beings seem to endorse the good sense in perceptual and moral modesty.

They seem to recognize the extent to which preferences are constructed, or developed, through a confrontation between preferences and actions that are inconsistent with them, and among conflicting preferences. Though they seek some consistency, they appear to see inconsistency as a normal and necessary aspect of the development and clarification of preferences. They sometimes do something for no better reason than that they must, or that someone else is doing it.

Human beings act as though some aspects of their beliefs are important to life without necessarily being consistent with actions, and important to the long-run quality of decision making without controlling it completely in the short run. They accept a degree of personal and social wisdom in simple hypocrisy.

They seem to recognize the political nature of argumentation more clearly and more personally than the theory of choice does. They are unwilling to gamble that God made those people who are good at rational argument uniquely virtuous. They protect themselves from cleverness, in themselves as well as in others, by obscuring the nature of their preferences.

What are the implications for our headmistress? Uncertainty about future consequences (the first guess) and human limitations in dealing with them lead decision makers, intelligently, to techniques of limited rationality. But what can a sensible decision maker learn from observations of preference ambig-

uity, beyond a reiteration of the importance of clarifying goals and an appreciation of possible human limits in achieving preference orderliness? Considerations of these complications in preferences, in fact, lead to a set of implications for the management of academies and other organizations, as well as for human choice more generally.

To begin with, we need to re-examine the function of decision. One of the primary ways in which individuals and organizations develop goals is by interpreting the actions they take, and one feature of good action is that it leads to the development of new preferences. As a result, decisions should not be seen as flowing directly or strictly from prior objectives. A headmistress might well view the making of decisions somewhat less as a process of deduction, and somewhat more as a process of gently upsetting preconceptions of what she is doing.

In addition, we need a modified view of planning. Planning has many virtues, but a plan can often be more effective as an interpretation of past decisions than as a blueprint for future ones. It can be used as part of our efforts to develop a new, somewhat consistent theory of ourselves that incorporates our recent actions into some moderately comprehensive structure of goals. A headmistress needs to be tolerant of the idea that the meaning of yesterday's action will be discovered in the experiences and interpretations of today.

Finally, we need to accept playfulness in action. Intelligent choice probably needs a dialectic between reason and foolishness, between doing things for no 'good' reason and discovering the reasons. Since the theory and ideology of choice are primarily concerned with strengthening reason, a headmistress is likely to overlook the importance of play.

Conflict

[. . .] Political perspectives on organizations emphasize the problems of using self-interested individuals as agents for other self-interested individuals. It is a set of problems familiar to studies of legislators, lawyers, and bureaucrats. If we assume that agents act in their own self-interest, then ensuring that the self-interest of agents coincides with the self-interest of principals becomes a central concern. This has led to extensive discussions of incentive and contractual schemes designed to assure such a coincidence, and to the development of theories of agency. It is clear, however, that principals are not always successful in assuring the reliability of agents. Agents are bribed or coopted. As a result, politics often emphasizes trust and loyalty, in parallel with a widespread belief that they are hard to find. The temptations to revise contracts unilaterally are frequently substantial, and promises of uncertain future support are easily made worthless in the absence of some network of favor giving.

Such complications lead to problems in controlling the implementation of decisions. Decisions unfold through a series of interrelated actions. If all conflicts of interest were settled by the employment contract, the unfolding would present only problems of information and coordination, but such problems are confounded by the complications of unresolved conflict. For example, one complication in control is that the procedures developed to measure performance in compliance with directives involve measures that can be manipulated. Any system of controls involves a system of accounts, and any system of accounts is a roadmap to cheating on them. As a result, control systems can be seen as an infinite game between controllers and the controlled in which advantage lies with relatively full-time players having direct personal interest in the outcomes.

Such features of organizations arise from one very simple modification of classical theories of choice: seeing decisions as being based on unreconciled preferences. It seems hard to avoid the obvious fact that such a description comes closer to the truth in many situations than does one in which we assume a consistent preference function. Somewhat more problematic is the second feature of much of the behavioral study of decision making — the tendency for the political aspects of decision making to be interminable. If it were possible to imagine a two-step decision process in which first we established (through side-payments and formation of coalitions) a set of joint preferences acceptable to a winning coalition and *then* we acted, we could treat the first stage as 'politics' and the second as 'economics'. Such a division has often been tempting (e.g. the distinction between policy making and administration), but it has rarely been satisfactory as a description of decision making. The decisions we observe seem to be infused with strategic actions and politics at every level and at every point.

An academy, like a business firm or government agency, is a political system of partly conflicting interests in which decisions are made through bargaining, power, and coalition formation. In general, there appear to be a few elementary rules for operating in a political system. Power comes from a favorable position for trading favors. Thus it comes from the possession of resources and the idiosyncrasy of preferences, from valuing things that others do not and having things that others value. If you have valued resources, display them. If you don't have them, get them — even if you don't value them yourself. Grab a hostage. Power comes from a reputation for power. Thus it comes from appearing to get what you want, from the trappings of power, and from the interpretations people make of ambiguous historical events. [. . .]

Rules
Theories of choice underestimate both the pervasiveness and sensibility of an alternative decision logic — the logic of obligation, duty and rules. Actual decisions seem often to involve finding the 'appropriate' rule as much as they do evaluating consequences in terms of preferences.

Much of the decision-making behavior we observe reflects the routine way in which people do what they are supposed to do. For example, most of the time, most people in organizations follow rules even when it is not obviously in their self-interest to do so. The behavior can be viewed as contractual, an implicit agreement to act appropriately in return for being treated appropriately, and to some extent there certainly is such a 'contract'. But socialization into rules and their appropriateness is ordinarily not a case of willful entering into an explicit contract. It is a set of understandings of the nature of things, of self-conceptions, and of images of proper behavior. It is possible, of course, to treat the word *rule* so broadly as to include any regularity in behavior, and sometimes that is a temptation too great to be resisted. But for the most part, we mean something considerably narrower. We mean regular operating procedures, not necessarily written but certainly standardized, known and understood with sufficient clarity to allow discourse about them and action based on them.

The proposition that organizations follow rules — that much of the behavior in an organization is specified by standard operating procedures — is a common one in the bureaucratic and organizational literature. To describe behavior as driven by rules is to see action as a matching of behavior with a position or situation. The criterion is appropriateness. The terminology is one of duties and roles rather than anticipatory decision making. The contrast can be characterized by comparing the conventional litanies for individual behavior.

Consequential action:
(1) What are my alternatives?
(2) What are my values?
(3) What are the consequences of my alternatives for my values?
(4) Choose the alternative that has the best consequences.

Obligatory action:
(1) What kind of situation is this?
(2) What kind of person am I?
(3) What is appropriate for me in a situation like this?
(4) Do it.

Research on obligatory action emphasizes understanding the kinds of rules that are evoked and used, the ways in which they fit together, and the processes by which they change.

The existence and persistence of rules, combined with their relative independence of idiosyncratic concerns of individuals, make it possible for societies and organizations to function reasonably reliably and reasonably consistently. Current rules store information generated by previous experience and analysis, even though the information cannot easily be retrieved in a form amenable to systematic current evaluation. [. . .] Insofar as action can be viewed as rule-following, decision making is not willful in the normal sense. It does not stem from the pursuit of interests and the calculation of future consequences of current choices. Rather it comes from matching a changing set of contingent rules to a changing set of situations. The intelligence of the process arises from the way rules store information gained through learning, selection, and contagion, and from the reliability with which rules are followed. The broader intelligence of the adaptation of rules depends on a fairly subtle intermeshing of rates of change, consistency, and foolishness. Sensibility is not guaranteed. At the least, it seems to require occasional deviation from the rules, some general consistency between adaptation rates and environmental rates of change, and a reasonable likelihood that networks of imitation are organized in a manner that allows intelligent action to be diffused somewhat more rapidly and more extensively than silliness.

In these terms, decision making in our headmistress's academy involves a logic of appropriateness. The issue is not what the costs and benefits are of an innovative new idea, but what a good headmistress does in a situation like this. The headmistress's role, like other roles, is filled with rules of behavior that have evolved through a history of experience, new year's resolutions, and imitation. There are rules about dress and decorum, rules about the treatment of staff members and guests, rules about dealing with grievances, rules about the kinds of equipment that should be provided and how it should be used. People in the organization follow rules: professional rules, social rules, and standard operating procedures. In such a world, some of the most effective ways of influencing decision outcomes involve the relatively dull business of understanding standard operating procedures and systems of accounting and control and intervening unobtrusively to make a particular decision a routine consequence of following standard rules.

Disorder

Theories of choice underestimate the confusion and complexity surrounding actual decision making. Many things are happening at once: technologies are changing and poorly understood; alliances, preferences, and perceptions are changing; problems, solutions, opportunities, ideas, people, and outcomes are mixed together in a way that makes their interpretation uncertain and their connections unclear.

Decision making ordinarily presumes an ordering of the confusions of life. The classic ideas of order in organizations involve two closely related concepts. The first is that events and activities can be arranged in chains of ends and means. We associate action with its consequences; we participate in making decisions in order to produce intended outcomes. Thus, consequential relevance arranges the relation between solutions and problems and the participation of decision makers. The second is that organizations are hierarchies in which higher levels control lower levels, and policies control implementation. Observations of actual organizations suggest a more confusing picture. Actions in one part of an organization appear to be only loosely coupled to actions in another. Solutions seem to have only a modest connection to problems. Policies are not implemented. Decision makers seem to wander in and out of decision arenas. In *Ambiguity and Choice in Organizations*, Pierre Romelaer and I described the whole process as a funny soccer game: 'Consider a round, sloped, multi-goal soccer field on which individuals play soccer. Many different people (but not everyone) can join in the game (or leave it) at different times. Some people can throw balls into the game or remove them. Individuals while they are in the game try to kick whatever ball comes near them in the direction of goals they like and away from goals they wish to avoid.'

The disorderliness of many things that are observed in decision making has led some people to argue that there is very little order to it, that it is best described as bedlam. A more conservative position, however, is that the ways in which organizations bring order to disorder is less hierarchical and less a collection of means-ends chains than is anticipated by conventional theories. There is order, but it is not the conventional order. In particular, it is argued that any decision process involves a collection of individuals and groups who are simultaneously involved in other things. Understanding decisions in one arena requires an understanding of how those decisions fit into the lives of participants.

From this point of view, the loose coupling that is observed in a specific decision situation is a consequence of a shifting intermeshing of the demands on the attention and lives of the whole array of actors. It is possible to examine any particular decision as the seemingly fortuitous consequence of combining different moments of different lives, and some efforts have been made to describe organizations in something like that cross-sectional detail. A more limited version of the same fundamental idea focuses on the allocation of attention. The idea is simple. Individuals attend to some things, and thus do not attend to others. The attention devoted to a particular decision by a particular potential participant depends on the attributes of the decision and alternative claims on attention. Since those alternative claims are not homogeneous across participants and change over time, the attention any particular decision receives can be both quite unstable and remarkably independent of the properties of the decision. The same decision will attract much attention, or little, depending on the other things that possible participants might be doing. The apparently erratic character of attention is made somewhat more explicable by placing it in the context of multiple, changing claims on attention.

Such ideas have been generalized to deal with flows of solutions and problems, as well as participants. In a garbage-can decision process it is assumed that there are exogenous, time-dependent arrivals of choice problems, solutions, and decision makers. Problems and solutions are attached to choices, and thus to each other, not because of their inherent connection in a means-end sense, but in terms of their temporal proximity. The collection of decision makers, problems, and solutions that come to be associated with a particular choice opportunity is orderly — but the logic of the ordering is temporal rather than hierarchical or consequential. At the limit, for example, almost any solution can be associated with almost any problem — provided they are contemporaries.

The strategies for a headmistress that can be derived from this feature of decision making are not complicated. First, persist. The disorderliness of decision processes and implementation means that there is no essential consistency between what happens at one time or place and what happens at another, or between policies and actions. Decisions happen as a result of a series of loosely connected episodes involving different people in different settings, and they may be unmade or modified by subsequent episodes. Second, have a rich agenda. There are innumerable ways in which disorderly processes will confound the cleverest behavior with respect to any one proposal, however important or imaginative. What such processes cannot do is frustrate large numbers of projects. Third, provide opportunities for garbage-can decisions. One of the complications in accomplishing things in a disorderly process is the tendency for any particular project to become intertwined with other issues simply by virtue of their simultaneity. The appropriate response is to provide irrelevant choice opportunities for problems and issues; for example, discussions of long-run plans or goals.

Symbols

Theories of choice assume that the primary reason for decision making is to make choices. They ignore the extent to which decision making is a ritual activity closely linked to central Western ideologies of rationality. In actual decision situations, symbolic and ritual aspects are often a major factor.

Most theories of choice assume that a decision process is to be understood in terms of its outcome, that decision makers enter the process in order to affect outcomes, and that the point of life is choice. The emphasis is instrumental: the central conceit is the notion of decision significance. Studies of decision arenas, on the other hand, seem often to describe a set of processes that make little sense in such terms. Information that is ostensibly gathered for a decision is often ignored. Individuals fight for the right to participate in a decision process, but then do not exercise the right. Studies of managerial time persistently indicate very little time spent in making decisions. Rather, managers seem to spend time meeting people and executing managerial performances. Contentiousness over the policies of an organization is often followed by apparent indifference about their implementation.

These anomalous observations appear to reflect, at least in part, the extent to which decision processes are only partly — and often almost incidentally — concerned with making decisions. A choice process provides an occasion:

- for defining virtue and truth, during which decision makers discover or interpret what has happened to them, what they have been doing, what they are going to do, and what justifies their actions.
- for distributing glory or blame for what has happened; and thus an occasion for exercising, challenging, or reaffirming friendship or trust relationships, antagonisms, power or status relationships.
- for socialization, for educating the young.
- for having a good time, for enjoying the pleasures connected with taking part in a choice situation.

In short, decision making is an arena for symbolic action, for developing and enjoying an interpretation of life and one's position in it. The rituals of choice infuse participants with an appreciation of the sensibility of life's arrangements. They tie routine events to beliefs about the nature of things. The rituals give meaning, and meaning controls life. From this point of view, understanding decision making involves recognizing that decision outcomes may often be less significant than the ways in which the process provides meaning in an ambiguous world. The meanings involved may be as grand as the central ideology of a society committed to reason and participation. They may be as local as the ego needs of specific individuals or groups.

Some treatments of symbols in decision making portray them as perversions of decision processes. They are presented as ways in which the gullible are misled into acquiescence. In such a portrayal, the witch doctors of symbols use their tricks to confuse the innocent, and the symbolic features of choice are opiates. Although there is no question that symbols are often used strategically, effective decision making depends critically on the legitimacy of the processes of choice and their outcomes, and such legitimacy is problematic in a confusing, ambiguous world. It is hard to imagine a society with modern ideology that would not exhibit a well elaborated and reinforced myth of choice, both to sustain social orderliness and meaning and to facilitate change.

The orchestration of choice needs to assure an audience of two essential things: first, that the choice has been made intelligently, that it reflects planning, thinking, analysis, and the systematic use of information; second, that the choice is sensitive to the concerns of relevant people, that the right people have had a word in the process. For example, part of the drama of organizational decision making is used to reinforce the idea that managers (and managerial decisions) affect the performance of organizations. Such a belief is, in fact, difficult to confirm using the kinds of data routinely generated in a confusing world. But the belief is important to the functioning of a hierarchical system. Executive compensation schemes and the ritual trappings of executive advancement reassure managers (and others) that an organization is controlled by its leadership, and appropriately so.

Thus, by most reasonable measures, the symbolic consequences of decision processes are as important as the outcome consequences; and we are led to a perspective that challenges the first premise of many theories of choice, the premise that life is choice. Rather, we might observe that life is not primarily choice; it is interpretation. Outcomes are generally less significant — both behaviorally and ethically — than process. It is the process that gives meaning to life, and meaning is the core of life. The reason that people involved in decision making devote so much time to symbols, myths, and rituals is that we (appropriately) care more about them. From this point of view, choice is a construction that finds its justification primarily in its elegance, and organizational decision making can be understood and described in approximately the same way we would understand and describe a painting by Picasso or a poem by T.S. Eliot.

As a result, a headmistress probably needs to see her activities as somewhat more dedicated to elaborating the processes of choice (as opposed to controlling their outcomes), to developing the ritual beauties of decision making in a way that symbolizes the kind of institution her academy might come to be. Just as educational institutions have libraries and archives of manuscripts to symbolize a commitment to scholarship and ideas, so also they have decision processes that express critical values. For example, if an important value of an organization is client satisfaction, then the decision process should be one that displays the eagerness of management to accept and implement client proposals, and one that symbolizes the dedication of staff to principles of availability and service.

Information and implications

These observations on decision making and theories of choice are not surprising to experienced decision makers. But they have some implications, one set of which can be illustrated by examining a classical problem: the design of an information system in an organization. In the case of our headmistress, there are issues of what information to gather and store, which archives to keep and which to burn, what information to provide to potential contributors, and how to organize the records so they are easily accessible to those who need them.

In most discussions of the design of information systems in organizations, the value of information is ordinarily linked to managerial decision making in a simple way. The value of an information source depends on the decisions to be made, the precision and reliability of the information, and the availability of alternative sources. Although calculating the relevant expected costs and returns is rarely trivial, the framework suggests some very useful rules of thumb. Don't pay for information about something that cannot affect choices you are making. Don't pay for information if the same information will be freely available anyway before you have to make a decision for which it is relevant. Don't pay for information that confirms something you already know. In general, we are led to an entirely plausible stress on the proposition that allocation of resources to information gathering or to information systems should depend on a clear idea of how potential information might affect decisions.

A notable feature of the actual investments in information and information sources that we observe is that they appear to deviate considerably from these conventional canons of information management. Decision makers and organizations gather information and do not use it; ask for more, and ignore it; make decisions first, and look for the relevant information afterwards. In fact, organizations seem to gather a great deal of information that has little or no relevance to decisions. It is, from a decision theory point of view, simply gossip. Were one to ask why organizations treat information in these ways, it would be possible to reply that they are poorly designed, badly managed, or ill-informed. To some extent, many certainly are. But the pervasiveness of the phenomenon suggests that perhaps it is not the decision makers who are inadequate, but our conceptions of information. There are several sensible reasons why decision makers deal with information the way they do.

Decision makers operate in a surveillance mode more than they do in a problem-solving mode. In contrast to a theory of information that assumes that information is gathered to resolve a choice among alternatives, decision makers scan their environments for surprises and solutions. They monitor what is going on. Such scanning calls for gathering a great deal of information that appears to be irrelevant to 'decisions'. Moreover, insofar as decision makers deal with problems, their procedures are different from those anticipated in standard decision theory. They characteristically do not 'solve' problems; they apply rules and copy solutions from others. Indeed, they often do not recognize a 'problem' until they have a 'solution'.

Decision makers seem to know, or at least sense, that most information is tainted by the process by which it is generated. It is typically quite hard to disaggregate social belief, including expert judgment, into its bases. The social process by which confidence in judgment is developed and shared is not overly sensitive to the quality of judgment. Moreover, most information is subject to strategic misrepresentation. It is likely to be presented by someone who is, for personal or subgroup reasons, trying to persuade a decision maker to do something. Our theories of information-based decision making (e.g. statistical decision theory) are, for the most part, theories of decision making with innocent information. Decision information, on the other hand, is rarely innocent, and thus rarely as reliable as an innocent would expect.

Highly regarded advice is often bad advice. It is easy to look at decision making and find instances in which good advice and good information were ignored. It is a common occurrence. Consequently, we sometimes see decision makers as perversely resistant to advice and information. In fact, much highly regarded advice and much generally accepted information is misleading. Even where conflict of interest between advice givers and advice takers is a minor problem, advice givers typically exaggerate the quality of their advice; and information providers typically exaggerate the quality of their information. It would be remarkable if they did not. Decision makers seem to act in a way that recognizes the limitations of 'good' advice and 'reliable' information.

Information is a signal and symbol of competence in decision making. Gathering and presenting information symbolizes (and demonstrates) the ability and legitimacy of decision makers. A good decision maker is one who makes decisions in a proper way, who exhibits expertise and uses generally accepted information. The competition for reputations among decision makers stimulates the overproduction of information.

As a result of such considerations, information plays both a smaller and a larger role than is anticipated in decision theory-related theories of information. It is smaller in the sense that the information used in decision making is less reliable and more strategic than is conventionally assumed, and is treated as less important for decision making. It is larger in the sense that it contributes not only to the making of decisions but to the execution of other managerial tasks and to the broad symbolic activities of the individual and organization.

If it is possible to imagine that life is not only choice but also interpretation, that they are heavily intertwined, and that the management of life and organizations is probably as much the latter as the former, it is possible to sketch some elements of the requirements for the design of useful management information systems.

We require some notion of the value of alternative information sources that is less tied to a prior specification of a decision (or class of decisions) than to a wide spectrum of possible decisions impossible to anticipate in the absence of the information; less likely to show the consequences of known alternatives for existing goals than to suggest new alternatives and new objectives; less likely to test old ideas than to provide new ones; less pointed towards anticipating uncertain futures than toward interpreting ambiguous pasts. [. . .]

More generally, research on how organizations make decisions leads us to a perspective on choice different from that provided by standard theories of choice, and may even provide some hints for an academy headmistress. The ideas are incomplete; the hints are rough. They point toward a vision of decision making that embraces the axioms of choice but acknowledges their limitations; that combines a passion for the technology of choice with an appreciation of its complexities and the beauties of its confusions; and that sees a headmistress as often constrained by sensibility and rules, but sometimes bouncing around a soccer field.

Questions about organizational structures have fascinated writers on organizations as much as they have baffled senior managers and administrators. Why do organizations come to arrange and co-ordinate their activities in such different ways? — and how should they do it? Indeed, this aspect of organizations may have attracted more attention than any other — the literature is labyrinthine. The considerable merit of the piece that follows is the broad overview it provides. It offers a plausible and simple explanation for the diversity of forms; and it highlights the areas of choice in the structuring of organizational activities and relationships — first, which of the basic options will be adopted (or what combination of them); and, second, in what ways will it be appropriate to implement that option (or mix of options)? The condensed and somewhat abstract style may make it less easy reading (no-one can accuse Galbraith of being long winded) but the basic ideas are straightforward — and very rewarding.

Organization Design: An Information Processing View

J.R. Galbraith

The information processing model

A basic proposition is that the greater the uncertainty of the task, the greater the amount of information that has to be processed between decision makers during the execution of the task. If the task is well understood prior to performing it, much of the activity can be preplanned. If it is not understood, then during the actual task execution more knowledge is acquired which leads to changes in resource allocations, schedules, and priorities. All these changes require information processing *during* task performance. Therefore *the greater the task uncertainty, the greater the amount of information that must be processed among decision makers during task execution in order to achieve a given level of performance.* The basic effect of uncertainty is to limit the ability of the organization to preplan or to make decisions about activities in advance of their execution. Therefore it is hypothesized that the observed variations in organizational forms are variations in the strategies of organizations to (1) increase their ability to preplan, (2) increase their flexibility to adapt their inability to preplan, or, (3) to decrease the level of performance required for continued viability. Which strategy is chosen depends on the relative costs of the strategies. The function of the framework is to identify these strategies and their costs.

The mechanistic model

This framework is best developed by keeping in mind a hypothetical organization. Assume it is large and employs a number of specialist groups and resources in providing the output. After the task has been divided into specialist subtasks, the problem is to integrate the subtasks around the completion of the global task. This is the problem of organization design. The behaviors that occur in one subtask cannot be judged as good or bad *per se*. The behaviors are more effective or ineffective depending upon the behaviors of the other subtask performers. There is a design problem because the executors of the behaviors cannot communicate with all the roles with whom they are interdependent. Therefore the design problem is to create mechanisms that permit coordinated action across large numbers of interdependent roles. Each of these mechanisms, however, has a limited range over which it is effective at handling the information requirements necessary to coordinate the interdependent roles. As the amount of uncertainty increases, and therefore information processing increases, the organization must adopt integrating mechanisms which increase its information processing capabilities.

1. Coordination by rules or programs

For routine predictable tasks March and Simon have identified the use of rules or programs to coordinate behavior between interdependent subtasks (March and Simon 1958, Chap. 6). To the extent that job related situations can be predicted in

Interfaces, Vol 4 No. 3, May 1974 pp.28-36. © Copyright 1974 the Institute of Management Sciences.

advance, and behaviors specified for these situations, programs allow an interdependent set of activities to be performed without the need for inter-unit communication. Each role occupant simply executes the behavior which is appropriate for the task related situation with which he is faced.

2. Hierarchy

As the organization faces greater uncertainty its participants face situations for which they have no rules. At this point the hierarchy is employed on an exception basis. The recurring job situations are programmed with rules while infrequent situations are referred to that level in the hierarchy where a global perspective exists for all affected subunits. However, the hierarchy also has a limited range. As uncertainty increases the number of exceptions increases until the hierarchy becomes overloaded.

3. Coordination by targets or goals

As the uncertainty of the organization's task increases, coordination increasingly takes place by specifying outputs, goals or targets (March and Simon 1958, p.145). Instead of specifying specific behaviors to be enacted, the organization undertakes processes to set goals to be achieved and the employees select the behaviors which lead to goal accomplishment. Planning reduces the amount of information processing in the hierarchy by increasing the amount of discretion exercised at lower levels. Like the use of rules, planning achieves integrated action and also eliminates the need for continuous communication among interdependent subunits as long as task performance stays within the planned task specifications, budget limits and within targeted completion dates. If it does not, the hierarchy is again employed on an exception basis.

The ability of an organization to coordinate interdependent tasks depends on its ability to compute meaningful subgoals to guide subunit action. When uncertainty increases because of introducing new products, entering new markets, or employing new technologies these subgoals are incorrect. The result is more exceptions, more information processing, and an overloaded hierarchy.

Design strategies

The ability of an organization to successfully utilize coordination by goal setting, hierarchy, and rules depends on the combination of the frequency of exceptions and the capacity of the hierarchy to handle them. As the task uncertainty increases the organization must again take organization design action. It can proceed in either of two general ways. First, it can act in two ways to reduce the amount of information that is processed. And second, the organization can act in two ways to increase its capacity to handle more information. The two methods for reducing the need for information and the two methods for increasing processing capacity are shown schematically in Figure 12.1. The effect of all these actions is to reduce the number of exceptional cases referred upward into the organization through hierarchical channels. The assumption is that the critical limiting factor of an organizational form is its ability to

handle the non-routine, consequential events that cannot be anticipated and planned for in advance. The non-programmed events place the greatest communication load on the organization.

1. Creation of slack resources

As the number of exceptions begin to overload the hierarchy, one response is to increase the planning targets so that fewer exceptions occur. For example, completion dates can be extended until the number of exceptions that occur are within the existing information processing capacity of the organization. This has been the practice in solving job shop scheduling problems (Pounds 1963). Job shops quote delivery times that are long enough to keep the scheduling problem within the computational and information processing limits of the organization. Since every job shop has the same problem standard lead times evolve in the industry. Similarly budget targets could be raised, buffer inventories employed, etc. The greater the uncertainty, the greater the magnitude of the inventory, lead time or budget needed to reduce an overload.

All of these examples have a similar effect. They represent the use of slack resources to reduce the amount of interdependence between subunits (March and Simon 1958, Cyert and March 1963). This keeps the required amount of information within the capacity of the organization to process it. Information processing is reduced because an exception is less likely to occur and reduced interdependence means that fewer factors need to be considered simultaneously when an exception does occur.

The strategy of using slack resources has its costs. Relaxing budget targets has the obvious cost of requiring more budget. Increasing the time to completion date has the effect of delaying the customer. Inventories require the investment of capital funds which could be used elsewhere. Reduction of design optimization reduces the performance of the article being designed. Whether slack resources are used to reduce information or not depends on the relative cost of the other alternatives.

The design choices are: (1) among which factors to change (lead time, overtime, machine utilization, etc.) to create the slack, and (2) by what amount should the factor be changed. Many operations research models are useful in choosing factors and amounts. The time-cost trade off problem in project networks is a good example.

2. Creation of self-contained tasks

The second method of reducing the amount of information processed is to change the subtask groupings from source (input) based to output based categories and give each group the resources it needs to supply the output. For example, the functional organization could be changed to product groups. Each group would have its own product engineers, process engineers, fabricating and assembly operations, and marketing activities. In other situations, groups can be created around product lines, geographical areas, projects, client groups, markets, etc., each of which would contain the input resources necessary for creation of the output.

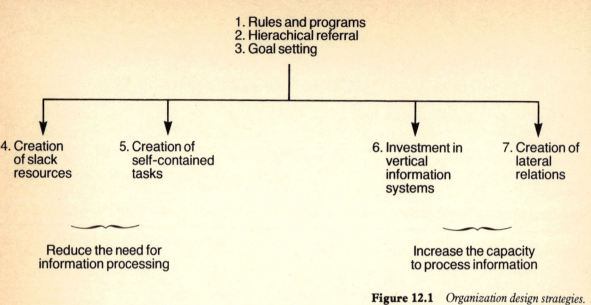

Figure 12.1   *Organization design strategies.*

The strategy of self-containment shifts the basis of the authority structure from one based on input, resource, skill, or occupational categories to one based on output or geographical categories. The shift reduces the amount of information processing through several mechanisms. First, it reduces the amount of output diversity faced by a single collection of resources. For example, a professional organization with multiple skill specialities providing service to three different client groups must schedule the use of these specialities across three demands for their services and determine priorities when conflicts occur. But, if the organization changed to three groups, one for each client category, each with its own full complement of specialities, the schedule conflicts across client groups disappears and there is no need to process information to determine priorities.

The second source of information reduction occurs through a reduced division of labor. The functional or resource specialized structure pools the demand for skills across all output categories. In the example above each client generates approximately one-third of the demand for each skill. Since the division of labor is limited by the extent of the market, the division of labor must decrease as the demand decreases. In the professional organization, each client group may have generated a need for one-third of a computer programmer. The functional organization would have hired one programmer and shared him across the groups. In the self-contained structure there is insufficient demand in each group for a programmer so the professionals must do their own programming. Specialization is reduced but there is no problem of scheduling the programmer's time across the three possible uses for it.

The cost of the self-containment strategy is the loss of resource specialization. In the example, the organization forgoes the benefit of a specialist in computer programming. If there is physical equipment, there is a loss of economies of scale. The professional organization would require three machines in the self-contained form but only a large time-shared machine in the functional form. But those resources which have large economies of scale or for which specialization is necessary may remain centralized. Thus, it is the degree of self-containment that is the variable. The greater the degree of uncertainty, other things equal, the greater the degree of self-containment.

The design choices are the basis for the self-containment structure and the number of resources to be contained in the groups. No groups are completely self-contained or they would not be part of the same organization. But one product divisionalized firm may have eight or fifteen functions in the division while another may have 12 or 15 in the divisions. Usually accounting, finance and legal services are centralized and shared. Those functions which have economies of scale, require specialization or are necessary for control remain centralized and not part of the self-contained group.

The first two strategies reduced the amount of information by lower performance standards and creating small autonomous groups to provide the output. Information is reduced because an exception is less likely to occur and fewer factors need to be considered when an exception does occur. The next two strategies accept the performance standards and division of labor as given and adapt the organization so as to process the new information which is created during task performance.

3. Investment in vertical information systems

The organization can invest in mechanisms which allow it to process information acquired during task performance without overloading the hierarchical communication channels. The investment occurs according to the following logic. After the organization has created its plan or set of targets for inventories, labor utilization, budgets and schedules, unanticipated events occur which generate exceptions requiring adjustments to the original plan. At some point when the number of exceptions becomes substantial, it is preferable to generate a new plan rather than make incremental changes with each exception. The issue is then how frequently should plans be revised — yearly, quarterly, or monthly? The greater the frequency of replanning the greater the resources, such as clerks, computer time, input-output devices, etc., required to process information about relevant factors.

The cost of information processing resources can be minimized if the language is formalized. Formalization of a decision-making language simply means that more information is transmitted with the same number of symbols. It is assumed that information processing resources are consumed in proportion to the number of symbols transmitted. The accounting system is an example of formalized language.

Providing more information, more often, may simply overload the decision maker. Investment may be required to increase the capacity of the decision maker by employing computers, various man-machine combinations, assistants-to, etc. The cost of this strategy is the cost of the information processing resources consumed in transmitting and processing the data.

The design variables of this strategy are the decision frequency, the degree of formalization of language, and the type of decision mechanism which will make the choice. This strategy is usually operationalized by creating redundant information channels which transmit data from the point of origination upward in the hierarchy where the point of decision rests. If data is formalized and quantifiable, this strategy is effective. If the relevant data are qualitative and ambiguous, then it may prove easier to bring the decisions down to where the information exists.

4. Creation of lateral relationships

The last strategy is to employ selectively joint decision processes which cut across lines of authority. This strategy moves the level of decision making down in the organization to where the information exists but does so without reorganizing around self-contained groups. There are several types of lateral decision processes. Some processes are usually referred to as the informal organization. However, these informal processes do not always arise spontaneously out of the needs of the task. This is particularly true in multi-national organizations in which participants are separated by physical barriers, language differences, and cultural differences. Under these circumstances lateral processes need to be designed. The lateral processes evolve as follows with increases in uncertainty.

4.1   *Direct contact* between managers who share a problem.

If a problem arises on the shop floor, the foreman can simply call the design engineer, and they can jointly agree upon a solution. From an information processing view, the joint decision prevents an upward referral and unloads the hierarchy.

4.2   *Liaison roles.* When the volume of contacts between any two departments grows, it becomes economical to set up a specialized role to handle this communication. Liaison men are typical examples of specialized roles designed to facilitate communication between two interdependent departments and to bypass the long lines of communication involved in upward referral. Liaison roles arise at lower and middle levels of management.

4.3   *Task forces.* Direct contact and liaison roles, like the integration mechanism before them, have a limited range of usefulness. They work when two managers or functions are involved. When problems arise involving seven or eight departments, the decision making capacity of direct contacts is exceeded. Then these problems must be referred upward. For uncertain, interdependent tasks such situations arise frequently. Task forces are a form of horizontal contact which is designed for problems of multiple departments.

The task force is made up of representatives from each of the affected departments. Some are full-time members, others may be part-time. The task force is a temporary group. It exists only as long as the problem remains. When a solution is reached, each participant returns to his normal tasks.

To the extent that they are successful, task forces remove problems from higher levels of the hierarchy. The decisions are made at lower levels in the organization. In order to guarantee integration, a group problem solving approach is taken. Each affected subunit contributes a member and therefore provides the information necessary to judge the impact on all units.

4.4   *Teams.* The next extension is to incorporate the group decision process into the permanent decision processes, that is, as certain decisions consistently arise, the task forces become permanent. These groups are labeled teams. There are many design issues concerned in team decision making such as at what level do they operate, who participates, etc. (Galbraith 1973, Chapters 6 and 7). One design decision is particularly critical. This is the choice of leadership. Sometimes a problem exists largely in one department so that the department manager is the leader. Sometimes the leadership passes from one manager to another. As a new product moves to the market place, the leader of the new product team is first the technical manager followed by the production and then the marketing manager. The result is that if the team cannot reach a consensus decision and the leader decides, the goals of the leader are consistent with the goals of the organization for the decision in question. But quite often obvious leaders cannot be found. Another mechanism must be introduced.

4.5   *Integrating roles.* The leadership issue is solved by creating a new role — an integrating role (Lawrence and Lorsch 1967, Chapter 3). These roles carry the labels of product managers, program managers, project managers, unit managers (hospitals), materials managers, etc. After the role is created, the design problem is to create enough power in the role to influence the decision process. These roles have power even when no one reports directly to them. They have some power because they report to the general manager. But if they are selected so as to be unbiased with respect to the groups they integrate and to have technical competence, they have expert power. They collect information and equalize power differences due to preferential access to knowledge and information. The power equalization increases trust and the quality of the joint decision process. But power equalization occurs only if the integrating role is staffed with someone who can exercise expert power in the form of persuasion and informal influences rather than exert the power of rank or authority.

4.6 *Managerial linking roles.* As tasks become more uncertain, it is more difficult to exercise expert power. The role must get more power of the formal authority type in order to be effective at coordinating the joint decisions which occur at lower levels of the organization. This position power changes the nature of the role which for lack of a better name is labeled a managerial linking role. It is not like the integrating role because it possesses formal position power but is different from line managerial roles in that participants do not report to the linking manager. The power is added by the following successive changes:

(a) The integrator receives approval power of budgets formulated in the departments to be integrated.

(b) The planning and budgeting process starts with the integrator making his initiation in budgeting legitimate.

(c) Linking manager receives the budget for the area of responsibility and buys resources from the specialist groups.

These mechanisms permit the manager to exercise influence even though no one works directly for him. The role is concerned with integration but exercises power through the formal power of the position. If this power is insufficient to integrate the subtasks and creation of self-contained groups is not feasible, there is one last step.

4.7 *Matrix organization.* The last step is to create the dual authority relationship and the matrix organization (Galbraith 1971). At some point in the organization some roles have two superiors. The design issue is to select the locus of these roles. The result is a balance of power between the managerial linking roles and the normal line organization roles. Figure 12.2 depicts the pure matrix design.

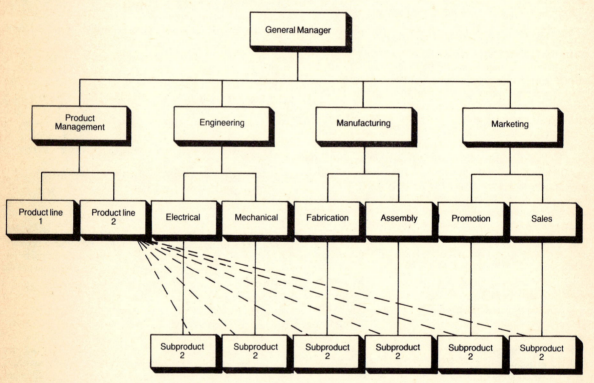

------- Technical authority over the product

——— Formal authority over the product (in product organization these relationships may be reversed)

Figure 12.2   *A pure matrix organization.*

Table 1

	Plastics	Food	Container
% new products in last ten years	35%	20%	0%

Integrating Devices	Rules
	Hierarchy
	Planning
	Direct
	   Contact
	Teams at 3
	   levels
	Integrating
	   Dept.
		Rules
		Hierarchy
		Planning
		Direct
		   Contact
		Task forces
		Integrators
			Rules
			Hierarchy
			Planning
			Direct
			   Contact

% Integrators/ Managers	22%	17%	0%

(Adapted from Lawrence and Lorsch 1967, pp. 86-138 and Lorsch and Lawrence 1968)

The work of Lawrence and Lorsch is highly consistent with the assertions concerning lateral relations (Lawrence and Lorsch 1967, Lorsch and Lawrence 1968). They compared the types of lateral relations undertaken by the most successful firm in three different industries. Their data are summarized in Table 1. The plastics firm has the greatest rate of new product introduction (uncertainty) and the greatest utilization of lateral processes. The container firm was also very successful but utilized only standard practices because its information processing task is much less formidable. Thus, the greater the uncertainty the lower the level of decision making and the integration is maintained by lateral relations.

Table 1 points out the cost of using lateral relations. The plastics firm has 22 per cent of its managers in integration roles. Thus, the greater the use of lateral relations the greater the managerial intensity. This cost must be balanced against the cost of slack resources, self-contained groups and information systems.

Choice of strategy

Each of the four strategies has been briefly presented. The organization can follow one or some combination of several if it chooses. It will choose that strategy which has the least cost in its environmental context. (For an example, see Galbraith 1970.) However, what may be lost in all of the explanations is that the four strategies are hypothesized to be an exhaustive set of alternatives. That is, if the organization is faced with greater uncertainty due to technological change, higher performance standards due to increased competition, or diversifies its product line to reduce dependence, the amount of information processing is increased. *The organization must adopt at least one of the four strategies when faced with greater uncertainty.* If it does

not consciously choose one of the four, then the first, reduced performance standards, will happen automatically. The task information requirements and the capacity of the organization to process information are always matched. If the organization does not consciously match them, reduced performance through budget overruns and schedule overruns will occur in order to bring about equality. Thus the organization should be planned and designed simultaneously with the planning of the strategy and resource allocations. But if the strategy involves introducing new products, entering new markets, etc., then some provision for increased information must be made. Not to decide is to decide, and it is to decide upon slack resources as the strategy to remove hierarchical overload.

There is probably a fifth strategy which is not articulated here. Instead of changing the organization in response to task uncertainty, the organization can operate on its environment to reduce uncertainty. The organization through strategic decisions, long term contracts, coalitions, etc., can control its environment. But these maneuvers have costs also. They should be compared with costs of the four design strategies presented above.

Summary

The purpose of this paper has been to explain why task uncertainty is related to organizational form. In so doing the cognitive limits theory of Herbert Simon was the guiding influence. As the consequences of cognitive limits were traced through the framework various organization design strategies were articulated. The framework provides a basis for integrating organizational interventions, such as information systems and group problem solving, which have been treated separately before.

References

Cyert, R. and March, J. (1963) *The Behavioral Theory of the Firm*, Prentice-Hall, Englewood Cliffs, New Jersey.

Galbraith, J. (1970) 'Environmental and technological determinants of organization design: a case study', in Lawrence, P. and Lorsch, J. (eds) *Studies in Organization Design*, Richard D. Irwin Inc., Homewood, Illinois.

Galbraith, J. (1971) 'Designing matrix organizations', *Business Horizons*, February, pp.29-40.

Galbraith, J. (1973) *Organization Design*, Addison-Wesley, Reading, Mass.

Lawrence, P. and Lorsch, J. (1967) *Organization and Environment*, Division of Research, Harvard Business School, Boston, Mass.

Lorsch, J. and Lawrence, P. (1968) 'Environmental factors and organization integration'. Paper read at the Annual Meeting of the American Sociological Association, 27 August, Boston, Mass.

March, J. and Simon, H. (1958) *Organizations*, John Wiley & Sons, New York.

Pounds, W. (1963) 'The scheduling environment', in Muth and Thompson (eds) *Industrial Scheduling*, Prentice-Hall, Englewood Cliffs, New Jersey.

Simon, H. (1957) *Models of Man*, John Wiley & Sons, New York.

13   Power in Organizations

In recent years the analysis of organizations as political systems has received greatly increased attention. It is a perspective that makes good sense to many managers and administrators whose day-to-day experience involves a considerable amount of lobbying and manoeuvring to promote or deflect particular initiatives. But central to any such analysis must be a treatment of topics like power, influence, authortiy and interests; phenomena which are notoriously slippery — and contentious. The following piece aims to provide a workable simplification of this difficult terrain.

Powers Visible and Invisible
R. Paton

Powers visible . . .

Anyone who must regularly attempt to get things done with and through other people has the problem of generating agreement, or perhaps just consent, or at least compliance, with regard to what will be done, how, when and on what terms. Characteristically, opinions will differ on the importance of the different goals and on what is an appropriate, or fair, basis to proceed. Such disagreements may be more or less significant and far reaching and conducted in a style ranging from the polite and circumspect to the openly threatening and coercive. But however it is done each side is attempting to influence the conduct of the other. And in doing so they will make use of whatever resources or means are available, and seem appropriate. Hence, to understand or anticipate the course of a particular conflict and its outcome, requires an appreciation of the different sorts of resources that those involved may use, or attempt to use. What follows is a brief catalogue of these different resources and the areas in which they may be used, starting with the more obvious ones that are regularly employed in relation to conflicts and disagreements that have 'surfaced' in the decision-making processes of the organization — that's to say, both sides know what's going on, even if it is not treated explicitly and is amicably handled and resolved. These more obvious 'visible' power resources provide a fairly straightforward way into a difficult topic. But it is worth emphasizing from the start that the power of individuals and groups in organizations will vary over different issues. A shop steward may be able to bring the entire plant to a halt on a matter concerning safety or manning levels, but this doesn't mean he or she can influence the decision to purchase a subsidiary or enter a new overseas market. So you shouldn't think of these different sorts of power as something that people can carry around to use whenever it suits them. The distribution of power is always *issue-specific*.

Position power

The most obvious source of power in organizations is that which stems from a person's formal position. In the first place, roles carry the right to make particular decisions. The head of a department may be entitled to say 'This is the way we're going to do it'; the issue — and any conflict associated with it — is closed (bar the grumblings, of course). Related to this formal authority is the status and respect often attributed to those in 'high' organizational positions. Someone from headquarters, for example, may be trusted and believed when the local manager is not; he or she must be in a position to know the full picture, someone of that calibre wouldn't do this unless it were absolutely necessary, and so on. Hence the prestige of a particular post may enable the incumbent to persuade and influence others even in areas that are not strictly within that person's authority.

Next, those in positions of authority can control the rewards of those they supervise — the foreman who allocates overtime, or the departmental head who can recommend promotions, salary increases, training courses and the like. This is sometimes called *reward power*.

Expert power

Organizations use specialist knowledge to cope with task and environmental uncertainty. This means that on certain issues they must rely on and accept the judgement of those who possess that knowledge. Experts — or rather, those who are seen as experts — thus possess a power resource which is more or less independent of their formal position in the organization. The middle-ranking research chemist who calmly says 'it just can't be done' can stop the marketing director of a chemical firm dead in his tracks. If the director is unwise enough to press the point he or she simply invites a lecture on, say, some finer points of polymer chemistry, whereupon — whether he or she pretends to understand and agree, or instead admits to not understanding and refuses to agree — the point is irretrievably lost.

The problem, essentially, is that no one can be an expert in all the activities of a complex organization. So some individuals will be formally superior to those whose expertise they cannot emulate. Hence, when the general manager disagrees with the head of one of his specialist departments it may be a straight tussle between position and expert power.

Such conflicts are now a distinctive characteristic of large-scale organizations of all sorts, including government ministries. Nevertheless, it remains very difficult to say with whom the advantage lies, unless one has very detailed knowledge of the particular case in question. To a large extent the expert's power will depend on the importance to the organization of the uncertainty on which the expert pronounces. Thereafter it is up to the expert to make the *best use* of such power.

Dependence power

When people join organizations it is because they want something from (or through) the organization and they are willing to contribute so long as they get what they want. Likewise, when recruiting employees or soliciting members, organizations offer inducements of one sort or another in order to gain what they want. So whatever else it represents, membership of an organization involves a straightforward *exchange; inducements* are offered in return for *contributions*. However, since each side wants what the other is offering, this exchange may also involve a measure of *dependence*.

The extent to which one side depends on the other is affected by a number of factors: how important is it to have what the other offers? Can it be obtained elsewhere? Are substitutes available? If the answers to these questions are 'very', 'no' and 'no', then the party concerned is very dependent *indeed* on the other party — *which need not be similarly dependent on the first party*. The final step is to point out that if someone depends on you for something then, for you, this is a source of power. Unless they do what you want, you may withhold what they want so badly.

So, starting from the basic and very general idea of an *exchange*, one can specify conditions for unequal exchanges and *dependence*, which itself is indicative of a *power relationship*, whether or not that power is actually used.

Such power is illustrated in strikes and other forms of industrial action. Union members withhold their labour, upon which management depend. The classic case is given by sequentially interdependent production operations in which a small group of employees can bring an entire plant, or perhaps several plants, to a standstill. However, this depends on the other workers refusing to 'man up' on jobs; on there being no alternative source of the components, or whatever; and on the union members having an alternative source of income sufficient for the duration of the strike — either savings or strike pay.

Although most common in industrial relations, dependence power may be used at other organizational levels: there have been occasions when a number of senior managers have blocked particular proposals by threatening to resign *en bloc*! The important point is that those in subordinate positions can under certain conditions, possess *very considerable power indeed*. So *dependence power* is the power of subordinates or peers arising from a dependence, not on their expertise or the rights of their position, but on their *willing cooperation*. It's worth pointing out, however, that the term can be applied much more generally — including, for example, expert power as the dependence of organizations on specialist knowledge. But a broad definition of dependence power would cover such a wide range of situations that one would immediately have to break it down into subcategories. So it is simpler to use it in a restricted sense as defined.

This sort of power has also been called 'negative power', but the term dependence relates it to the idea of exchanges. This has advantages when some of its more subtle manifestations are considered later.

Personal power

The attributes of many organizational roles — such as outward confidence, decisiveness and an authoritative tone — are often mistakenly seen as personal qualities. The new head of department may start off pretending still to be one of the lads but it won't last long; in no time he or she will be adopting the style and mannerisms expected of someone in that position. There may be nothing about it in the job description, but it's an almost inescapable part of the job nonetheless. A doctor's 'bed-side manner' is a classic example; calm, sympathetic, reassuring, but serious and authoritative — these look like personal qualities but they are clearly the learned patterns expected of someone in that role.

Personal power does not refer to these apparently personal qualities that more or less 'come with the job'. Nor to those reputations for dynamism and charisma that tell us little about the person concerned, but a great deal about the public relations business. It refers to those abilities and qualities which enable some people to make the most of whatever other power resources they have. Charm, intelligence and a silver tongue are obviously useful in many situations. Likewise sensitivity to the progress of a meeting can mean success for a well-timed proposal that would have been rejected if it had been made at the start. Similarly, the ability to 'take the role of the other' and anticipate the reactions of potential opponents is characteristic of successful negotiators. This form of power also overlaps a bit with expert power — training exists in negotiation and interpersonal skills. Nevertheless, some people have these capacities, without training, far more than others who have been trained.

To start with, then, four forms of 'visible' power have been loosely distinguished. The first, position power, involves several elements (formal authority, status, and control of rewards) that may be associated with particular, and especially the more senior, positions in a hierarchy. The second, expert power, referred to the use of appeals to expertise to influence others. The third, dependence power, draws attention to the fact that those who lack other forms of power may still be able to influence peers or superiors by suspending or threatening to suspend, an exchange those others have come to depend on. Finally, the term personal power was used to cover those personal qualities (of leadership and the like) which make some individuals far more influential than others with otherwise comparable power resources. So far, so good; but this much is only the beginning.

... And invisible

The preceding discussion considered the various forms of power that may be employed when a contentious issue appears on the agenda of organizational decision-making. They concern *whose solution will be accepted*, to resolve a given problem. But there are three other ways in which power may be exercised. In the first place, how an issue is presented can affect the way it is treated; secondly, many organizational practices develop informally and are not dealt with in an explicit decision-making process; thirdly, if power is exercised when a group ensures, against opposition, that its preferred option is selected, then power is also excercised if that group ensures that an option detrimental to its interests is *not even considered* by the parties to a conflict.

These three less obvious arenas for the exercise of power are considered in turn and reveal important additional dimensions of position and dependence power in particular.

The following quotation provides a clear example of how an issue can be presented in a way that favours a particular outcome:

> The marketing manager of an insurance company was on the brink of launching a large product development campaign. At the next management meeting, it had been decided to discuss poor profit performance in the previous two quarters. At issue was whether to deploy resources to expanding sales or to cutting costs by increasing automation (via electronic data processing). He knew that if this issue were to be raised at the meeting, he would be outvoted by a small majority of peers who leaned toward investing the funds in automation. However, he was convinced that automation didn't sell insurance! Therefore, he needed to find an issue that would rearrange the coalition structure currently against him. He realized that the key issue that he would prefer to have discussed was market share and not profits, so he did three things. First, he sent a report to all the management committee members that showed how losses in market share could be regained by his proposal. Second, he sent to all members of the management committee a memo asking them to consider ways in which his proposed product development program could be carried out effectively and at a lower cost. Third, he persuaded the chief executive to place his project proposal first on the agenda. When the meeting started, the issue was not whether the product launch should take place or not, but what funds would be required to launch the product; the automation proposal was postponed, because some marginal members of the automation coalition had become committed to the marketshare issue.[2]

In this case the marketing manager's efforts were directed at focusing attention on certain questions at the expense of others. Although he did not decide the agenda for the meeting himself, he recognized its importance and was able to influence the Chief Executive. In general, position power — through control of information and agendas — also allows a person to affect the terms on which an issue will be discussed. But as this example shows, those who hold position power may themselves be influenced (in this case, presumably by the marketing manager's expert and personal power). The meeting before the meeting is often the one that matters. Hence the apparent paradox of a chairperson who is immensely influential, and yet scrupulously impartial in the conduct of meetings.

These aspects of position power are also relevant to clashes or tensions between 'experts' and 'generalists' (the latter relying primarily on position power). Even if the uncertainty on which the expert's power is based is considerable, the generalist still has a number of cards to play. In the first place because he or she usually holds a higher position in the organization, the generalist can often determine the areas in which the expert will operate, the questions they must answer and the assumptions they will make. Moreover, the generalist may be able to break down the various specialist tasks into smaller units which only he or she can coordinate. If need be, one expert can then be played off against another. Finally, the generalist may actually be able to choose the expert concerned; since experts often disagree this can allow the appointment to the job of a 'sympathetic' expert. Hence it may very well be the case that experts only possess power on issues which directly and substantially concern them, while on more general matters *they exist as a resource to be tapped by others*. Certainly, many operations research practitioners have claimed that when their reports are used it is often only to provide a convenient 'scientific' rationale for what the generalist wanted to do anyway.

The second domain in which power may be exercised 'invisibly' is that of the gradual, informal evolution of working practices and arrangements. The idea of 'dependence power' was introduced earlier with the example of strikes, and related forms of industrial action.

The power in such cases derives from the employer's dependence on what is primarily an economic exchange with employees — cash in return for time and effort. But other sorts of exchange pervade organizational life: they are largely informal *social* exchanges, typically an exchange of *favours* of one sort or another. It is worth quoting from the classic analysis of the way in which social exchanges can be a power resource in shaping organizational practices:

> Thus dependence together with the manipulation of the dependency relationship is the key to the power of lower participants.

A number of examples can be cited which illustrate the preceding point. Scheff, for example, reports on the failure of a state mental hospital to bring about intended reform because of the opposition of hospital attendants. He noted that the power of hospital attendants was largely a result of the dependence of ward physicians on attendants. This dependence resulted from the physician's short tenure, his lack of interest in administration, and the large amount of administrative responsibility he had to assume. An implicit trading agreement developed between physicians and attendants, whereby attendants would take on some of the responsibilities and obligations of the ward physician in return for increased power in decision-making processes concerning patients. Failure of the ward physician to honor his part of the agreement resulted in information being withheld, disobedience, lack of cooperation, and unwillingness of the attendants to serve as a barrier between the physician and a ward full of patients demanding attention and recognition. When the attendant withheld cooperation, the physician had difficulty in making a graceful entrance and departure from the ward, in handling necessary paper work (officially his responsibility), and in obtaining information needed to deal adequately with daily treatment and behavior problems. When attendants opposed change, they could wield influence by refusing to assume responsibilities officially assigned to the physician.

Similarly, Sykes describes the dependence of prison guards on inmates and the power obtained by inmates over guards. He suggests that although guards could report inmates for disobedience, frequent reports would give prison officials the impression that the guard was unable to command obedience. The guard, therefore, had some stake in ensuring the good behavior of prisoners without use of formal sanctions against them. The result was a trading agreement whereby the guard allowed violations of certain rules in return for cooperative behavior. A similar situation is found in respect to officers in the Armed Services or foremen in industry. To the extent that they require formal sanctions to bring about cooperation, they are usually perceived by their superiors as less valuable to the organization. For a good leader is expected to command obedience, at least, if not commitment.[3]

Dependence power is thus a pervasive feature of organizations and it can be a formidable resource. It sets the limits on position power so that every organization represents a negotiated order. Such negotiation is usually tacit or even unspoken, but most bosses recognize that it will do them no good at all to push too hard. Not cooperating can make another person's life very difficult.

The third way in which power can be exercised is by *preventing* particular issues or conflicts of interest from being considered. In other words, power is exercised not only in relation to matters that have become the subject of disagreement and dispute; it may also be exercised in relation to what does *not* become an issue. This can happen in a number of ways considered briefly below; but it should be emphasized that this is a contentious area. It raises some difficult questions concerning, for example, the notion of 'real interests' (are people sometimes unaware of what is in their own interests?). In fact, most people do seem prepared to say that certain others (though not themselves, of course) are mistaken about what is in their interests — as a result of propaganda or 'social conditioning'. But where there is disagreement is over which groups are mistaken, and what the 'real interests' really are. In short, this, more than any

other, is an area where social and political ideology can colour organizational analysis, but a thorough treatment of these topics is well beyond the scope of this paper.

The first way in which issues can can be suppressed is by latent intimidation: for example a belief that certain proposals are completely unacceptable and would provoke outright, unrestrained opposition, may be enough to ensure that demands are well tailored within a range that is 'acceptable'. In authoritarian organizations, as in totalitarian countries, certain matters are not worth discussing, indeed even to raise such issues (for example, concerning the formation and recognition of an independent trade union; but at management level questioning a particular policy commitment) may be a recklessly deviant act. Note, too, that such a state of affairs does *not* require explicit and frequent threats or demonstrations of determination by those in power: a belief that some form of punishment or coercion would follow may derive from past conflicts, may be maintained by very occasional and implicit threats, and may be sufficient to prevent it having to be used.

Thus, the fact that in the normal course of disagreements superiors do not threaten to dismiss a number of subordinates does not mean that the power to do so is irrelevant — as one-third of Harold MacMillan's cabinet discovered one famous evening when he sacked them. Of course, the most colourfully ruthless examples of determined coercion are associated with employers' resistance to the unionization of their employees. In many respects the story of 'Solidarity' in Poland is a good example but the American South, even in quite recent years, has seen some spectacular conflicts in which physical intimidation and outside agencies (the police, the courts and the local press) have been used to break strikes or prevent unionization. Events which also highlight the extent to which controllers of an organization may be particularly well placed to enlist the support of elements in the organization's environment, for support in a conflict. However, the point of such cases is that although they are exceptional, *their impact may live on* in shaping people's beliefs about what is 'realistic'. So the earlier discussion of 'visible power' has to be seen in a much wider context if it is not to be seriously limited and naive. For example, it was suggested in discussing dependence power that every organization can be seen as representing a 'negotiated order' — there will always be some measure of give and take, of mutual accommodation, simply because it is patently provocative and self-defeating to trample roughshod over subordinates and 'lower participants' in organizations. But it should now be clear that this tacit 'negotiation' and mutual accommodation occurs within very definite limits, and in normal times those in power may only have to use a small fraction of the resources they have at their disposal.

However, this is still a long way from being the full story. The fact that employees *pragmatically* accept — because they see no realistic alternative — a regime that they do not consider fair or legitimate, provides a somewhat fragile basis for organizational order. Given a reservoir of grievances and resentment, even a comparatively small incident can be the trigger for a fierce dispute — as many paternalistically autocratic family businesses have discovered (similar eruptions occur in totalitarian regimes and in both cases the angry but puzzled response of the power holders is to credit a few 'dissidents' and 'trouble-makers' with an astonishing talent for organization and persuasion). A much more stable order exists where there is a *normative* acceptance by subordinates and employees of the organizational arrangements — that's to say they are seen as fair and legitimate. This suggests another area of 'invisible' power; the use of an organization's resources deliberately to promote values and beliefs that legitimize particular practices and policies can reduce the areas of disagreement to the point where only marginal adjustments are at issue.

In promoting such attitudes and beliefs the organization's controllers may be able to appeal to, or take advantage of, ideas and values that are dominant in the wider society (concerning, say, 'the needs of the economy' or 'excessive' trade union power') — and which indeed, they may also have been well placed to promote. Needless to say, trade unions also attempt to win the 'hearts and minds', — and not just trade unions; in 1982 middle managers at British Airways tried to use the press to discredit the Directors' plans for restructuring and rationalization. But arguably the resources and scope for subordinates to do so is more limited; for, as the following passage makes plain, this conflict of meanings and perspectives is not conducted solely through rival announcements and newsheets. It was extracted from an internal document of a major British company.

> The core of the approach is the *work group* structure. This is both a fundamental and radical concept — our basic answer to a whole range of (at present wholly intractable) problems ranging from genuine participation without anarchy to increased employee productivity. Essentially, and we should recognize this, it is not an industrial concept at all, but a socio-political one, applied in the industrial context. It represents, in fact, a capitalist version of the Marxist 'cell' structure. . . .
>
> The full development of so radical a concept will necessarily be long and difficult. Certain immediate steps, however, can already be identified under each of the elements of the personnel plan.
>
> Under *redeployment*, intensive efforts must be made to identify the *natural* work group leaders for subsequent training and indoctrination, and to retrain the new supervisors and superintendents . . .
>
> Under *retraining and development*, we therefore need to put a heavy emphasis on the development of work group leaders on the one hand and the new supervision on the other, so that these two classes become, in fact, capitalist equivalents to the Marxist 'cadres'. We should not be frightened to admit that this means specifically the exploitation of training and development schemes for *indoctrination* as well as technical training.
>
> Under *pay*, we must provide the group with a monetary system of group penalties and rewards which means, in fact, that the group itself will lean on any of its members who fall short because they will lose solid cash for the group as a whole; that is, *group self-discipline*.
>
> Under *organization structure*, the key work unit should be pushed down as close as possible to the shop floor (away from abstractions like 'the company' or 'the union') — starting first with the unit and then proceeding down to the basic work group. The basic unit of organization should thus be based on

the *natural* work unit (a common group organized around a common task).

> Under *organization style*, the attempt must be made to withdraw *exterior* discipline to those areas where it will be recognized by the group as legitimate (targeting, criteria and group sanctions and, to substitute for this within the group, 'group self-discipline'). British tradition is still so firmly based on the 'warders and convicts' syndrome that, at this stage, extending the right to consultation on the appointment of the work group leader to the group as a whole will be seen as a genuine management concession to industrial democracy . . .
>
> The new 'consultation' structure must be progressed in step with the development of the work group concept so as to provide a new system of worker representation as an alternative to the union system.

Apart from the promotion of 'congenial' values and beliefs, this extract also points to another aspect of 'invisible' power; in the longer term the controllers of an organization may have the opportunities to structure the work or relationships among the workforce, in ways that will minimize the likelihood of effective opposition. 'Divide and rule' is the most familiar way this can be done and there are numerous instances where it has been suggested that managers have been able to play on divisions within a workforce (for example between skilled and unskilled workers, between office and manual workers, between separate plants) in order to prevent concerted opposition emerging. Also under this same general heading are such decisions as the automation of particular jobs among the reasons for which may be a concern to reduce dependence on particular skilled and well-organized workers. Or decisions to transfer production of particular items to another country. Such decisions reflect in part a strategic concern to preserve or enhance control over the workforce by shaping the context of and terms on which any future conflicts will be played out.

Finally, invisible power also appears in the form of what has been called 'institutional bias'. The point is that organizations provide individuals and groups with scope for the pursuit of certain sorts of goals, and they restrict the scope for pursuing others. For example, as numerous writers on industrial relations have pointed out, an unfocused frustration with, say, repetitive machine-paced work is not something one can easily negotiate about. Negotiations, by their nature, end in a bargained compromise; and that means the sorts of things that can be dealt with must be quantitative: wage rates, hours of work, days of holiday, and so on. If people did want autonomy and variety in their jobs, or better working relationships, it's hard to see these goals being attained by incremental changes achieved in annual negotiations. Industrial relations practices, therefore, have an inherent bias towards the resolution of certain sorts of demands, while others are, in effect, screened out. Comparable 'biases' occur in other organizations: secondary and tertiary education are biased towards certain sorts of teaching and learning — crudely, that which can be readily assessed — while other sorts and styles of learning are restricted, or even denied altogether. Such 'biases' can be considered an aspect of 'invisible power' because they may benefit some of the 'stakeholders' in an organization far more than others, namely, those whose interests are well served through the existing arrangements. Normally, such groups will be the dominant groups, but this is not always or necessarily the case, since on occasions they may be the ones who are attempting to promote changes. On such occasions the biases and inertia of particular institutional arrangements may be a significant obstacle; expectations, motivational patterns, beliefs, identities and loyalties may be affected gradually by the sorts of deliberate methods already described, but in no way can they be reconstructed at will. Militants and radicals are not the only people who bemoan the difficulties of inducing systemic changes.

In summary, the idea of 'invisible power' is a general one that has been used to refer to the indirect or informal exercise of power that occurs outside of the accepted decision-making process, and which may not be recognized by some of those concerned. It was suggested that invisible power can be exercised in three domains:

■ first, through the scope for shaping the terms on which a contentious matter will be dealt with; typically, the control of information and agendas, associated with particular positions, is important.

■ second, through the scope for the informal development (or corruption) of working practices to suit those involved; typically, this reflects the dependence power of subordinates that can arise from social exchanges, as when cooperation over some matters is given in return for autonomy over others.

■ third, through the scope for preventing potential conflicts from emerging.

This last area is the most difficult but it was suggested that potential conflicts could be suppressed, obscured, avoided or screened out in the following ways:

■ by latent intimidation;

■ by promoting values and beliefs to legitimize arrangements that may otherwise be contested;

■ by structuring work and relationships so as to prevent, avoid or divide any significant opposition;

■ as a result of 'institutional biases' whereby those whose concerns can be met through existing arrangements are at an enormous advantage compared to those whose concerns can only be met by changing the arrangements.

Overall, the aim has been to catalogue the principal resources that may allow people to exercise power; and to indicate the different areas and ways in which they may exercise it.

It should be clear that there may be a great deal more to the conflicts and struggles for control that occur in organizations than appears on the surface. And while many of the examples have been drawn from the area of industrial relations which is well documented, it would be naive to pretend that ruthlessness and a concern for strategic advantage in relation to others, do not also occur at all levels in organizations, including the boardroom.

References

1. MacMillan, I.C. (1978) *Strategy Formulation: Political Concepts*, West Publishing Co., p.7.
2. Ibid. pp. 61-62.
3. Mechanic, D. (1962) 'Sources of power of lower participants in complex organizations', *Administrative Science Quarterly*, **7**, December.

The idea that an organization (or a Society) is like an organism — in being a richly interconnected and inter-dependent whole, displaying subtle regulatory processes — has had a long, not to say chequered, career. Critics have claimed that such an analogy lends itself to uncritical, conservative perspectives in which conflict and major changes are poorly treated — or seen as pathological. Its essentially 'unitary' assumptions means the following piece clearly falls in the 'organic' tradition, but, arguably, it goes some way towards meeting the usual criticisms. Not only are the authors concerned with conflict and the way second-order changes are managed in organizations, but the perspective they develop provides (later in their book) the basis for a sub-stantial critique of the usual pattern of organizational relationships. In any event, the idea of organizational learning is becoming increasingly popular among both organizational commentators and practitioners — and it's a refreshingly lucid piece of writing.

What is an Organization that it may Learn?
C. Argyris and *D. Schön*

The question

There has probably never been a time in our history when members, managers, and students of organizations were so united on the importance of organizational learning. Costs of health care, sanitation, police, housing, education, and welfare have risen precipitously, and we urge agencies concerned with these services to learn to increase their productivity and efficiency. Governments are torn by the conflicting demands of full employment, free collective bargaining, social welfare, and the control of inflation; we conclude that governments must learn to understand and accommodate these demands. Corpor-ations have found themselves constrained by a web of increas-ingly stringent regulations for environmental protection and consumer safety, at the same time that we are most sensitive to the need for jobs and for economic growth. Government and business must learn, we say, to work together to solve these problems.

Sometimes our demands for learning turn back on our history, as when politicians and planners ask, 'What have we learned from the last 20 years of housing policy?' 'What have we learned from the Great Depression?' 'What have we learned from Vietnam?' In a bicentennial article on 'The American Experiment', Daniel Moynihan begins by asking, 'What have we learned?' (Glazer and Kristol 1976).

It is not only that we are poignantly aware of our dilemmas and of the need for learning. We are also beginning to notice that there is nothing more problematic than solutions. Some of our most agonizing problems have been triggered by our solutions to slum eradication and urban renewal, by the success of the labor movement in achieving income security for workers, by rising expectations consequent to our economic growth, by the unwanted consequences of technological innovations. We begin to suspect that there is no stable state awaiting us over the horizon. On the contrary, our very power to solve problems seems to multiply problems. As a result, our organizations live in economic, political, and technological environments which are predictably unstable. The require-ment for organizational learning is not an occasional, sporadic phenomenon, but is continuous and endemic to our society.

Nevertheless, it is not at all clear what it means for an organization to learn. Nor is it clear how we can enhance the capacity of organizations to learn.

The difficulty has first to do with the notion of learning itself. When we call for learning or change, we seem to be calling for something good. But there are kinds of change which are not good, such as deterioration, regression and stagnation. And there are kinds of learning, such as government's learning to deceive and manipulate society, which are no better. So we need to spell out both the kinds of change we have in mind when we speak of learning, and the kinds of learning we have in mind when we call for more of it.

Further, it is clear that organizational learning is not the same thing as individual learning, even when the individuals

Argyris, C. and Schön, D. *Organizational learning* (© 1978), Chapter 1, pp.8-29, Addison-Wesley Publishing Co., Reading, Mass. Reprinted with permission.

who learn are members of the organization. There are too many cases in which organizations know *less* than their members. There are even cases in which the organization cannot seem to learn what every member knows. Nor does it help to think of organizational learning as the prerogative of a man at the top who learns *for* the organization; in large and complex organizations bosses succeed one another while the organization remains very much itself, and learns or fails to learn in ways that often have little to do with the boss.

There is something paradoxical here. Organizations are not merely collections of individuals, yet there is no organization without such collections. Similarly, organizational learning is not merely individual learning, yet organizations learn only through the experience and actions of individuals.

What, then, are we to make of organizational learning? What is an organization that it may learn?

Theory of action

In our earlier book, *Theory in Practice* (Argyris and Schön 1974), we set out to understand how practitioners of management, consultation, and intervention might learn to become more competent and effective. Our concern was especially directed to learning about interpersonal interaction. In that context, we found it useful to look at professional practice as informed by *theories of action:*

'All human beings — not only professional practitioners — need to become competent in taking action and simultaneously reflecting on this action to learn from it. The following pages provide a conceptual framework for this task by analyzing theories of action that determine all deliberate human behavior, how these theories are formed, how they come to change, and in what senses they may be considered adequate or inadequate'. (p. 4)

When we attributed theories of action to human beings, we argued that all deliberate action had a cognitive basis, that it reflected norms, strategies, and assumptions or models of the world which had claims to general validity. As a consequence, human learning, we said, need not be understood in terms of the 'reinforcement' or 'extinction' of patterns of behavior but as the construction, testing, and restructuring of a certain kind of knowledge. Human action and human learning could be placed in the larger context of knowing.

We found it necessary to connect theories of action to other kinds of theory:

'. . . whatever else a theory of action may be, it is first a theory. Its most general properties are properties that all theories share, and the most general criteria that apply to it — such as generality, centrality, and simplicity — are criteria that apply to all theories.' (p.4)

And we also found it necessary to differentiate theories of action from theories of explanation, prediction, and control:

'A full schema for a theory of action, then, would be as follows: in situation *S*, if you want to achieve consequence *C*, under assumptions *a . . . n*, do *A . . .* A theory of action is a theory of deliberate human behavior which is for the agent a theory of

control but which, when attributed to the agent, also serves to explain or predict his behavior.' (p.6)

Because we wished to do empirical research into human learning in situations of interpersonal interaction, we distinguished espoused theory from theory-in-use:

'When someone is asked how he would behave under certain circumstances, the answer he usually gives is his espoused theory of action for that situation. This is the theory of action to which he gives allegiance and which, upon request, he communicates to others. However, the theory that actually governs his actions is his theory-in-use, which may or may not be compatible with his espoused theory; furthermore, the individual may or may not be aware of the incompatibility of the two theories.' (p.7)

From the directly observable data of behavior, we could then ground our construction of the models of action theories which guided interpersonal behavior. And we could relate these models to the capacity for types of learning in professional practice.

It is tempting to apply this line of thought to the problem of understanding organizational learning. Perhaps organizations also have theories of action which inform their actions, espoused theories which they announce to the world and theories-in-use which may be inferred from their directly observable behavior. If so, then organizational learning might be understood as the testing and restructuring of organizational theories of action and, in the organizational context as in the individual one, we might examine the impact of models of action theories upon the capacity for kinds of learning.

But this path is full of obstacles. It is true that we do apply to organizations many of the terms we also apply to individuals. We speak of organizational action and organizational behavior. We speak also of organizational intelligence and memory. We say that organizations learn, or fail to learn. Nevertheless, a closer examination of these ways of speaking suggests that such terms are metaphors. Organizations do not literally remember, think, or learn. At least, it is not initially clear how we might go about testing whether or not they do so.

It is even puzzling to consider what it means for an organization to act or behave — notions which are essential to the construction of organizational theories of action. Does an organization act whenever one of its members acts? If so, there would appear to be little difference between an organization and a collection of individuals. Yet it is clear that some collections of people are organizations and others are not. Furthermore, even when a collection of people is clearly an organization, individual members of the organization do many things (such as breathe, sleep, gossip with their friends) which do not seem, in some important sense, to be examples of organizational action.

If we are to speak of organizational theories of action, we must dispel some of the confusion surrounding terms like organizational intelligence, memory, and action. We must say what it means for an organization to act, and we must show how organizational action is both different from and conceptually connected to individual action. We must say what it means for an organization to know something, and we must spell out the metaphors of organizational memory, intelligence, and learning.

Perspectives on organization

Let us begin by exploring several different ways of looking at an organization. An organization is:

a government, or *polis*;
an agency;
a task system.

Each of these perspectives will illuminate the sense in which an organization may be said to act. Further, an organization is:

a theory of action;
a cognitive enterprise undertaken by individual members;
a cognitive artifact made up of individual images and public maps.

Each of these descriptions will reveal the sense in which an organization may be said to know something, and to learn.

Consider a mob of students protesting against their university's policy. At what point do they cease to be a mob and begin to be an organization?

The mob is a collectivity. It is a collection of people who may run, shout, and mill about together. But it is a collectivity which cannot make a decision or take an action in its own name, and its boundaries are vague and diffuse.

As the mob begins to meet three sorts of conditions, it becomes more nearly an organization. Members must devise procedures for: (1) making decisions in the name of the collectivity, (2) delegating to individuals the authority to act for the collectivity, and (3) setting boundaries between the collectivity and the rest of the world. As these conditions are met, members of the collectivity begin to be able to say 'we' about themselves; they can say, 'We have decided,' 'We have made our position clear,' 'We have limited our membership.' There is now an organizational 'we' that can decide and act.

When the members of the mob become an identifiable vehicle for collective decision and action, they become, in the ancient Greek sense of the term, a *polis*, a political entity. Before an organization can be anything else, it must be in this sense political, because it is as a political entity that the collectivity can take organizational action. It is individuals who decide and act, but they do these things *for* the collectivity by virtue of the rules for decision, delegation, and membership. When the members of the collectivity have created such rules, they have organized.

Rule making need not be a conscious, formal process. What is important is that members' behaviour by rule-governed in crucial respects. The rules themselves may remain tacit, unless for some reason they are called into question. So long as there is continuity in the rules which govern the behavior of individuals, the organization will persist, even though members come and go. And what is most important for our purposes, it now becomes possible to set up criteria of relevance for constructing organizational theory-in-use. Organizational theory-in-use is to be inferred from observation of organizational behavior — that is, from organizational decisions and actions. The decisions and actions carried out by individuals are organizational insofar as they are governed by collective rules for decision and delegation. These alone are the decisions and actions taken in the name of the organization.

Through such a process, a mob becomes an organization. But if we are interested in organizational theory of action, we must ask what *kind* of an organization it becomes.

If a collection of people begins to decide and to act on a continuing basis, it becomes an instrument for continuing collective action, an *agency*. In this sense, the collections of workers involved in the labor movement organized from time to time to form unions, and collections of individual investors organized to form limited liability corporations. Such agencies have functions to fulfill, work to do. Their theories-in-use may be inferred from the ways in which they go about doing their work.

Generally speaking, an agency's work is a complex task, continually performed. The agency — an industrial corporation, a labor union, a government bureau, or even a household — embodies a strategy for decomposing that complex task into simpler components which are regularly delegated to individuals. Organizational roles — president, lathe-operator, shop steward — are the names given to the clusters of component tasks which the agency has decided to delegate to individual members. The organization's *task system*, its pattern of interconnected roles, is at once a design for work and a division of labor.

An agency is thus the solution to a problem. It is a strategy for performing a complex task which might have been carried out in other ways. This is true not only for the design of the task system, the division of labor, but also for the selection of strategies for performing component tasks.

We can view a sugar refining company, for example, as an answer to questions such as these: What is the best way to grow and harvest cane? How should it be refined? How is it best distributed and marketed? For each subquestion the organization is an answer. The company's way of growing cane reflects certain strategies (for the cultivation of land, for harvesting and fertilizing), certain norms (for productivity and quality, for the use of labor), and certain assumptions (about the yields to be expected from various patterns of cultivation). The norms, strategies, and assumptions embedded in the company's cane-growing practices constitute its *theory of action* for cane-growing. There are comparable theories of actions implicit in the company's ways of distributing and marketing its products. Taken together, these component theories of action represent a theory of action for achieving corporate objectives. This global theory of action we call 'instrumental'. It includes norms for corporate performance (for example, norms for margin of profit and for return on investment), strategies for achieving norms (for example, strategies for plant location and for process technology), and assumptions which bind strategies and norms together (for example, the assumption that maintenance of a high rate of return on investment depends on the continual introduction of new technologies).

The company's instrumental theory of action is a complex

system of norms, strategies, and assumptions. It includes in its scope the organization's patterns of communication and control, its ways of allocating resources to goals, and its provisions for self-maintenance — that is, for rewarding and punishing individual performance, for constructing career ladders and regulating the rate at which individuals climb them, and for recruiting new members and instructing them in the ways of the organization.

Like the rules for collective decision and action, organizational theories of action need not be explicit. Indeed, formal corporate documents such as organization charts, policy statements, and job descriptions often reflect a theory of action (the *espoused theory*) which conflicts with the organization's *theory-in-use* (the theory of action constructed from observation of actual behavior) — and the theory-in-use is often tacit. Organizational theory-in-use may remain tacit, as we will see later on, because its incongruity with espoused theory is *undiscussable*. Or it may remain tacit because individual members of the organization know more than they say — because the theory-in-use is *inaccessible* to them. Whatever the reason for tacitness, the largely tacit theory-in-use accounts for organizational identity and continuity.

Consider a large, enduring organization such as the U.S. Army. Over 50 years or so, its personnel may turn over completely, yet we still speak of it as 'the Army'. It is no longer the same collection of people, so in what sense is it still the same? Suppose we wanted to discover whether it was in fact the same organization. How would we proceed? We might examine uniforms and weapons, but in 50 years these might have changed entirely. We might then study the 50-year evolution of military practices — that is, the norms for military behavior, the strategies for military action, the assumptions about military functioning. We would then be studying the evolution of the Army's theory-in-use. And we might learn that certain features of it — for example, the patterns of command, the methods of training, the division into regiments and platoons — had remained essentially unchanged, while other features of it — battle strategies, norms for performance — had evolved continuously from earlier forms. We might conclude that we were dealing with a single organization, self-identical, whose theory-in-use had evolved considerably over time.

It is this theory-in-use, an apparently abstract thing, which is most distinctively real about the Army. It is what old soldiers know and new ones learn through a continuing process of socialization. And it is the history of change in theory-in-use which we would need to consult in order to inquire into the Army's organizational learning.

In order to discover an organization's theory-in-use, we must examine its practice, that is the continuing performance of its task system as exhibited in the rule-governed behavior of its members. This is, however, an outside view. When members carry out the practices appropriate to their organization, they are also manifesting a kind of knowledge. And this knowledge represents the organization's theory-in-use as seen from the inside.

Images and maps

Each member of the organization constructs his or her own representation, or image, of the theory-in-use of the whole. That picture is always incomplete. The organization members strive continually to complete it, and to understand themselves in the context of the organization. They try to describe themselves and their own performance insofar as they interact with others. As conditions change, they test and modify that description. Moreover, others are continually engaged in similar inquiry. It is this continual, concerted meshing of individual images of self and others, of one's activity in the context of collective interaction, which constitutes an organization's knowledge of its theory-in-use.

An organization is like an organism each of whose cells contain a particular, partial, changing image of itself in relation to the whole. And like such an organism, the organization's practice stems from those very images. Organization is an artifact of individual ways of representing organization.

Hence, our inquiry into organizational learning must concern itself not with static entities called organizations, but with an active process of organizing which is, at root, a cognitive enterprise. Individual members are continually engaged in attempting to know the organization, and to 'know themselves' in the context of the organization. At the same time, their continuing efforts to know and to test their knowledge represent the object of their inquiry. Organizing is reflexive enquiry.

From this perspective, organizational continuity is a considerable achievement. But we could not account for organizational continuity if the cognitive enterprise of organizing were limited to the private inquiry of individuals. Even when individuals are in face-to-face contact, private images of organization erode and diverge from one another. When the task system is large and complex, most members are unable to use face-to-face contact in order to compare and adjust their several images of organizational theory-in-use. They require external references. There must be public representations of organizational theory-in-use to which individuals can refer.

This is the function of organizational maps. These are the shared descriptions of organization which individuals jointly construct and use to guide their own inquiry. They include, for example, diagrams of work flow, compensation charts, statements of procedure, even the schematic drawings of office space. A building itself may function as a kind of map, revealing patterns of communication and control. Whatever their form, maps have a dual function. They describe actual patterns of activity, and they are guides to future action. As musicians perform their scores, members of an organization perform their maps.

Organizational theory-in-use, continually constructed through individual inquiry, is encoded in private images and in public maps. These are the media of organizational learning.

Organizational learning

As individual members continually modify their maps and

images of the organization, they also bring about changes in organizational theory-in-use.

Not all of these changes qualify as learning. Members may lose enthusiasm, become sloppy in task performance, or lose touch with one another. They may leave the organization, carrying with them important information which becomes lost to the organization. Or changes in the organization's environment (a slackening of demand for product, for example) may trigger new patterns of response which undermine organizational norms. These are kinds of deterioration, sometimes called organizational entropy.

But individual members frequently serve as agents of changes in organizational theory-in-use which run counter to organizational entropy. They act on their images and on their shared maps with expectations of patterned outcomes, which their subsequent experience confirms or disconfirms. When there is a mismatch of outcome to expectation (error), members may respond by modifying their images, maps, and activities so as to bring expectations and outcomes back into line. They detect an error in organizational theory-in-use, and they correct it. This fundamental learning loop is one in which individuals act from organizational theory-in-use, which leads to match or mismatch of expectations with outcome, and thence to confirmation or disconfirmation of organizational theory-in-use.

Quality control inspectors detect a defect in product, for example; they feed that information back to production engineers, who then change production specifications to correct that defect. Marketing managers observe that monthly sales have fallen below expectations; they inquire into the shortfall, seeking an interpretation which they can use to devise new marketing strategies which will bring the sales curve back on target. When organizational turnover of personnel increases to the point where it threatens the steady performance of the task system, managers may respond by investigating the sources of worker dissatisfaction; they look for factors they can influence — salary levels, fringe benefits, job design — so as to reestablish the stability of their work force.

Single-loop learning

In these examples, *members of the organization respond to changes in the internal and external environments of the organization by detecting errors which they then correct so as to maintain the central features of organizational theory-in-use.* These are learning episodes which function to preserve a certain kind of constancy. As Gregory Bateson has pointed out (Bateson 1972), the organization's ability to remain stable in a changing context denotes a kind of learning. Following his usage, we call this learning single-loop (Bateson 1960). There is a single feedback loop which connects detected outcomes of action to organizational strategies and assumptions which are modified so as to keep organizational performance within the range set by organizational norms. The norms themselves — for product quality, sales, or task performance — remain unchanged.

These examples also help to make clear the relationship between individual and organizational learning. The key to this distinction is the notion of *agency. Just as individuals are the agents of organizational action, so they are the agents for organizational learning.* Organizational learning occurs when individuals, acting from their images and maps, detect a match or mismatch of outcome to expectation which confirms or disconfirms organizational theory-in-use. In the case of disconfirmation, individuals move from error detection to error correction. Error correction takes the form of inquiry. The learning agents must discover the sources of error — that is, they must attribute error to strategies and assumptions in existing theory-in-use. They must invent new strategies, based on new assumptions, in order to correct error. They must produce those strategies. And they must evaluate and generalize the results of that new action. 'Error correction' is shorthand for a complex learning cycle.

But in order for *organizational* learning to occur, learning agents' discoveries, inventions, and evaluations must be embedded in organizational memory. They must be encoded in the individual images and the shared maps of organizational theory-in-use from which individual members will subsequently act. If this encoding does not occur, individuals will have learned but the organization will not have done so.

Suppose, for example, that the quality control inspectors find a product defect which they then decide to keep to themselves, perhaps because they are afraid to make the information public. Or suppose that they try to communicate this information to the production engineers, but the production engineers do not wish to listen to them. Or suppose that the interpretation of error requires collaborative inquiry on the part of several different members of the organization who are unwilling or unable to carry out such a collaboration. (Indeed, because organizations are strategies for decomposing complex tasks into task/role systems, error correction normally requires collaborative inquiry.) In all of these instances, individual learning may or may not have occurred, but individuals do not function as agents of organizational learning. What individuals may have learned remains as an unrealized potential for organizational learning.

From this it follows both that there is no organizational learning without individual learning, and that individual learning is a necessary but insufficient condition for organizational learning. We can think of organizational learning as a process mediated by the collaborative inquiry of individual members. In their capacity as agents of organizational learning, individuals restructure the continually changing artifact called organizational theory-in-use. Their work as learning agents is unfinished until the results of their inquiry — their discoveries, inventions, and evaluations — are recorded in the media of organizational memory, the images and maps which encode organizational theory-in-use.

If we should wish to test whether organizational learning has occurred, we must ask questions such as these: Did individuals detect an outcome which matched or mismatched the expectations derived from their images and maps of organizational theory-in-use? Did they carry out an inquiry which yielded discoveries, inventions, and evaluations pertaining to organizational strategies and assumptions? Did these results become embodied in the images and maps employed for purposes such as control, decision, and instruction? Did members subsequently act from these images and maps so as to carry out new organizational practices? Were these changes in images, maps, and organizational practices regularized so that they were unaffected by some individual's departure? Do new members learn these new features of the organizational theory of action as part of their socialization to the organization?

Each of these questions points to a possible source of failure in organizational learning, as well as to the sources of organizational learning capacity. So far, however, we have limited ourselves to the kind of learning called single-loop. Let us now consider learning of another kind.

Double-loop learning

Organizations are continually engaged in transactions with their internal and external environments. Industrial corporations, for example, continually respond to the changing pattern of external competition, regulation and demand, and to the changing internal environment of workers' attitudes and aspirations. These responses take the form of error detection and error correction. Single-loop learning is sufficient where error correction can proceed by changing organizational strategies and assumptions within a constant framework of norms for performance. It is concerned primarily with effectiveness — that is, with how best to achieve existing goals and objectives and how best to keep organizational performance within the range specified by existing norms. In some cases, however, error correction requires an organizational learning cycle in which organizational norms themselves are modified.

Consider an industrial firm which has set up a research and development division charged with the discovery and development of new technologies. This has been a response to the perceived imperative for growth in sales and earnings and the belief that these are to be generated through internally managed technological innovation. But the new division generates technologies which do not fit the corporation's familiar pattern of operations. In order to exploit some of these technologies, for example, the corporation may have to turn from the production of intermediate materials with which it is familiar to the manufacture and distribution of consumer products with which it is unfamiliar. But this, in turn, requires that members of the corporation adopt new approaches to marketing, managing, and advertising; that they become accustomed to a much shorter product life cycle and to a more rapid cycle of changes in their pattern of activities; that they, in fact, change the very image of the business they are in. And these requirements for change come into conflict with another sort of corporate norm, one that requires predictability in the management of corporate affairs.

Hence, the corporate managers find themselves confronted with conflicting requirements. If they conform to the imperative for growth, they must give up on the imperative for predictability. If they decide to keep their patterns of operations constant, they must give up on the imperative for growth, at least insofar as that imperative is to be realized through intern-

ally generated technology. A process of change initiated with an eye to effectiveness under existing norms turns out to yield a conflict in the norms themselves.

If corporate managers are to engage this conflict, they must undertake a process of inquiry which is significantly different from the inquiry characteristic of single-loop learning. They must, to begin with, recognize the conflict itself. They have to set up a new division which has yielded unexpected outcomes; this is an error, in the sense earlier described. They must reflect upon this error to the point where they become aware that they cannot correct it by doing better what they already know how to do. They must become aware, for example, that they cannot correct the error by getting the new division to perform more effectively under existing norms; indeed, the more effective the new division is, the more its results will plunge the managers into conflict. The managers must discover that it is the norm for predictable management which they hold, perhaps tacitly, that conflicts with their wish to achieve corporate growth through technological innovation.

Then the managers must undertake an inquiry which resolves the conflicting requirements. The results of their inquiry will take the form of a restructuring of organizational norms, and very likely a restructuring of strategies and assumptions associated with those norms, which must then be embedded in the images and maps which encode organizational theory-in-use.

We call this sort of learning *double-loop*. There is in this sort of episode a double feedback loop which connects the detection of error not only to strategies and assumptions for effective performance but to the very norms which define effective performance.

Single-loop learning, as we have defined it, consists not only of a change in organizational strategies and assumptions but of the particular sort of change appropriately described as learning. In single-loop learning, members of the organization carry out a collaborative inquiry through which they discover sources of error, invent new strategies designed to correct error, produce those strategies and evaluate and generalize the results. Similarly, double-loop learning consists not only of a change in organizational norms but of the particular sort of inquiry into norms which is appropriately described as learning.

In organizational double-loop learning, incompatible requirements in organizational theory-in-use are characteristically expressed through a conflict among members and groups within the organization. In the industrial organization, for example, some managers may become partisans of growth through research and of a new image of the business based upon research, while others may become opponents of research through their allegiance to familiar and predictable patterns of corporate operation. Double-loop learning, if it occurs, will consist of the process of inquiry by which these groups of managers confront and resolve their conflict.

In this sense, the organization is a medium for translating incompatible requirements into interpersonal and intergroup conflict.

Members of the organization may respond to such a conflict

in several ways, not all of which meet the criteria for organizational double-loop learning. First, the members may treat the conflict as a fight in which choices are to be made among competing requirements, and weightings and priorities are to be set on the basis of prevailing power. The 'R & D faction', for example, may include the chief executive who wins out over the 'old guard' through being more powerful. Or the two factions may fight it out to a draw, settling their differences in the end by a compromise which reflects nothing more than the inability of either faction to prevail over the other.

In both of these cases, the conflict is settled for the time being, but not by a process that could be appropriately described as learning. The conflict is settled not by inquiry but by fighting it out. Neither side emerges from the settlement with a new sense of the nature of the conflict, of its causes and consequences, or of its meaning for organizational theory-in-use.

On the other hand, parties to the conflict may engage the conflict through inquiry of the following kinds:

They may invent new strategies of performance which circumvent the perceived incompatibility of requirements. They may, for example, succeed in defining a kind of research and development addressed solely to the existing pattern of business, which offers the likelihood of achieving existing norms for growth. They will then have succeeded in finding a single-loop solution to what at first appeared as a double-loop problem.

They may carry out a 'trade-off analysis' which enables them to conclude jointly that so many units of achievement of one norm are balanced by so many units of achievement of another. On this basis, they may decide that the prospects for R & D payoff are so slim that the R & D option should be abandoned, and with that abandonment there should be a lowering of corporate expectations for growth. Or they may decide to limit R & D targets so that the disruptions of patterns of business operation generated by R & D are limited to particular segments of the corporation.

Here there is a compromise among competing requirements but it is achieved through inquiry into the probabilities and values associated with the options for action.

In the context of the conflict, the incompatible requirements may not lend themselves to trade-off analysis. They may be perceived as incommensurable. In such a case, the conflict may still be resolved through inquiry which gets underneath the members' starting perceptions of the incompatible requirements. Participants must then ask why they hold the position they do, and what they mean by them. They may ask, what factors have led them to adopt these particular standards for growth in sales and earnings, what their rationale is, and what are likely to be the consequences of attempting to achieve them, through any means whatever? Similarly, they may ask what kinds of predictability in operations are of greatest importance, to whom they are most important, and what conditions make them important.

Such inquiry may lead to a significant restructuring of the configuration of corporate norms. Or it may lead to the invention of new patterns of incentives, budgeting and control which take greater account of requirements for both growth and predictability.

We will give the name 'double-loop learning' to those sorts of organizational inquiry which resolve incompatible organizational norms by setting new priorities and weightings of norms, or by restructuring the norms themselves together with associated strategies and assumptions.

In these cases, individual members resolve the interpersonal and intergroup conflicts which express incompatible requirements by creating new understandings of the conflicting requirements, their sources, conditions, and consequences — understandings which then become embedded in the images and maps of organization. By doing so, they make the new, more nearly compatible requirements susceptible to effective realization.

There are three observations we wish to make about distinction between single- and double-loop organizational learning.

First, it is often impossible, in the real-world context of organizational life, to find inquiry cleanly separated from the uses of power. Inquiry and power-play are often combined. Given such mixtures, we will want to differentiate the two kinds of processes which are often mixed in practice so that we may speak of those aspects of interpersonal and intergroup conflict which involve organizational learning and those which do not.

Second, while we have described the *kinds* of inquiry which are essential to single- and double-loop learning, we have not yet dwelt on the *quality* of inquiry. Two different examples of double-loop learning, both of which exhibit detection of error and correction of error through the restructuring of organizational norms, may be of unequal quality. The same is true of single-loop learning. Organizations may learn more or less well, yet their inquiries may still qualify as learning of the single- or double-loop kind.

Finally, we must point out that the distinction between single- and double-loop learning is less a binary one than might first appear. Organizational theories-in-use are systemic structures composed of many interconnected parts. We can examine these structures from the point of view of a particular, local theory of action, such as the industrial firm's theory of action for quality control, or we can attend to more global aspects of the structure, such as the firm's theory of action for achieving targeted return on investment. Furthermore, certain elements are more fundamental to the structure and others are more peripheral. For example, the industrial firm's norms for growth and for predictability of management are fundamental to its theory of action — in the sense that if they were changed, a great deal of the rest of the theory of action would also have to change — and it is their fundamental status which gives a special poignancy to their conflict. On the other hand, a particular norm for product quality may be quite peripheral to the organization's theory of action; it could change without affecting much of the rest of the theory of action.

Now, an inquiry into a *strategy* fundamental to the firm's theory of action, such as the strategy of measuring divisional performance by monthly profit-and-loss statements, will be likely to involve much of the rest of the organization's theory of action, including its norms. But an inquiry into a *norm* peripheral to the organization's theory of action may involve very little of the rest of its theory of action. From this, two conclusions may be drawn. First, in judging whether learning is single- or double-loop, it is important to notice where inquiry goes as well as where it begins. Second, it is possible to speak of organizational learning as *more or less* double-loop. In place of the binary distinction we have a more continuous concept of depth of learning.

It is possible, we think, to make clear distinctions between relatively deep and relatively peripheral examples of organizational learning. We will continue to call the former double- and the latter single-loop learning. Our examples of double-loop learning will involve norms fundamental to organizational theories of action, for these are the examples we believe to be of greatest importance. The reader should keep in mind, however, that we speak of these categories as discrete when they are actually parts of a continuum.

With these *caveats*, we can return to our main line of argument.

Deutero-learning

Since World War II, it has gradually become apparent not only to business firms but to all sorts of organizations that the requirements of organizational learning, especially for double-loop learning, are not one-shot but continuing. There has been a sequence of ideas in good currency — such as 'creativity', 'innovation', 'the management of change' — which reflect this awareness.

In our earlier example, to take one instance, managers of the industrial firm might conclude that their organization needs to learn how to restructure itself, at regular intervals, so as to exploit the new technologies generated by research and development. That is, the organization needs to learn how to carry out single- and double-loop learning.

This sort of learning to learn Gregory Bateson has called *deutero-learning* (that is, second-order learning). Bateson illustrates the idea through the following story:

'A female porpoise . . . is trained to accept the sound of the trainer's whistle as a "secondary reinforcement". The whistle is expectably followed by food, and if she later repeats what she was doing when the whistle blew, she will expect again to hear the whistle and receive food.

The porpoise is now used by the trainers to demonstrate "operant conditioning" to the public. When she enters the exhibition tank, she raises her head above the surface, hears the whistle and is fed . . .

But this pattern is (suitable) only for a single episode in the exhibition tank. She must break that pattern to deal with the *class* of such episodes. There is a larger context of contexts which will put her in the wrong . . .

When the porpoise comes on stage, she again raises her head. But she gets no whistle. The trainer waits for the next piece of conspicuous behavior, likely a tail flip, which is a common expression of annoyance. This behavior is then reinforced and repeated (by giving her food).

But the tail flip was, of course, not rewarded in the third performance.

Finally the porpoise learned to deal with the context of contexts — by offering a different or new piece of conspicuous behavior whenever she came on stage.'

Each time the porpoise learns to deal with a larger class of episodes, she learns *about* the previous contexts for learning. Her creativity reflects deutero-learning.

When an organization engages in deutero-learning, its members learn, too, about previous contexts for learning. They reflect on and inquire into previous episodes of organizational learning, or failure to learn. They discover what they did that facilitated or inhibited learning, they invent new strategies for learning, they produce these strategies, and they evaluate and generalize what they have produced. The results become encoded in individual images, and maps and are reflected in organizational learning practice.

The deutero-learning cycle is relatively familiar in the context of organizational learning curves. Aircraft manufacturers, for example, project the rate at which their organizations will learn to manufacture a new aircraft and base cost estimates on their projections of the rate of organizational learning. In the late 1950s, the Systems Development Corporation undertook the 'cogwheel' experiment, in which members of an aircraft spotting team were invited to inquire into their own organizational learning and then to produce conditions which would enable them more effectively to learn to improve their performance (Chapman and Kennedy 1956).

In these examples, however, deutero-learning concentrates on single-loop learning; emphasis is on learning for effectiveness rather than on learning to resolve conflicting norms for performance. But the concept of deutero-learning is also relevant to double-loop learning. How, indeed, can organizations learn to become better at double-loop learning? How can members of an organization learn to carry out the kinds of inquiry essential to double-loop learning? What are the conditions which enable members to meet the tests of organizational learning? And how can they learn to produce those conditions?

Organizations are not only theories of action. They are also small societies composed of persons who occupy roles in the task system. What we have called the internal environment of an organization is the society of persons who make up the organization at any given time. These societies have their own characteristic behavioral worlds. These enable us to recognize a person as 'an army man', 'a government man', 'a General Electric man'. Within these societies, members tend to share characteristic languages, styles, and models of *individual* theory-in-use for interaction with others. In the light of these behavioral worlds, we can and do describe organizations as more or less 'open', 'experimental', 'confronting', 'demanding', or 'defensive'. These behavioral worlds, with their characteristic models of individual theory-in-use, may be more or less conducive to the kinds of collaborative inquiry required for organizational learning.

Hence, if we wish to learn more about the conditions that facilitate or inhibit organizational learning, we must explore the ways in which the behavioral worlds of organizations affect the capacity for inquiry into organizational theory-in-use.

Summary

Organizational learning is a metaphor whose spelling out requires us to re-examine the very idea of organization. A collection of individuals organizes when its members develop rules for collective decision delegation and membership. In their rule-governed behavior, they act for the collectivity in ways that reflect a task system. Just as individual theories of action may be inferred from individual behavior, so organizational theories of action may be inferred from patterns of organizational action. As individuals have espoused theories which may be incongruent with their (often tacit) theories-in-use, so with organizations.

Organizational learning occurs when members of the organization act as learning agents for the organization, responding to changes in the internal and external environments of the organization by detecting and correcting errors in organizational theory-in-use, and embedding the results of their inquiry in private images and shared maps of organizations.

In organizational single-loop learning, the criterion for success is effectiveness. Individuals respond to error by modifying strategies and assumptions within constant organizational norms. In double-loop learning, response to detected error takes the form of joint inquiry into organizational norms themselves, so as to resolve their inconsistency and make the new norms more effectively realizable. In both cases, organizational learning consists of restructuring organizational theory of action.

When an organization engages in deutero-learning its members learn about organizational learning and encode their results in images and maps. The quest for organizational learning capacity must take the form of deutero-learning; most particularly about the interactions between the organization's behavioral world and its ability to learn.

References

Argyris, C. and Schön, D. (1974) *Theory in Practice*, Jossey-Bass, San Francisco.
Bateson, G. (1958) *Naven*, Stanford University Press, Stanford, California. Bateson borrows the term from Ashby, W.R. (1960) *Design for a Brain*, Wiley, New York.
Bateson, G. (1972) *Steps to an Ecology of Mind*, Ballantine, New York.
Chapman, R.L. and Kennedy, J.L. (1956) *Background and Implications of Systems Research Laboratory Studies*, Rand Corporation Report.
Glazer, N. and Kristol, I. (eds) (1976) Introduction: 'The American experiment', in *The American Commonwealth — 1976*, Basic Books, New York.

15 Interorganizational Relations

This is an area that has only recently been receiving the attention it deserves in organizational analysis. Too often organizations have been represented as passively adapting to their environments — rather than attempting actively to intervene in and shape their environments. The first of the two pieces that follow describes the different ways in which organizations attempt to control other organizations, or actively to manage their dealings with them. The second piece considers the nature of the economic system created by such activity and ultimately it is concerned with the dangers of oversimplifying as one moves up to a higher level of complexity. At each level of complexity it is usual to assume that differences at a lower level can be ignored. For example, in considering a firm it is useful to be able to neglect the differences in the internal organization of, say, the marketing and production departments. The more complex the organization being considered the more these assumptions are required to keep discussions tractable, and the more dubious they become.

So Galbraith questions the conventional assumptions made regarding the national economy. Rather than see the economy as a single organized system he regards it as comprised of two systems, each with significantly different characteristics, problems and goals.

15(a)   Organization and environment
M. Blunden

Organizations are likely to be greatly affected by the behaviour of other formally independent organizations with which they interact, and develop strategies for managing these often problematical relationships. The degree of interdependence between an organization and others in its environment will vary widely. In general, interdependence between organizations has increased, and is increasing. Sayles and Chandler, authors of a study of the National Aeronautics and Space Administration (NASA), which at its peak in the mid 1960s received inputs from 20,000 different organizations, argue that ever increasing interdependency between organizations is an obvious characteristic of modern society:

> For example, improving safety in air transportation involves the development of new avionics and air transport equipment, perhaps by government research centres working with private industry. This equipment will have to be produced by private companies, certified by the Federal Aviation Agency, accepted by commercial airlines, and fitted into the existing airport and navigation-communication system, which are regulated by local authorities and by national and international agencies.[1]

Peter Drucker[2] has predicted that the world of the future will be one in which highly differentiated, specialized organizations are bound to and must 'use' one another, and where the lateral relationships that tie them together are as important as, or more important than, the more frequently analysed relationships within organizations.

This paper examines some of the commonly encountered strategies which organizations use to try to manage relationships with other organizations in their environment. It is concerned particularly with relationships which involve fairly frequent interactions between organizations, that is, a high degree of interdependency. Where interactions between organizations are infrequent, or not so important, the relationship can usually be managed through the familiar processes of bargaining and negotiating. The paper concentrates on co-operative rather than competitive relationships between organizations. These relationships between broadly collaborative organizations are examined in terms of informal control mechanisms and strategies to promote mutual understanding by interpenetration. By these means, organizations try to avoid or reduce uncertainty. As Pfeffer and Salancik[3] remark, 'Rather than accepting uncertainty as an unavoidable fate, organizations seek to create around themselves more stable and predictable environments.'

Strategies for managing relationships with *competing* organizations — either formal mechanisms for restricting competition, as in the formation of cartels, or informal strategies, such as a tacit adherence to certain standard practices — are not the concern of this paper.

In relationships between formally independent but collaborative organizations, attempts to control must of necessity be informal rather than formal, covert rather than overt. Bonis[4] uses the analogy of disguised Imperialism to describe this process:

> A kind of disguised Imperialism results when the organization seeks to control the external elements: customers, suppliers, subcontractors, members of other organizations, politicians and political organizations, the press, public opinion, pressure groups, etc.

An organization will, in Bonis' view, often achieve 'disguised Imperialism', or informal control, by creating various kinds of dependencies in associated organizations. Whereas the concept of 'interdependence' refers to the quality of interactions between organizations, the concept of 'dependency' refers to the quality of such relationships, and the differing status of the organizations involved. Simple economic dependencies can be created by an organization which generates a massive supply or demand of products, or by one which produces or requires a highly specialized product. The extent of an organization's economic dependence on another in this sense can be measured by calculating the proportion of its total support provided by this particular source. Sayles and Chandler report that, in some large Japanese enterprises, managers were able to run down a list of their contractors and give the exact degree of dependency for each.[5]

An organization may put to various uses the economic dependency of other organizations upon it. Perrow, for instance, observed that General Motors' power over its automotive suppliers was such that it could not only make demands about permissible prices but also enforce demands to audit the suppliers' books and ensure that they were not making excessive profits.[6]

The obvious counter strategy to economic dependency is diversification. Pfeffer and Salancik observe that:

> The most effective strategies for dealing with dependence which arises from reliance on a single product or market are those which alter the purposes and structure of the organization so that it no longer requires only a limited range of inputs or serves only a few markets.

On the other hand, high levels of dependency may persist in an apparently stable relationship between organizations for long periods of time. The Kanban system, operated by Toyota in Japan, an example of very great interdependency, is a case in point. Under the Kanban system, component suppliers and the final car assembler (Toyota) integrate their production lines so that there is virtually a continuous flow from primary manufacture to final assembly, crossing formally independent organizational boundaries, with only very low stocks being maintained at each stage. In principle, Toyota withdraws components from the subcontractor factories; in practice, the subcontractor generally delivers the parts to Toyota, to a specified receiving gate, perhaps as many as eight times a day. The costs of such frequent deliveries may be reduced by a 'round tour mixed loading system'. For example, four subcontracting companies, A, B, C and D, located in the eastern area, must bring their products to Toyota four times a day in small lots. This is accomplished as follows. The first delivery at 9 o'clock would be made by subcontractor A, also picking up on the way products from companies B, C and D. The second delivery at 11 o'clock could be made by company B, similarly picking up the products of A, C and D on the way.[7] The Kanban system reflects both an exceptionally high level of interdependency, and high levels of economic dependency. It must also rest on sophisticated ideological penetration, in the sense of shared beliefs about the way to do things, both amongst the component suppliers and between them and their main customer.

The example of the Kanban system raises an interesting issue — is dependence necessarily a bad thing, from the point of view of the dependent organization? General Motors' exploitation of dependence power implied that a state of dependency was an undesirable one. The Toyota example suggests, on the contrary, that it has its compensations. Clearly, in this case, high-trust relationships have developed and everyone is prepared to take a long-term view. Status differentials between organizations seem to be accepted without anxiety and security achieved through dependence. So organizations confronted with dependency power may have a clear strategic choice — to embrace the compensations of a dependent position, or to escape it by diversification.

Technical dependency — the reliance of one organization on the technical expertise of another — may reinforce or cut across simple economic dependencies. A particular technological practice can, for instance, establish an effective community of interests between producers and consumers, reinforcing the dependence power of the major partner and making it too expensive for the dependent partner to withdraw, should things go wrong. On the other hand, superiority in technical expertise can outweigh small size. Sayles and Chandler describe how 'a very small but top-quality optical-coating subcontractor returned the designs of its main customer, a large aerospace firm, and insisted on doing its own. If the mammoth concern would not agree to this arrangement, the tiny company confidently predicted a delay of months or even a year.'[8]

The creation of financial dependencies, for instance through stockholding in linked organizations, or special credit arrangements, may extend almost to a total control over suppliers, subcontractors or customers. Bonis considers that there is also a strategy of creating psychological dependencies: in this strategy, an organization forms strong personal links, social as well as professional, between its own staff and the staff of associated organizations. 'There is no doubt', says Bonis, 'that this is an effective way to establish a situation of dependency between the organization and the environment.'[9]

The strategy of dependency creation, whatever form it may take, is a limited option for most organizations, in that it may involve obligations and responsibilities as well as conferring dependence power. As Sayles and Chandler point out, 'Few, if any organizations, can afford to have the majority of their relationships in the high-dependency category, especially in the sense of having others highly dependent on them.'[10]

The fostering of strong professional links across organizational boundaries can be seen as an informal control mechanism. Alternatively it can be seen as a mechanism for creating mutual understanding between organizations to smooth and reduce conflict and assist mutual adjustment. This is what Stern calls 'the interpenetration mechanisms'. An organization can 'penetrate' other linked organizations in a variety of ways. It can for instance achieve 'penetration' by collaborating with another organization on a common task, what Pennings calls 'coalescing'[11]. Joint programmes have traditionally been thought of as devices for securing some of the advantages of a merger (for instance, economies of scale) while at the same time preserving the identity and autonomy of the organizations concerned. But Stern sees joint programmes primarily as mechanisms for reducing conflict between organizations: 'The arranging of interorganizational collaboration on a common task jointly accepted as worthwhile and involving personal association of individuals as functional equals should result in lessened hostility among the organizations.'[12]

The development of one of the Swedish prefabricated firms described by Broden[13] illustrates how joint programmes may work. The organization, A.B. Götene Traindustri, began in 1967 to manufacture large prefabricated elements such as whole walls and floors. As a result of a joint venture with a large building contractor, measurements were standardized, with resulting large production benefits, and joint programmes were subsequently initiated with a few other large contractors. The joint venture clearly involved rationalization across organizational boundaries — such as would have taken place under a formal merger — but without paying the price of a loss of autonomy. The joint programme also effectively reduced potential conflict between the component manufacturer and the building contractor — for instance, conflict over the measurement of building components — and probably helped to reduce status differences between the staff of the two organizations.

Interpenetration mechanisms may, on the other hand, take the form of a formal exchange of staff for a specified length of time. This can occur at different levels in an organization. A period spent working in a linked organization, such as a supplier or customer or marketing agent could, for instance, form part of the training programme of a new recruit. Interpenetration at high levels across organizational boundaries is very marked in certain sectors of private industry in Britain. Non-executive directors, working part-time on the boards of several companies simultaneously, may generate contacts, information or enhanced legitimacy for these organizations, as well as, in some cases, contributing specific skills. The recruitment of a part-time, non-executive director, may be a strategy for penetrating certain influential areas of an organization's environment, or enhancing mutual understanding. For instance Towco, a private building services group with a turnover in 1983 of £12 million, looked for two new non-executive directors as part of a plan to join the Unlisted Securities Market as a broad ranging building maintenance services and fitting group. The managing director wanted to take on to the board a man who could 'open doors in the City'. The organization for the Promotion of Non-Executive Directors found him an ex-director of Lloyds Bank, 'regarded both highly and affectionately in the City'.[14] The new board member might confidently be expected to smooth the path of Towco's interactions with the City's financial institutions, and prove a successful exercise in interpenetration.

Interpenetration mechanisms may, on the other hand, rely exclusively on the activities of 'boundary people' that is, those people within an organization who are concerned primarily with external relations with other organizations. Some boundary people may actually carry out work on the premises of a linked organization. For instance, computer manufacturers may station personnel for a long time at a customer's installation to perform engineering work. In any event, boundary people are likely to form particularly close links with their opposite members or 'role partners' in other organizations; the relationship may involve a social as well as a strictly functional dimension. The social dimension is also functional, not in terms of formal job specification but in terms of 'ideological penetration', or persuading staff of the other organization to think in similar terms.

The creation of shared criteria of success, or at least of acceptable levels of performance, are particularly important. Shared standards are most obviously needed where there are material flows between organizations, as in the case of component suppliers and final product assemblers. Some Japanese electronics firms operating within the EEC have been reluctant to buy the expected proportion of locally manufactured components largely because of different criteria of performance between themselves and European components suppliers. Their differing expectations about component reject rates, or about the relative importance of product reliability versus an efficient follow-up maintenance service, reflect not just different expectations, norms and managerial rationalities, in the sense of beliefs about the best way of doing things, but different concepts. Quality control may, for instance, be seen as the responsibility of every operator in a factory (the Japanese concept) or as the specialist responsibility of a quality control department at the end of the line. Quality can be seen as resting essentially on high reliability (as in Japan, which has traditionally catered for geographically distant markets, correspondingly expensive for maintenance provision) or on lower and less expensive standards of reliability, supported by generous guarantee terms. Cross-cultural ideological penetration, to reduce conflicting perceptions and rationalities between organizations, is clearly not impossible but it is complex.

Finally it is useful to look at a very distinctive kind of interpenetration mechanism which has attracted a good deal of attention — this is cooptation. Cooptation was defined by Selznick, in a classic study of the Tennessee Valley Authority, as 'the process of absorbing new elements into the leadership or policy-determining structure of an organization as a means of averting threats to its stability or existence'.[15]

Cooptation is essentially a defensive strategy. Like other forms of overlapping membership between organizations, such as the recruitment of non-executive directors, the strategy involves an organization taking an outsider into itself, that outsider being simultaneously a member of another organization. Whereas the motive for overlapping directorships can be simply to facilitate contacts or enhance legitimacy, the motive for cooptation is to transform the attitudes of the coopted member, to reduce the threat which his or her organization represents. The object is to bring the modes of thought of the coopted member more into line with the dominant rationalities of the coopting organization. What Stern calls 'ideological penetration' is at the heart of cooptation. Pfeffer and Salancik write that: 'The aim of bringing in potentially hostile outsiders is to socialize them and to commit them to provide assistance to the focal organization.'[16]

It is possible of course that both coopting and coopted organizations may each be seeking the ideological transformation of the other. Ideological transformation can work either way; and the support which cooptation secures may have a high price. Selznick described how interests initially hostile to the Tennessee Valley Authority were coopted and convinced to support the project; but the original aims of the project were diverted in the process. Local conservative farming interests, originally opposed to the project, were coopted and gave support. However, as a result, many of the New Deal's objectives for the programme were subverted and many of the project's activities benefited, not the poor and landless, but those well-established farming interests.

Cooptation doesn't always work. It may create a semblance of communication without effective communication really existing; and manipulated or fictitious cooptation only conceals the need for real communication and influence. Alternatively the person coopted may be repudiated by his or her former organization. The cooptation of worker directors on to the boards of companies, for instance, may fail for either of these reasons.

It is clear that cooptation, originally introduced as an interpenetration mechanism, or means of reducing conflict between organizations, can equally well be considered as a control strategy — an attempt to increase control over other organizations — or as a counter control strategy — an attempt to reduce the control of other organizations. Although a distinction was made at the beginning of the paper between two categories, control strategies and strategies for mutual understanding, reality is not so clear cut and many of the strategies discussed here can be seen as being in either category or in both. The strategies themselves may well overlap; dependency, for instance, usually involves some interpenetration as the Kanban system clearly shows. The distinctions made in this paper and summarized in Figure 15.1 are useful tools of analysis, but they necessarily simplify the rich variety of ways in which organizations seek to cope with their unpredictable or even turbulent environments.

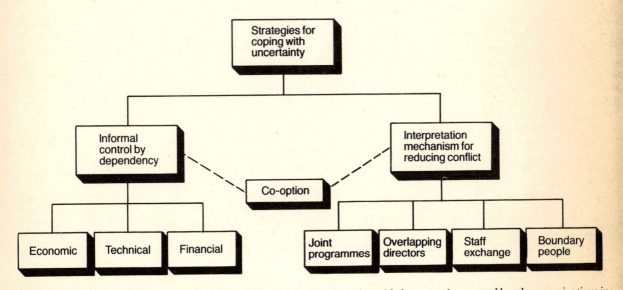

Figure 15.1 *Illustrating the range of strategies used by organizations in coping with the uncertainty created by other organizations in the environment.*

References

1. Sayles, L.R. and Chandler, M.K. (1971) *Managing Large Systems*, Harper & Row, New York, p.2.
2. Drucker, P. (1969) *The Age of Discontinuity*, Harper & Row, New York, Chapter 1.
3. Pfeffer, J. and Salancik, G.R. (1978) *The External Control of Organizations*, Harper & Row, New York, p.282.
4. Bonis, J. (1980) 'Organization and environment', Lockett, M. and Spear, R., *Organizations as Systems*, Open University Press, Milton Keynes, p.163.
5. Sayles and Chandler, op. cit., p.72.
6. Cited Pfeffer and Salancik, op. cit., p.72.
7. Monden, Y. (1981) 'Adaptable Kanban system helps Toyota maintain Just-in-Time production', *Industrial Engineering*, **13**, 5, p.40.
8. Sayles and Chandler, op. cit., p.73.
9. Bonis, op. cit., p.164.
10. Sayles and Chandler, op. cit., p.84.
11. Pennings, J.M. (1981) 'Strategically Interdependent Organizations', in Nystrom, P.C. and Starbuck, W.H., *Handbook of Organizations Design*, vol. 1, p.433, Oxford University Press.
12. Stern, L.W. (1980) 'Potential conflict management mechanisms in distribution channels: an interorganizational analysis', in Lockett, M. and Spear, R, *Organizations as Systems*, Open University Press, p.174.
13. *The Handbook of Organizations Design*, p.37.
14. *The Observer*, 23 January, p.20.
15. Selznick, P. (1949) *TVA and the Grass Roots*, University of California Press, Berkeley, p.13.
16. Pfeffer and Salancik, op. cit., p.110.

15(b)   The Valid Image of the Modern Economy
J.K. Galbraith

I am here concerned to see if I can provide a comprehensive and integrated view of the principal problems of economic management in our time. In doing so, I shall offer an alternative picture of the structure of modern economic society. This will compress into brief and, I trust, sharp form without obscuring detail what I have hitherto written about at much greater length.[1] Finally, I shall attempt to apply this model to some contemporary problems.

In considering the image of modern industrial society, one must have clearly in mind two factors that act strongly and persistently to distort the economist's view of that reality.

The first of these distorting factors is the very great inclination to think of the ultimate subject matter with which we deal in static terms. Physics, chemistry and geology deal with an unchanging subject matter. What is known and taught about them changes only as information is added or interpretation is revised. They are, all agree, sciences. It is the great desire of nearly all economists to see their subject as a science too. Accordingly, and without much thought, they hold that its matter is also fixed. The business firm, the market, the behaviour of the consumer, like the oxygen molecule or the geologist's granite, are given. Economists are avid searchers for new information, eager in their discussion of the conclusions to be drawn. But nearly all of this information is then fitted into a fixed, unchanging view of the role of business firms, markets, labor relations, consumer behavior, and the economic role of the government. It is not an accident that economists who see their subject in evolutionary terms are a minority in the profession.

This is not a small methodological point. You will not doubt its importance if, in fact, the institutions with which economics deals are not stable, if they are subject to change. In truth, they *are*, and the first step toward a more valid perception of economic society and its problems is an appreciation of the very high rate of movement that has been occurring in basic economic institutions. The business corporation is the greatest of the forces for such change. In consequence of the movement it initiates, there has been a rapid alteration in the nature of the labor market and of trade union organization. Also in the class structure of modern economic society and in the resulting patterns of consumption. Also in the services and responses of the modern state. The ultimate effect of these changes is, in fact, to make the economic knowledge of one generation obsolete in the next. And also the prescription and policy based on that knowledge.

The second factor that distorts economic understanding is the very great social and political convenience — or so it seems — of the wrong image of economic society. I can best give substance to this abstraction by proceeding to the structure of the modern industrial economy.

The presently accepted image of this economy is, of course, of numerous entrepreneurial firms distributed as between consumer- and producer-goods industries, all subordinate to their market and thus, ultimately, to the instruction of the consumer. Being numerous, the firms are competitive; any tendency to overprice products by one firm is corrected by the undercutting of a competitor. A similar corrective tendency operates, if less perfectly, in the purchase of materials and labor. Being entrepreneurial, the firm has a simple internal structure. Authority, power within the firm, lies with the entrepreneur, on whom, overwhelmingly, achievement depends. The entrepreneur being the owner, the partial owner or the direct instrument of the owner, the motivation is also simple and straightforward. It is to maximize return.

To say that the firm is subordinate to the market is to say that it submits to prices that it does not control and that it submits, ultimately, to the will of the consumer. Decision originates with the consumer, and this decision, expressed through the market, is sovereign. If the consumer has sovereign power, the firm cannot have any important power at all in the market; there cannot be two possessors of sovereign power. The business firm is also, by assumption rather than by evidence, without organic power in the state.

In one exception, the firm has influence over prices and output; that is the case of monopoly or oligopoly, or their counterparts, in the purchase of materials and components, products for resale or labor. But monopoly — the control of prices and production in an industry by one firm — and oligopoly — control by a few firms — are never the rule in this image; they are always the exception. They are imperfections in the system. The use of the word imperfection, which is the standard reference to monopoly and oligopoly, affirms that these are departures from the general competitive rule.

To any economist the broad image of economic society that I have just sketched will not seem replete with novelty. It is also admirable proof of the resistance of the subject to change. In the last hundred years the notion of oligopoly has been added to that of monopoly, and the notion of monopoly has been widened to include partial monopoly in brands, services or the like — monopolistic competition. On occasion, there is now in basic economic instruction some bow to the managerial as distinct from the entrepreneurial character of the modern great corporation. Otherwise the basic structure — competitive entrepreneurial firms, the supremacy of the market, the flawing exception of monopoly — is not very different in the modern textbook from that described in Alfred Marshall's *Principles of Economics*, which was first published in the year 1890. Anyone not deeply conditioned by conventional economic instruction must wonder, as he or she reflects on the extent of economic change in our time, if so static a theory of basic economic arrangements can be valid. It is right to do so.

The image is not valid. But it does contribute both to the tranquility of the economist's existence and to the social and political convenience of modern corporate enterprise.

The service of the accepted image of economic life to the political needs of the business firm — the large corporation in particular — is, in fact, breathtaking. Broadly speaking, it removes from the corporation all power to do wrong and leaves with it only the power to do right.

Are its prices too high? The corporation is blameless. Prices are set by the market. Are profits unseemly? They are too deter-mined by the market. Are products deficient in safety, durability, design, usefulness? They only reflect the will of the sovereign consumer. The function of the firm is not to interpose its judgment, only to accept that of the consumer. Is there adverse effect on the environment? If so it reflects (with some minor effect from external diseconomies) the higher preference of people for the goods being produced as opposed to the protection of air, water or landscape. Is there criticism of the influence of corporations on the state — of the devastating foreign policy of Lockheed in Italy, Japan, Holland? These are abberations, for an organic relationship between the business firm and the state does not exist.

One sees how great are the political and social advantages of this image of economic life. It is not easy to think of the accepted economics as the handmaiden of politics. Most economists suppress the thought. None should.

However, self-delusion also has its cost — and this is great. Specifically, this image conceals from us the workings of the modern economic system, the reasons for its successes and its failures and the nature of the needed remedial action. Among the victims of this concealment are those most intimately involved — those with the greatest need to understand the correct image — and they are businessmen themselves. And there is a damaging public effect. People cannot accept as valid an image of modern society that makes the great corporation the helpless, passive instrument of market forces and itself a force of minimal influence in the state. This is too deeply at odds with common sense. So they come to believe that there is something intrinsically deceptive about the modern corporation, and perhaps also about the economics that projects the conventional image. Better and safer the truth.

The valid image of the economic system is not, in fact, of a single competitive and entrepreneurial system. It is of a double or bimodal system. The two parts are very different in structure but roughly equal in aggregate product. In the United States, reflecting the force of the corporation for change in the last century around 1000 to 2000[2] firms contribute about half of all private economic product. In 1967, for example, 200 manufacturing corporations (out of 200,000) shipped 42 percent of all manufactured goods by value. Later figures suggest further concentration. Of 13,687 commercial banks in 1971, 50 had 48 percent of all assets; of 1805 life insurance companies, the 50 largest had 82 percent of all assets.[3] Set against this half of the economy is the dispersed sector: depending on what is called a firm, this consists, in the United States, of between 10 and 12 million small businesses — farms, service and professional enterprises, construction firms, artistic enterprises, small traders. They contribute the other half of product. The division in other advanced industrial countries is roughly similar. Thus the valid image of modern economic society is the division of the productive task between a few large firms that are infinitely large and many small firms that are infinitely numerous.

The large corporation differs organically from the small; the burden of proof cannot seem excessive for the individual who asserts that there is a fundamental difference in organization and structure between General Motors, Shell or Volkswagen and the small farm, neighborhood restaurant, cafe or retail flower shop. The coexistence of these two very different structures and the resulting economic behavior are themselves features of the greatest importance. But first a further word on the corporate sector — what I have elsewhere called the planning system.[4]

The most obvious characteristic of the corporate half of the economy is the great size of the participating units. In the United States a handful of industrial corporations — General Motors, Exxon, Ford, a couple of others at most — have sales equal to all agriculture. Size in turn contributes to the two features of the modern large firm that differentiate it from the entrepreneurial and competitive enterprise and explain its impact on the society. The first of these is its deployment of market and political power. The second — one that is less noticed — is its diffusion of personal power.

The deployment of market and political power is diverse and, except as described in economic instruction, also commonplace. The modern large corporation has extensive influence over its prices and over its costs. It supplies much of its capital from its own earnings. It strongly influences the tastes and behavior of its consumers; even professional economists when looking at television have difficulty concealing from themselves the impact of modern advertising, although many succeed. And it exists in the closest relationship with the modern state.

The government gives the corporation legal existence; establishes the environmental and other parameters within which it functions; monitors the quality and safety of its products and certain of the advertising claims it makes for them; supplies, in the manner of highways to the automobile industry, the services on which sale of its products depends. Also — an increasingly important function — the government is the safety net into which the firm falls in the event of failure. Above a certain size — as the recent history of some large American banks, the eastern railroads in the United States, the Lockheed Corporation, Rolls-Royce, British Leyland, British Chrysler, Krupp and the vast agglomerations of IRI in Italy all show — a very large corporation is no longer allowed to go out of business. The social damage is too great. Modern socialism is extensively the adoption by reluctant governments, socialist and otherwise, of the abandoned offspring of modern capitalism. Being thus so dependent, the corporation must seek power in the state. This power, like that in the market, is not plenary. But its existence can be denied only by those who are trained extensively to ignore it.

As earlier noted, the role of the modern great corporation in diffusing personal power is less celebrated than its deployment of market and public power, but it is not, I believe, less important. In its fully developed form, the corporation, as others have emphasized, removes power from the ownership interest, the traditional locus of capitalist authority. In doing so, it removes it from the representatives of the stockholders — the board of directors. No director of General Motors, Exxon or IBM who is not a member of management — I speak carefully here — has any continuing effective influence on company operations. The ceremony which proclaims that power — usually of aged, occasionally senile men meeting for a couple of hours on complex matters six times a year — is almost wholly implausible except to the participants. Directors do not make decisions; they ratify them. But to remove power from the owners and their alleged representatives — from the capitalists — is only a part of a larger process. That larger process involves extensive diffusion of such power. As power passes from capitalist to management in the large firms, this diffusion occurs in three ways.

First, decisions being numerous and complex, they must be delegated and redelegated, and the decision-making process passes down into the firm. This all recognize to be necessary. Nothing so criticizes an executive as the statement, 'He cannot delegate responsibility'.

Second, decisions being technically and socially complex, they become the shared responsibility of specialists — engineers, scientists, production men, marketing experts, lawyers, accountants, tax specialists. Power, in other words, passes from individuals to groups — to what I have called the technostructure of the modern corporation.

Finally, where there is no participation in decision, organization takes form to influence it. Thus the trade union. Union power is the natural answer to the power of the corporation. Only in the rarest cases in the developed industrial world is there a large corporation where labor is not organized.

The diffusion of power extends beyond the boundaries of the corporation, for the corporation brings into existence a vast array of supporting professions and services — law firms to advise on, or sometimes bend, the law; accountants to record, and sometimes create, its earnings; universities, colleges and business schools to train its executives and specialists or those who will so pass; dealers to sell its products; repairmen to service the products or advise that they are beyond repair. Marx held that, in its final stages of development, the capitalist firm devoured the small entrepreneur. This may well be true as regards small competitors. But the modern corporation also nurtures and sustains a large penumbra of independent firms. These peripheral groups and firms also assert their right to power. Lawyers and accountants have their special claims on decisions. So do consulting firms and custodians of expert knowledge from the universities. Dealer relations departments exist to consider the rights of those who sell and service the products. All have a claim on power.

We should not test our image of the economic system by its political convenience, or we should not if we are interested in analytical serviceable truths. We should see, instead, whether our image accords with observed circumstance, observed need.

The first test of the system I have just been describing has to do with the foremost problem of our time, the disagreeable and persistent tendency for severe unemployment in the modern industrial society to be combined with severe inflation.

If one accepts the competitive and entrepreneurial image of economic society, this combination does not and cannot occur. There can be inflation. But by conventional macroeconomic monetary and fiscal policy — restricting bank lending and tightening the public budget — the aggregate demand for goods and services in the economy can be reduced. Since, in this image, no firm controls prices, production is affected only as prices fall —

that is what brings to the firm the message of declining demand. So, as the first effect, prices will cease to rise, which is to say the inflation will come to an end. Later, as prices and earnings fall, production may be curtailed and there may be unemployment. But unemployment and inflation do not and cannot co-exist. One is cured before the other is caused.

Similarly, if there is unemployment, aggregate demand in the economy can be expended by monetary and fiscal action — more public expenditure, reduced taxes, easier lending and thus more spending from borrowed funds. The initial effect will be more sales, more jobs. Prices may then rise. But, once again, that is because unemployment has been cured or, at a minimum, is by way of being cured.

In the bimodal image of the economy, a combination of inflation and unemployment must be expected at least for so long as fiscal and monetary policy are the sole instruments of economic management. Trade unions, as we have seen, have power over their wages in the corporate sector of the economy. Corporations, having power in their markets, have the ability to offset concessions to trade unions with higher prices. Modern collective bargaining has lost much of its old-fashioned acerbity for a very simple reason: as an alternative to confrontation, unions and management can reach agreement and pass the resulting cost on to the public. Complaints over the cost of wage settlements now rarely come from employers. Almost invariably they come from the government, which is concerned over the inflationary effect, or from the public, which has to pay the higher price.

When this wage-price inflation is attacked by the traditional methods — monetary and budget restraint to reduce demand — prices do not automatically fall. The firm has the power to maintain its prices. The first industrial effect is, instead, on sales, output and employment. And if unions continue to press for higher wages, prices will continue to increase. Only when unemployment is very severe — so severe as to deter the unions from pressing for wage increases and the corporations from exercising their power to raise prices — do the traditional monetary and fiscal measures begin to bite. Meanwhile unemployment and inflation, as in the world today, do co-exist.

Before monetary and fiscal policy act on the corporate sector, however, they work on the competitive and entrepreneurial sector of the economy. Here, as before, prices do respond to monetary and fiscal measures to restrain demand. Also in this half of the economy are industries — housing and construction being the notable cases — that exist on borrowed funds, which makes them uniquely vulnerable to monetary action, to restrictions on bank lending. (This vulnerability is in contrast with the position of the large corporation, which has resort to retained earnings for capital and which, in the event of outside need, is a priority customer at the banks.) So, while inflation continues in the corporate half of the economy, there can be falling farm prices and a painful recession in the entrepreneurial and competitive sector. That too accords fully with recent or present circumstances. Beginning in 1974, monetary restriction was brought sharply to bear on the then serious inflation. There followed a serious recession, the worst, in fact,

since the Great Depression. Farm prices fell. Housing, where output fell by more than a third, was seriously depressed. Unemployment rose to around 10 percent of the labor force. And industrial prices — those of the corporate sector — kept right on rising.

The practical conclusion is that inflation cannot now be arrested by fiscal and monetary policy alone unless there is willingness to accept a very large amount of unemployment. There remains only one alternative; that is to restrain incomes and prices not by unemployment but by direct intervention — by an incomes and prices policy. Such action is not a substitute for orthodox monetary and fiscal management of demand but an essential supplement to it. [. . .]

The bimodal view also explains the increasingly unequal development of the modern economy and the measures that governments find themselves taking to deal with it. The corporate half of the economy combines advanced organization, high technical skills and relatively ample capital with the ability to persuade the consumer and the state as to their need for its products. In consequence, in all industrial countries, automobiles, lethal weapons, household appliances, pharmaceuticals, alcohol, tobacco and cosmetics are amply supplied. The very notion of shortage, inadequacy, in these commodities would strike all as distinctly odd. The contemporary experience with oil shortages is deeply traumatic. But in the competitive entrepreneurial sector, where organization, technology, capital and persuasion are less available or absent, inadequacy is assumed. Housing, health care, numerous consumer services and, on occasion, the food supply are a source of complaint or anxiety in all of the developed countries. All governments find themselves seeking ways to compensate for the inadequacies of private enterprise in this half of the bimodal economy. The conventional economics has only one explanation for this unequal development: it reflects consumer choice, which is to say that the consumer is unaware of his — or her — needs. Where housing, health care and food are concerned, this is hard to believe.

The bimodal image of the economy serves also our understanding of inequality of opportunity and reward in the modern economy and its consequences. In the conventional image of the economy, inequality is the result of differences in talent, luck or choice of ancestors. But between occupations it is constantly being remedied by movement from lower- to higher-income jobs. If this remedy is to work, people must, of course, be able to move.

The corporate sector of the economy deserves more approval than it receives for the income it provides. In the United States it is doubtful if any union member with full time employment in this sector falls below the poverty line. But there are grave barriers to movement into this area. In particular, so long as inflation is the chief problem and monetary and fiscal policy are the remedies, there will be unemployment in this sector — either chronic or recurrent. If there is unemployment, there obviously cannot be easy movement of new workers into its higher paid employment. The old unemployed have first chance.

In the entrepreneurial part of the economy, by contrast,

employment can often be found either by taking a lower self-employment return or possibly low pay in an industry that has no union. There is, accordingly, a continuing source of inequality between the two parts of the economy derived from the occluded movement between them. We have here another reason for forgoing exclusive reliance on monetary and fiscal policy for controlling inflation. The resulting unemployment is also a source of occluded movement and thus of further inequality as between the different sectors of the economy. [. . .]

There are further tests of the image of the economy I am here describing. Let me conclude by combining several into one. In removing power from owners, diffusing it through the techno-structure and accepting and even nurturing the organized response of workers, the modern corporation does more than diffuse power. It takes a long step, if not toward a classless society, at least toward one in which class lines are extensively blurred. This, in turn, has a major effect on consumption patterns. Specifically, there is no longer in the corporate sector of the economy full acceptance by any group that it was meant by the nature of its occupation to consume less. And this acceptance will continue to erode. The pressure so exerted both for private goods and services and the requisite wages is one source of inflation. Pressure for such public services as education, health care and public transportation is another source. The thrusts for more private income and consumption and for more public goods and services have, we see, the same sources and can be equally strong. They are associated with the power — the power diffused by the corporation — to make the claim effective. In consequence, to cut consumption of private goods through taxes or for that matter through an incomes policy or to cut the consumption of public goods through reduced public outlays is very difficult. The bimodal image of economic society helps explain the new budget pressures with their inflationary effect as well as the new sources of inflation in the wage-price spiral. And it tells us also why control is politically and socially so difficult.

The business units in the corporate sector of the economy, becoming large, become international. The modern corporation internationalizes its income and wage standards as entrepreneurial industry never did. It also creates an international civil service — men who, like the servants of the Holy Church, are at home in all lands, who differ only in owing their ultimate allegiance not to Rome but to IBM. The international corporation defends relative freedom from tariff barriers and other constraints on trade. That is because competition is rarely cut-throat between large firms; they are restrained by oligopolistic convention. And international competition is never serious if you own the international competitor. It was the growth of the corporate sector of the modern economy that made possible the Common Market — made it necessary, perhaps, because intra-European trade barriers had become only a nuisance for the large corporation. Agriculture and other entrepreneurial enterprises have not changed their attitude on international trade. Their instinct is still protective. Farmers and other small producers would never have brought the EEC into existence. They are the source of at least 90 percent of its problems. Again the bimodal image fits the history.

Footnotes

1. In Galbraith, J.K. (1973) *Economics and the Public Purpose*, Houghton Mifflin, Boston.
2. The statistical difference between 1000 and 2000 is not, in fact, great, for the contribution of the second thousand is small as compared with that of the first.
3. Hughes, J.R.T. (1977) *The Governmental Habit: Economic Controls from Colonial Times to the Present*, Basic Books, New York, p.203. William Leonard, adjusting for some underreporting — the tendency to assign some manufacturing activities to mining for tax reasons — puts the share of manufacturing employment of the largest 200 corporations at 60 percent in 1974. 'Mergers, industrial concentration, and antitrust policy', *Journal of Economic Issues*, **X**, 2, June 1976, pp. 354-381.
4. In Galbraith, J.K. (1978) *The New Industrial State*, 3rd edition, Houghton Mifflin, Boston and *Economics and the Public Purpose*.

Index